Safer by Design

Second Edition

Design Council

The Design Council is the UK's national authority on design. Its main activities are:

- commissioning research on design-related topics, particularly stressing design effectiveness to improve competitiveness;
- communicating key design effectiveness messages to industry and government; and
- working to improve both design education and the role of design in education generally.

The Design Council is working with Gower to support the publication of work in design management and product development. For more information about the Design Council please phone 0171 208 2121. A complete list of book titles is available from Gower Publishing on 01252 331551.

Safer by Design

Second Edition

A guide to the management and law of designing for product safety

Howard Abbott
and
Mark Tyler

Gower

First edition published 1987 by The Design Council.

Published by
Gower Publishing Limited
Gower House
Croft Road
Aldershot
Hampshire GU11 3HR
England

Gower
Old Post Road
Brookfield
Vermont 05036
USA

Howard Abbott and Mark Tyler have asserted their rights under the Copyright, Designs and Patents Act 1988 to be identified as the author of this work.

British Library Cataloguing in Publication Data
Abbott, Howard
    Safer by design. – 2nd ed.
    1. Products liability – England
    I. Title   II. Tyler, Mark
    344.2′0638

    ISBN 0 566 07707 8

Library of Congress Cataloging-in-Publication Data
Abbott, Howard.
    Safer by design / Howard Abbott. Mark Tyler. – 2nd ed.
        p.   cm.
    Includes index.
    ISBN 0–566 07707–8 (cloth)
    1. Product safety–Law and legislation.   2. Products liability. 3. Design.
Industrial–Law and legislation.   4. Design. Industrial–Management.   5.
Product safety–Law and legislation–Great Britain.   6. Products liability–Great
Britain.   7. Design. Industrial–Law Britain–Management.   I. Tyler, Mark.   II.
title.
K953.A73   1997
346.03′8–dc20
[342.638]   96-34694
                                                                                      CIP

Phototypeset in Baskerville 11 on 14 pt by Intype London Ltd
Printed in Great Britain by Biddles Ltd, Guildford.

Contents

List of figures

List of tables

List of abbreviations

ALARP	as low as reasonably practicable
AIOC	Amoco International Oil Company
ATP	Automatic Train Protection
BATNEEC	best available techniques not involving excessive cost
BL	British Leyland
CDM	construction, design and management
CENELEC	Comité Européen de Normalisation Electrotechnique
CEPA	Consumer Electronic Products Association
CPSC	Consumer Product Safety Commission (USA)
EHLASS	European Home and Leisure Accident Surveillance System
EIAJ	Electronic Industry Association of Japan
EPA	Environmental Protection Agency
ESREDA	European Safety and Reliability Data Association
ETSI	European Telecommunications Standards Institute
FDA	Food and Drug Administration (USA)
FIRA	Furniture Industry Research Association
FMEA	Failure Mode and Effect Analysis
FMECA	Failure Mode Effect and Criticality Analysis
FTA	Fault Tree Analysis
GPS	General Product Safety
HACCP	Hazard Analysis Critical Control Point
HADD	Home Accident Death Database
HASS	Home Accident Surveillance System
HAZOP	Hazard and Operability Study
HSWA	Health and Safety at Work etc Act
IEC	International Electrical Commission
IMO	International Maritime Organization

IMQ	Istituto Italiano del Marchio di Qualita
ISO	International Standards Organisation
KWm²	kilowatts per square metre
LASS	Leisure Accident Surveillance System
NBS	National Bureau of Standards
NEISS	National Electronic Injury Surveillance System USA
NES	Normal Engineering Standard
OEM	original equipment manufacturer
OFT	Office of Fair Trading
OSHA	Occupational Safety and Health Administration (USA)
PE	polyethylene
PVC	polyvinyl chloride
RAPEX	rapid exchange of information procedure
SOLAS	International Convention for the Safety of Life at Sea
UCTA	Unfair Contract Terms Act 1977
UL	Underwriters' Laboratories

Acknowledgements

We owe a debt of gratitude to many people who provided information and inspiration on the new material that has gone into this second edition.

We greatly appreciated help from P. J. Booker, the Secretary of the Institution of Engineering Design; Geoff Dessent of the Consumer Safety Unit of the Department of Trade and Industry; Bill Gulliver of the Furniture Industry Research Association; Ian Hodgskinson of Lloyd's Register Quality Assurance Ltd; Bob Malins of Raychem Limited and Tim Watt of the Consumers' Association.

We also benefited from the advice of Kathie Claret of S. G. Archibald, Paris; Jocelyn Kellam of Clayton Utz, Sydney; Dennis Neutze of Shook Hardy & Bacon, London and Simon Thomas of McKenna & Co, London. Christopher Hodges kindly took time to read drafts and suggest improvements.

Our editor Suzie Duke provided us with careful guidance and our special thanks go to Debbie Jenkins who skilfully and patiently co-ordinated our work and prepared manuscripts.

Howard Abbott
Mark Tyler

Introduction

People have a right to expect products to be safe, even though this has to be an unattainable absolute in every case. A significant cause of product failure is design which makes a fundamental contribution to product safety, and there have been some spectacular design disasters. From a corporate point of view design should be managed and taken out of the understairs cupboard where it is sometimes kept.

In this new edition of *Safer by Design* Part 1, 'The Management of Design Risks' has been considerably updated and rewritten. Chapter 2, 'Product Databases', and Chapter 3, 'Identification of Risks', which are crucial, have been enlarged.

Since the first edition of this book was published in 1987 the legal position has changed greatly. Part 2, 'The Legal Background' has been entirely rewritten by Mark Tyler to cover the current legislation which is critical for the designer. The personal responsibilities and liability of the individual designer are dealt with in Chapter 11.

The case histories in Part 3 have been significantly changed: half of them are new and the remainder have been updated. 'The Lessons from History' now review the 22 design failures and show that there is a commonality of failure modes to which designers are vulnerable, whatever their product. The case histories are directly linked to the Management of Design Risks in Part 1 and the Legal Background in Part 2 by reference numbers, to illustrate what happened in a corresponding real-life situation.

The management of design risks ultimately concerns us all, both at work and at home. Yet there is a general reluctance on the part of companies to discuss the topic—particularly designing for safety. This is true of manufacturers of safety-critical products, which could make a valuable contribution to the debate. It is almost as if they feel that it would be tempting the devil to give even general information about the procedures they use to prevent people getting hurt.

This second edition represents an attempt to go some way towards rectifying the situation. It is not concerned with the scientific or engineering aspects of design safety. Rather it draws attention to how the *management* of design can help make products safer.

We have endeavoured to state the legal position, as at July 1996.

Howard Abbott

Part One
THE MANAGEMENT OF
DESIGN RISKS

1
The Management Strategy

Introduction

The new product liability laws in Europe and elsewhere give design a new dimension. Too much can be at stake to leave the responsibility for design in the hands of a single department, let alone one person. The case histories in Part 3 illustrate the seriousness of design defects only too clearly: the costs in terms of lives and money can be alarmingly high (see Case History 18).

It is the simple word 'defect' that creates difficulty. What it precisely means depends on the training and experience one has received. Broadly, there is a dichotomy between the lawyers on the one hand and the engineers and scientists on the other. Because he cannot know all the situations in which it will be used a lawyer needs an 'expanding suitcase' definition; he needs a catch-all to cover washing powder, a microchip, an office chair and a ferry – as Case Histories 5, 13, 14 and 20 show.

Problems with definitions and claims

Article 6 of the Directive on Liability for Defective Products 1985 states that a product is defective when 'it does not provide the safety which a person is entitled to expect, taking all the circumstances into account'. Article 2 of the General Product Safety Directive 1992 says that a safe product is one 'which, under normal or reasonably foreseeable conditions of use, including duration, does not present any risk or only the minimum risks compatible with the product's use, considered as acceptable and consistent with a high level of protection for the safety and health of persons', taking into account certain factors.

Section 6 of the Health and Safety at Work etc Act 1974, imposes on designers a duty to ensure, so far as is reasonably practicable, that articles and substances for use at work are safe and without risks to health when properly used. The Sale and Supply of Goods Act 1994 amended the Sales of Goods Act 1979 by replacing the old-fashioned term 'merchantable quality' with 'satisfactory quality' for all goods sold under contract. The new Act makes it clear that, as well as fitness for purpose, aspects of quality include freedom from minor defects, appearance and finish, safety and durability. The designer will find these definitions difficult to put into practice as they stand, for they are open to interpretation.

Similarly, superlatives and comparatives by themselves provide little guidance to the designer: they have to relate to something specific to gain perspective (see Case History 4). Expressions such as 'best quality', 'highest standard' and 'largest capacity' have no real meaning unless they refer to graduated degrees of quality, standards or capacities. In the same way, 'guaranteed 100 per cent pure', 'no deleterious substances present', 'no danger when used according to the instructions' and 'completely safe for children' are all impossible absolutes.

The claim 'guaranteed 100 per cent pure' gives no benchmark against which the purity has been measured, nor does it specify the quantity which is claimed to be pure. Is it 10 tonnes, a milligram or a tested sample from what volume? 'No deleterious substances present' might mean that the manufacturer did not find any in the sample he checked. Nowadays no designer can accurately claim 'no danger when used according to the instructions' or 'completely safe for children'. These phrases carry with them an unattainable aura of omniscience, because every product must have some danger for someone, somewhere, sometime. The fact that a manufacturer has never received a complaint about his product does not mean that there have not been any.

Safety targets

The criteria for safety involve a variety of social, political and technical judgements. One expert[1] has suggested that if a risk of hazard is so low that only one person in 10 million is likely to be killed every year then action to reduce that hazard further is not justified. The choice of this figure is based on the fact that risks of this level – equivalent to the probability of being killed by lightning strikes, falling aircraft, snake and insect bites – are considered to be so low that action to reduce them would be absurd. A further perspective is provided by the example that the general risk of death in a fire or explosion caused by a gas leak in the home is one in a million; this, in turn, has the same probability of picking up a single grain of sugar from a one pound bag which contains about one million grains.

Acceptance of this view that we cannot avoid every conceivable accident leads to an examination of numerical methods for helping to decide a level of acceptable risk – in other words, we have to decide just how 'safe' a product should be. Obviously some hazards have to be eliminated because their risks are too high, while others have to be reduced to a minimum. But what is the minimum?

The definition of safety becomes difficult when we try to measure it in terms of how much it is worth, for this ultimately leads to putting a value on a human life. British Rail assessed individual safety projects comparatively and if the cost was more than £2 million per life saved they would rarely go ahead.[2] The ATP (Automatic Train Protection) proposal, designed to prevent trains going through a red signal, was recommended by the Clapham rail crash enquiry. However, at £700 million it was dropped, because it would cost £14 million per life saved and was being overtaken by more advanced technology. The Department of Transport has valued the marginal reduction in the risk of a road fatality at £683 000.[3] The RAC estimated that a death caused by a road accident cost £744 000, a serious injury £84 262 and a minor injury £6540.

These are deep waters and raise many moral dilemmas and

ethical questions which have no place in this book. The Health and Safety Executive[4] has adopted a risk management approach called ALARP or 'as low as reasonably practicable'. In this concept there is an upper boundary above which risk is judged intolerable under any circumstances and a lower boundary below which risk is considered broadly acceptable and undeserving of further significant investment. Between these two boundaries is the region within which risk must be reduced until it is as low as reasonably practicable. However, a cost-benefit exercise alone is unlikely to be the sole determining factor because socio-political considerations also have to be taken into account.

A definition of that troublesome phrase 'reasonably practicable' was given by Asquith LJ in *Edwards* v. *National Coal Board* 1949. He said:

> Reasonably practicable is a narrower term than physically possible, and implies that a computation must be made in which the quantum of risk is placed in one scale, and the sacrifice, whether in money, time or trouble, involved in the measures necessary to avert the risk, is placed in the other; and that, if it be shown that there is a gross disproportion between them, the risk being insignificant in relation to the sacrifice, the person upon whom the duty is laid discharges the burden of proving that compliance was not reasonably practicable. This computation falls to be made at a point of time anterior to the happening of the incident complained of.

The fundamental difficulty here for designers is that there are no factual markers by which they can determine whether or not they have fulfilled their obligations. The courts are reluctant to lay down principles of law for general application, where there is a factual question which has to be determined on a case-by-case basis. Moreover, demonstrating that what has been done is the universal practice in an industry is not of itself proof that a duty has been discharged so far as is reasonably practicable. It will only be one factor to be weighed in the evidence.[5]

The Inspectorate of Pollution uses an approach to risk management called BATNEEC – Best Available Techniques Not Entailing Excessive Cost. In this approach the costs and benefits of pollution control and environmental protection are balanced: the upper boundary of tolerability reflects specified environmental quality objectives and the lower boundary of broad acceptability is defined by action levels. The zone between the two limits is the BATNEEC area.

For many designers any of these approaches will be difficult to adopt because of a lack of data and the resources to achieve them. Large national undertakings and regulatory bodies operate in a different field, remote from the individuals in a commercial enterprise with shareholders. Yet all are concerned with promoting safety and preventing people getting hurt.

The complexities of some common products increase apace without failure rates being known. As is illustrated by Case History 13, software introduces its own problems as it is impossible to confirm that a program is completely reliable and safe in every circumstance. However, at the same time there is an increasing demand to ensure that products are safer.

For most products we cannot set a finite safety target nor can we require that it is completely safe. The alternative is to establish a programme which will make a product as safe as possible by using an approach which accepts the realities of product safety in a pragmatic way. It is advantageous to be able to prove that all due diligence was exercised and that all reasonable precautions were taken.

Sources of defect

There are three sources of a product failure:

- design defect
- manufacturing error
- failure of information.

In this book we are only concerned with design defect, which is perhaps the principal source of product failure, bearing in mind that it can have a significant influence on the other two factors. The need to manage safety in product design is clear and what follows is the outline of a course to achieve that end.

To do this effectively a strategy is needed to provide a framework which ensures that the company's requirements are met. It establishes the infrastructure to direct the tactics which will manage the potential product design exposures. There can be no fixed rules, for each company has a unique combination of products, people and markets. However, we will examine the more common factors, remembering that they have to be in place for some time before they can influence the course of events.

It will be seen that the management of safety in product design includes functions other than those normally associated with design. The need for this wider contribution is a reflection of the wider consequences of a design failure today. The techniques of yesterday will need modification to be effective in the new situation.

Key elements of strategy

The four key elements of the strategy are briefly reviewed below, before being examined in subsequent chapters.

1 *Identify the product risks.* If the risks have not been identified they cannot be managed. The danger is that managers familiar with the product will assume that they already know its hazards and the risks they present. But that very familiarity is a hazard because, as we will see in Part 2, the climate of risk has changed. The marketplace in which the product is sold will take on a new dimension, so a fresh approach to the whole question of risk identification is required.

2 *Risk reduction programme.* The next element of the strategy is active risk reduction, possibly as part of a design review system. As this programme develops, some of the risk identification techniques may be used to help evaluate the success of the risk reduction activity.

3 *Risk transfer programme.* As no product can be absolutely safe, any risk reduction programme will leave residual product risks. Some of these, once they have been identified, can be trans-

ferred to third parties by such mechanisms as insurance or contract.

4 *Risk retention programme.* However successful the previous elements of the strategy, some residual product risk will have to be retained within the company. An active programme will provide more protection than a passive one.

The strategy follows classic risk management principles, applied to a special requirement. There is a further element, risk avoidance, which is not considered in this book. An example would be a product for use in a hostile environment which had to reduce to the minimum the possibility of a spark; in certain circumstances one way of achieving this would be to avoid the risk of an electric spark by using a hydraulic form of energy. Another way of avoiding risk would be to stop making a product which had too many risks associated with it. Risk avoidance is more of a negative concept in product safety than it is in other risk management applications, such as occupational safety and health in the chemical industry. It is assumed that risk avoidance is folded into risk reduction for product safety.

Summary

No product can be absolutely safe, and some industries set safety targets against an agreed scale. Achieving an acceptable degree of product safety requires a strategy to manage design, as this is probably the principal source of product failures. Given the lack of failure data for many products, it is proposed that the strategy should have four elements: risk identification, risk reduction, risk transfer and risk retention.

References

1 Kletz, T. A. (1982), 'Hazard analysis – a review of criteria', *Reliability Engineering*, **3** (4), pp. 325–38.
2 'Costing Lives', *Economist*, 12 September 1992.

3 'Transport safety and the high price of human life', *Financial Times*, 5 October 1992.
4 Goats, G. C. and Ball, D. J. (1994), 'The management of risks posed by food chemical contaminants', Centre for Environmental and Risk Management, University of East Anglia, September.
5 Hodges C. Tyler, M. and Abbott, H. (1996), *Product Safety*, London: Sweet & Maxwell.

2
Product Databases: Sources of Information on Product-related Accidents

Introduction

Surprisingly there are few sources of data on which end-products are most likely to cause injury. Designers would be the first to benefit from a database which would warn them of those products which required their greatest attention. Even more useful would be a source of information which could reveal why a particular product caused an accident. Some companies have this facility, as far as their own products are concerned, but such data are very confidential. Insurers and insurance brokers may have some information on which products are most likely to cause harm, but it would be of little use to a designer seeking serious scientific and engineering facts. The insurance industry needs information to set premiums not to establish detailed product design criteria.

The Home Accident Surveillance System (HASS)

The closest to a valuable source for end-products is to be found in the Home Accident Surveillance System (HASS) and its associated systems. In the UK more people are killed in accidents in the home than on the roads. Home accidents account for over 4000 deaths per year – for example, every week one person is killed and about 100 injured in a home accident with a ladder. About 40 per cent of all fatalities and approximately one-third of all accidents treated in hospital occur at home. Three million people each year seek medical treatment as a result of non-fatal home accidents.

It is important to appreciate that the HASS deals with products *involved* in accidents – not those *responsible* for them. The system dates back to a 1973–74 feasibility study undertaken for the Home Office which then looked after consumer safety. Today, the Consumer Safety Unit of the Department of Trade collects data on the essential characteristics of home and leisure accidents and, in particular, the involvement of consumer products. Accidents are classified according to these characteristics and recorded in the HASS and LASS (Leisure Accident Surveillance System). Data on fatal accidents are recorded in the HADD (Home Accident Death Database). The two linked databases of the HASS and LASS hold records of accidents involving injury or suspected injury, including details of associated factors and consequences. The records represent a sample of all home accidents and outdoor product accidents, in which the victim was treated in the Accident and Emergency (A&E) Unit of selected hospitals. Data collection takes place in 18 of these Units, which are representative of the 400 in the country as a whole. A statistical process selects the HASS hospitals, using stratification of the population of all eligible hospitals into groups, within which a random selection is made.

Details of accidents are recorded at the hospitals by specially trained interviewers. They use a standard interviewing questionnaire, but do not deal with occupational or road accidents. Completed questionnaires are entered on a HASS/LASS-dedicated computer in the hospital and are subsequently transferred to the central database at the Consumer Safety Unit through an exchange of magnetic tapes.

All historical data, from the introduction of the HASS in 1976, have been converted to the system. A separate database for the HADD is maintained for all fatal accidents in England and Wales. By computing the proportion of all UK A&E attendances represented by the HASS hospitals, national estimates are derived and published annually. There are 41 article categories of home and leisure accidents covering over 1500 different products, articles and features (see Tables 2.1–2.4).

The Consumer Safety Unit analyses the data in the HASS, LASS and HADD to identify key factors. Short reports are produced, which frequently form the first stage of further research work and lead directly to initiatives for accident prevention. There are 36 Data Analyses published on products ranging from toys to bottles to Christmas decorations and sunbeds. Other projects include work on dishwasher fires, clothing flammability, domestic electrical appliances and mountain bikes. Detailed reports on 60 products are available with another 11 from the Laboratory of the Government Chemist.

Table 2.1   Home accidents in the United Kingdom

Location	Treated in Hospital %	Treated by GP %	All Medically Treated %
Home	30	40	34
Work	24	21	23
Sports	14	14	14
Road	10	8	9
Other	22	17	20

Source: Report on 1994 Accident Data and Safety Research, Consumer Safety Unit, Department of Trade and Industry.

Table 2.2 HASS: general categories of home accidents

Article Category	National Estimate (000s)
Construction feature	832
Electrical wiring/accessories	12
Lighting equipment	8
Water/sanitary system	48
Heat/cooling equipment	33
Recording/communication equipment	24
Furniture	350
Furnishings	125
Miscellaneous household item	18
Cooking/kitchen equipment	145
Washing/cleaning equipment	54
Washing/cleaning products	15
Ladder/support equipment	41
DIY, etc tools/machines	81
Garden/farm equipment	33
Sewing/knitting equipment	14
Office/school equipment	18
Building/raw materials	169
Fuel/chemical	15
Transport	76
Toy/game/novelty	39
Leisure/hobby equipment	2
Sports equipment	52
Fair/playground	20
Clothing/footware	199
Personal/care/items	74
Mobility aid	22
Carrying equipment	8
Safety equipment	14
Animal's items	6
Food/drink	119
Medicine	33
Container/wrapping	69
Person	249
Animal/insect	113
Outdoor surface	172
Plant/tree	37
Natural feature	24
Built feature	60
Miscellaneous article	131
Unspecified article	380
Total accidents	2,658

Source: *Report on 1994 Accident Data and Safety Research*, Consumer Safety Unit, Department of Trade and Industry.

Table 2.3   LASS: General categories of leisure accidents

Article Category	National Estimate (000s)
Construction feature	361
Electrical wiring/accessories	0
Lighting equipment	0
Water/sanitary system	5
Heat/cooling equipment	5
Recording/communication equipment	0
Furniture	70
Furnishings	12
Miscellaneous household item	0
Cooking/kitchen equipment	12
Washing/cleaning equipment	5
Washing/cleaning products	0
Ladder/support equipment	6
DIY, etc tools/machines	16
Garden/farm equipment	5
Sewing/knitting equipment	0
Office/school equipment	12
Building/raw materials	110
Fuel/chemical	6
Transport	273
Toy/game/novelty	12
Leisure/hobby equipment	4
Sports equipment	458
Fair/playground	72
Clothing/footware	241
Personal care/items	19
Mobility aid	15
Carrying equipment	19
Safety equipment	13
Animal's items	0
Food/drink	57
Medicine	0
Container/wrapping	23
Person	571
Animal/insect	161
Outdoor surface	925
Plant/tree	36
Natural feature	81
Built feature	116
Miscellaneous article	106
Unspecified article	703
Total accidents	3,187

Source: *Report on 1994 Accident Data and Safety Research*, Consumer Safety Unit, Department of Trade and Industry.

Table 2.4 HADD: general categories of home accidents

Categories	Number of Accidents
Baby and child furniture	8
Baby and child transport	1
Cleaning equipment	4
Cleaning products	5
Clothing and clothing accessories	65
Communication equipment	5
Constructional features of the house	604
Containers/wrappings	7
Cooking appliances	34
DIY/house maintenance	70
Dust/dirt/wood particles	0
Electric equipment	21
Flammable/corrosive liquids	12
Food and drink	359
Footwear	0
Freezing/refrigerating equipment	1
Garden equipment/tools	5
Imprecisely specified articles	17
Heating and ventilation equipment	105
Household fixtures	49
Household furnishings	23
Household furniture	177
Household linen	26
Hot liquids	73
Ignition (source)	539
Kitchen utensils	23
Laundry equipment	7
Leisure activities (adults)	0
Lighting	13
Luggage	0
Medicines/tablets	378
Miscellaneous household equipment	9
Outside environment	32
Personal items	29
Pets' articles	0
Plants and trees	6
Playthings/toys	8
Sewing/knitting	0
Stationery/writing equipment	4
Vehicles	31
Walking aids	6
Wall and floor coverings	0
Waste disposal	3
Pets/insects	0
Sports equipment	4
Unspecified	1,595
Total	4,358
Total accidents	3,841

Source: Report on 1994 Accident Data and Safety Research, Consumer Safety Unit, Department of Trade and Industry.

The European Home and Leisure Accident Surveillance System (EHLASS)

The European Home and Leisure Accident Surveillance System (EHLASS) was operated on a trial basis from 1986, in a similar way to the HASS and LASS in the UK. The Council of Ministers then established it to run for five years, from 1994 to 1999, to collect data on accidents at home and its immediate surroundings as well as during leisure activities, including sport and at school. The data comes from 11 of the HASS hospitals in the UK, from eight hospitals in France, seven each in Italy and the Netherlands, six in Portugal, five in Denmark, four each in Belgium and Greece and two in Ireland. Data is collected by means of household surveys in Germany, Spain and Luxembourg. Individual EU Member States prepare an annual EHLASS report on the basis of national data. It is possible to compare national distributions of accidents within a category, such as the product involved or the accident mechanism. Most of the countries publish their own EHLASS data, and a summary of the national reports is published by the EU Director of Consumer Policy, DG 224.

The US National Electronic Injury Surveillance System (NEISS)

The US Consumer Product Safety Act requires a National Injury Information Clearing House 'to collect, investigate, analyse, and disseminate injury data and information relating to the causes and prevention of death, injury, and illness associated with consumer products'. One of the principal resources of the Clearing House is the National Electronic Injury Surveillance System (NEISS), which operates in a similar manner to the UK's HASS and LASS.

The NEISS began operation in 1972 and gathers data from a sample of hospitals that are statistically representative of the emergency departments in the USA and its territories. Estimates are made of product-related injuries associated with, but not necessarily caused by, consumer products. Terminals in the emergency departments transmit data to a central computer with each injury cited against one or two of the 900 product codes. Each product-related injury is assigned a severity value ranging from 10 to 2516, based primarily on three factors: injury diagnosis, body part involved and disposition of the case. The estimated mean severity is an average severity value for an estimated number of injuries. Table 2.5 gives examples of the highest value recorded of the estimated mean severity, selected from some of the 15 product groupings.

Table 2.5 US National Electronic Injury Surveillance System: injuries associated with selected consumer products treated in hospital emergency departments, 1994

Product Group Example	*Estimated Mean Severity Highest Value Recorded
Nursery products	52
Toys	33
Swimming equipment	104
Barbecue equipment	73
Sound equipment	38
Cigarettes etc	189
Power lawn equipment	74
Welding, soldering, cutting tools	108
Cleaning agents	78
Cookers, etc.	102
Heaters	101

Source: US Consumer Product Safety Commission. * See text above, this page.

The Clearing House publishes hazard analyses, special studies and data summaries to identify hazards, accident patterns and types of products. The data are available in various computer formats. Among the clients of the Clearing House are manufacturers and industry associations who study the hazard patterns, consumer groups and lawyers seeking background information on injuries. About 6000 requests for information are dealt with each year.

The European Safety and Reliability Data Association

Assessing reliability and safety requires reliable and relevant data on the components and sub-assemblies that comprise the end-product. Maintenance regimes, operational and environmental factors over long surveillance times will be important. Although much of this type of data may be lurking in company records, its ready availability may be less than satisfactory.

An example of this type of database is that of AEA Technology which participates in the European Safety and Reliability Data Association (ESReDA). AEA has a failure event database of raw data drawn from specific collection campaigns, which analyses the performance of components against a variety of factors. The component reliability database provides average failure rates, failure on demand probabilities and repair times for components at different population sizes under various operating conditions. This database has 4000 component populations representing 1.3 billion component years of experience for over 300 component classifications. The components and subsystems are divided into four categories: mechanical, electrical, control and instrumentation and other.

There are a number of additional AEA databases available which cover over 14 000 accidents. They include the Major Hazards Incident Database of 6000 incidents worldwide, the Explosives Incidents Database which has about 3000 incidents, the Environmental Incident Database with 600 incidents and the Accident and Incident Database which has 2600 workplace accidents.

The EU Rapid Exchange of Information Procedure (RAPEX)

In 1978 the European Commission set up an informal information exchange system on the safety of foodstuffs which was operated, during the 1980s, on an experimental basis for nearly all consumer products. Following this, the General Product Safety

Directive 1992 formally established the Rapid Exchange of Information Procedure (RAPEX) for any dangerous consumer products. If there is a serious and immediate risk to the health and safety of consumers, which could extend beyond a Member State's national boundaries, the Commission has to be informed. The Commission will then relay the information to the relevant authorities in the other Member States and may, in exceptional circumstances, initiate an investigation of its own and convene the Committee on Product Safety Emergencies. In 1990 there were 16 notifications which rose to 96 the following year, but only from Belgium, Spain and the UK.

As the barriers to trade come down in Europe, and goods move more freely throughout the 15 countries, this procedure grows in significance for designers.

Summary

There is a surprising lack of information on those products which are responsible for accidents. In the UK and USA there are well established systems which record information on which products are *involved* in home and leisure accidents. The EU operates a similar system. These systems provide raw data for the regulatory and legislative bodies and publish reports on selected individual products. Individual databases on the reliability and safety of components and sub-assemblies are maintained by members of the European Safety and Reliability Data Association. The EU Rapid Information Exchange Procedure disseminates among Member States information on consumer products which pose a serious and immediate risk to health and safety.

3
Identification of Risks: Hazard Analysis and Risk Assessment Techniques

Introduction

We are exposed to a variety of hazards in every aspect of life: physical from the forces of nature and human activity; chemical from acute and chronic poisons; biological from infectious organisms; and psychological from social relationships. The most dramatic and most easily recognized are often the visible physical hazards because of the immediate and obvious connection between cause and effect: the fatal outcome of a lightning strike is instantaneous whereas exposure to blue asbestos can take decades to achieve the same effect.

As a result of universal media coverage of the latest disasters and the efforts of the community to cope with them, public interest in, and concern with, hazards has grown. But physicists', biologists' and psychologists' views on risks are by no means identical, while statisticians, epidemiologists, doctors and economists can each add further perspectives. In 1983 the Royal Society published a survey of risk assessment which was probably the first attempt to cover the many different disciplines involved. It was updated in 1992[1] and provides a pragmatic introduction to risk reduction, puts the subject into perspective and explains why there can be no single answer.

The report classifies risks as those

■ for which statistics of identified casualties are available

- for which there may be some evidence, but where the connection between suspected cause and injury cannot be traced
- which are experts' best estimates of probabilities of events that have yet to happen
- which were not foreseen.

All systems have a probability of failure, and engineers and scientists have to work to reduce that probability to an acceptable level. An anticipatory approach based on judgement and experience will be subject to substantial uncertainties due to the inadequacies of data and knowledge. A deterministic approach implies that there is a probability of failure that is acceptable for design purposes, without quantifying it. It incorporates implicit value judgements and describes hazards in terms of risk of failure and the associated consequences. This enables the decision on acceptability to be externalized from the design process.

A vital component of risk estimation is the identification of hazards. But this itself has a potential source of error as all the possibilities may not have been named. It is against these qualifications that this chapter must be read. It reviews some of the hazard analysis and risk assessment techniques which designers can use. Advice[2] from some years ago still has great validity today:

> Hazard analysis is a sophisticated technique for good organisations who wish to allocate their resources sensibly and improve their standards. It should not be used unless the basic management is satisfactory. If [management] do not run a 'tight ship', if the people are not trained, if there are no instructions, if no one cares or monitors, then the error rates will be much higher and hazard analysis a waste of time. First improve the management. Is the result of the hazard analysis in accordance with experience and common sense? If not, the hazard analysis must be wrong.

Hazard or risk?

First, we have to establish that 'hazard' and 'risk' are not synonyms, even if the *Oxford English Dictionary* thinks that they are. For our purposes we need more precise definitions.

Hazard   a set of conditions in the operation of a product or system with the potential for initiating an accident sequence (BS 4778 13.3.1); a potential source of harm.

Risk   the combined effect of the probability of occurrence of an undesirable event, and the magnitude of that event (BS 4778 13.3.2); a measure of the probability and severity of harm.

If we look at hazards by themselves we have no way of knowing what threat they present. We will not know what the chances are of the threat becoming a reality, or how serious the outcome would be.

The identification of hazards depends on the knowledge, experience and imagination of the analyst. Checklists of hazards are not an alternative to thinking, but should be regarded more as *aidesmémoire*. Each analyst should develop a list which concentrates on his or her company's own products. A very open mind is necessary, with a facility for lateral thinking being a considerable advantage. One may well dismiss 'flying objects' from the hazards that could be presented by a television set, but one television repair man had the sight of one eye damaged by a spring-loaded control which flew off a set he was servicing and hit him in the face.

In risk assessment, subjective values can be based on a simple scoring system and the judgement of the analyst. There are also databases (Chapter 2) which have been developed within various industries and cover a wide range of components, systems and instruments. These databases provide statistical measurements of reliability derived from a large number of actual instances. Their use needs care because of the great variety of practice in categorization and allocation, and the proprietary nature of much of the material.

Remember that hazard analysis and risk assessment techniques are aids to management. They are not a substitute for the pragmatic engineer or scientist.

Two of the principal techniques can be characterized as the top-down method and bottom-up method. In the first an adverse event is the starting point and the analyst works towards discovering what failures could cause it to happen. In the second the individual components or subsystems are examined and the consequences of a failure or a series of failures developed. The first method is Fault Tree Analysis and the second is Failure Mode and Effect Analysis.

Fault Tree Analysis (FTA)

FTA is defined as:

> The study of the possible sequence of events constituting the failure of a system using the diagrammatic method of algorithms. (BS 4778 17.9)

Originally developed by Bell Telephones in 1961, the technique was used by NASA in the space programmes of the 1960s and 1970s and has been extensively used in the nuclear industry. It is a convenient way of representing the logical connection between the failure modes of a system. The top of the tree, the top event, can be evaluated both qualitatively and quantitatively, with the aid of a computer where appropriate (see, further, Case History 19).

The first step is to define the system that is to be analysed, to prevent the tree from becoming too complex. Because a tree can only analyse one top event, a number of them may be needed for one product. A system can be divided into its phases, such as start-up, run, and shut-down, for separate analysis.

The next step is the selection of the top event, which is the undesirable event, such as a fire, explosion or the failure of a system, subsystem or assembly. The tree then develops by the identification of the logical combination of the failure modes that would result in the occurrence of the top event.

The modes of failure can have a variety of causes, such as the breakdown of an individual component, operator error, the failure of a test procedure or a maintenance programme. The failure modes are combined in a number of ways which are called gates. The most common are the OR gate and the AND gate, which represent a particular condition or failed state within the

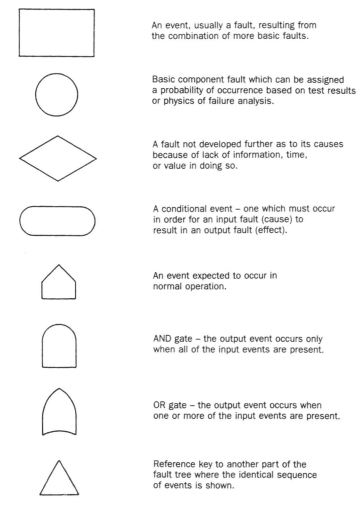

An event, usually a fault, resulting from
the combination of more basic faults.

Basic component fault which can be assigned
a probability of occurrence based on test results
or physics of failure analysis.

A fault not developed further as to its causes
because of lack of information, time,
or value in doing so.

A conditional event – one which must occur
in order for an input fault (cause) to
result in an output fault (effect).

An event expected to occur in
normal operation.

AND gate – the output event occurs only
when all of the input events are present.

OR gate – the output event occurs when
one or more of the input events are present.

Reference key to another part of the
fault tree where the identical sequence
of events is shown.

Figure 3.1   Some basic Fault Tree symbols

system. An OR gate will satisfy the logic if any one failure mode
connected to the gate exists.

For an AND gate all the failure modes feeding into the gate
must exist to satisfy the logic. There are other types of gate that
can be used, some of which have specialized applications.

Basic fault tree symbols are shown in Figure 3.1. A rectangle
is used to represent an output event caused by the inputs from
the level below; it is at the same time an input to the level above.
A circle is a basic fault event, such as a component failure or a

human error, and ends its particular branch of the tree because it has no output. A diamond symbolizes a secondary factor which could lead to the primary failure. A house represents an event that always occurs.

The analyst identifies the events on the next level down that could cause the top event, and determines whether they will happen as an AND function or an OR function. He or she continues to develop the tree in this manner, using the symbols, until the lowest possible level is reached and the basic failure event identified. Having completed the tree the analyst will now evaluate it to discover what specific actions are required and make the appropriate recommendations. Figure 3.2 is an example of a simple fault tree.

The construction of the fault tree should follow a methodical procedure by first identifying general events – that is, failure states – which, when logically combined, will result in the undesired top event. These events can be considered as the second level of the fault tree. Each event on this second level should be developed in the same methodical manner until all of the basic failure modes of the analysis have been included. These failure modes are often referred to as components of the fault tree. Computer codes exist which will convert network diagrams into fault trees.

A useful means of identifying the failure modes which should be included in the fault tree is through a Failure Modes and Effect Analysis (FMEA) (see opposite). Although an FMEA does not in itself establish the logical connection between failure modes, it is a process which traces the effects of a failure and, as such, it is a useful tool in the construction of the fault tree, particularly where the same component failure appears in more than one branch of the tree.

Failure Mode and Effect Analysis (FMEA)

The mental discipline that a designer should go through during the design process is reflected in an FMEA. It aims at anticipating potential failures so that their source can be eliminated. It is basic

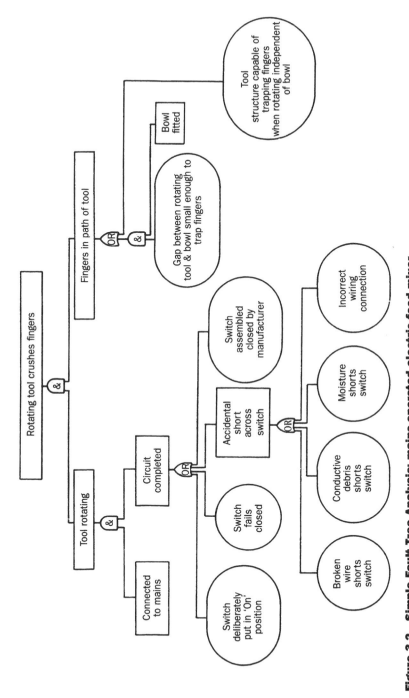

Figure 3.2 Simple Fault Tree Analysis: mains-operated electric food mixer

Source: Boswell, D. and Brewer, R., *Guide to The Management of Product Safety and Occupational Health and Safety* (draft BSI publication).

hazard analysis which was originally developed from reliability estimating procedures, to which risk considerations have been added (see, further, Case History 2). FMEA is defined as:

> The study of the potential failures that might occur in any part of a system to determine the probable effect of each on all the other parts of the system and on probable operational success. (BS 4778 17.7)

To be correct we should distinguish between FMEA and FMECA – that is Failure Mode Effect and Criticality Analysis – which is defined as:

> The study of the potential failures that might occur in any part of a system to determine the probable effect of each on all the other parts of the system and on probable operational success, the results of which are ranked in order of seriousness. (BS 4778 17.8)

The difference between FMEA and FMECA lies in the ranking of the results, which is part of the latter exercise but not the former. However, we will follow common practice and use FMEA to cover both techniques.

Many companies claim to use FMEA, although fewer probably use it in reality. The pioneers of the technique were in the defence, aerospace, automotive and nuclear industries. Today companies in such industries stipulate that their suppliers should use FMEA as part of their contractual requirements. Often a procedure document will lay down how the FMEA should be performed, who should be part of the evaluation team, the method of results presentation and how corrective action is to be effected.

An FMEA is not an addition to an engineer's workload but a disciplined technique that enables him to perform his job more effectively. A good FMEA is one which:

- identifies known and potential failure modes
- identifies the causes and effects of each failure mode
- give each identified failure mode a priority number according to the probability and severity of its risk and the chance of detection before failure occurs
- provides for corrective action.

Table 3.1 Failure Mode and Effect Analysis: Part of vehicle engine mounting system

Component	Failure Mode	Effect of Failure	Cause of Failure	1	2	3	4	Corrective Action
Tie bar bracket	Bracket fractures	Stabilizing function of tie bar removed. All motion of engine transferred to mountings.	Inadequate specification of hole-to-edge distance	1	7	10	70	Test suitability of specification.
	Bracket corrodes	As above	Inadequate specification for preparation of tie bracket.	1	5	10	50	Test suitability of specification.
	Fixing bolts loosen	As above	Bolt torque inadequately specified.	5	5	8	200	Test for loosening.
			Bolt material or thread type inadequate.	1	5	10	50	Test suitability of specification.
	Fixing bolts fracture	As above	Bolts incorrectly specified.	4	7	10	280	Test bolts for fracture.
			Bolt torque specification too high.	5	7	8	280	Test suitability of torque specification.
	Bracket bends	As above	Material thickness inadequately specified.	1	5	10	50	Test suitability of specification.
			No flexibility in bracket to the bar when rotational loads applied.	7	5	10	350	Redesign bush to allow for flexibility under rotational loads.

Notes:

1 = Occurrence: *Score:* 1 = very low probability; 10 = near certainty.
2 = Severity. *Score:* 1 = minor nuisance; 10 = serious safety hazard.
3 = Chance of detection. *Score:* 1 = very high probability; 10 = very low probability
4 = Risk priority number. 1 × 2 × 3

Special forms and ranking tables are used to carry out an FMEA. A simple example is given in Tables 3.1 and 3.2, and the key elements of the information it contains are described below.

- **Failure mode**. The analyst has to anticipate how the part being considered could fail. It is not a question of whether it *will* fail but rather how it *could* fail. Consider a tie bar bracket which is part of a vehicle engine mounting system which stabilizes all movement of the engine. The bracket could have a number of failure modes – for example bracket fractures, bracket corrosion, loosening fixing bolts, fracturing fixing bolts, bending bracket and so on. These are all listed and each possibility is then analysed under the following headings.

- **Effect of failure**. The result of the first failure mode, of the bracket fracturing, would be the removal of its stabilizing function and the transfer of all motion of the engine to its mountings. The same effect would be produced by the other failure modes, but the cause would not necessarily be the same in each case.

- **Cause of failure**. The analyst has to anticipate what could cause the failure mode to occur and describe the conditions that bring it about. In the example the brackets could fracture because of an inadequate specification of hole-to-edge distance for the fixing bolts. The cause of the bracket corroding could be the inadequate specification for the preparation of the bracket, such as the type of coating.

- **Occurrence of failure**. The analyst must now use his or her knowledge and experience to estimate the probability of the bracket actually failing. He or she has to assess the likelihood of occurrence using an evaluation scale of 1 to 10, with 1 indicating a very low probability of occurrence and 10 indicating a near certainty of occurrence. The score for the first failure mode in the example is given as 1: very low probability of occurrence, theoretically possible only.

- **Severity of failure**. The question here is: what is the consequence of failure? How severe will it be? The same evaluation scale is used, with 1 indicating a minor nuisance and 10 a serious consequence. The score in the example is given as 7:

Table 3.2 Failure Mode and Effect Analysis ranking table: Tie bar bracket, stabilizing all movement engine

Rating	Occurrence	Severity	Detection
1	Very low probability of occurrence; thereoretically possible only.	Visual non-functional failure only. Hardly noticeable.	Almost certain to be detected during test or inspection before item reaches user.
2	Low probability of occurrence during design life.		Very likely to be detected.
3			Likely to be detected.
4			
5	Moderate.	Failure causes reduction in engine mounting stabilization and requires attention.	Could be detected.
6			
7		Failure causes total loss of engine mounting stabilization. Further use could cause eventual safety-critical failure of engine mountings.	
8	High.		Unlikely to be detected.
9		Vehicle unusable but not safety-critical.	Very unlikely to be detected before item reaches customer.
10	Very high probability of occurrence. Very likely to occur during design life.	Safety-critical failure. Vehicle off road after catastrophic failure.	Almost impossible to detect before item reaches customer.

failure causes total loss of engine mounting stabilization. Further use could cause eventual safety-critical failure.

■ **Detection of failure**. The analyst has to estimate the chance of a potential failure being detected before the end-user finds it. The evaluation scale is still 1 to 10 but the weighting is reversed, with 1 indicating a very high probability that failure would be detected before it reached the end-user and 10 showing a very low probability of detection. The score in the example is given as 10: almost impossible to detect before the item reaches the customer.

■ **Risk priority number**. This is the product of the estimates of occurrence, severity and detection and provides a relative priority of the failure mode. The higher the number the more serious is the failure mode. The list of risk priority numbers will highlight the top priority areas for action. The risk priority number for the failure of the bracket caused by inadequate hole specification is $1 \times 7 \times 10 = 70$.

■ **Corrective action**. The follow-up is critical to the use of an FMEA. The analyst must provide sound corrective actions to deal with the potential failure modes that have been identified in the analysis.

The above example is a simple explanation of an FMEA but more sophisticated variations are used, some developed to meet the requirements of particular products. Fault Tree Analysis (see above) can provide a filter with which to discover the most critical failure modes before applying FMEA. The classification of failure frequency is at the heart of FMEA, and the most reliable information will come from the databases (Chapter 2). Care is needed to establish that the particular application and life cycle under analysis are compatible with the database failure rate. A simple classification system can be used for a first pass to isolate the critical areas for more detailed analysis.

Severity scales can be developed to fit the product line of the company. The extremes of a scale are usually fairly easy to determine, but the levels in between may require much consideration. If a scale of commercial damage is measured in money for the purposes of graduation, the severity of the loss of £1 million will depend on the financial viability of the company. The threshold of ruin is unique to each company. A multinational would scarcely notice such a sum but it could spell disaster for a small company.

The severity of an injury can be measured in a number of ways, such as cost, time off work or the assignment of a medical value; the UK Home Accident Surveillance System and the US National Electronic Injury Surveillance System use different methods for measuring severity (see Chapter 2).

There is another factor that can be taken into account – the degree of imperilment can be classified where appropriate. The concept is concerned with the spontaneity of failure. Some failures are progressive and give plenty of warning that they are going to happen, so that their effect is limited. Other failures occur instantaneously and produce a catastrophe without any warning at all. Yet other failures present no hazard whether they occur slowly or spontaneously. One ranking of imperilment has four levels:

- rapid or spontaneous – no effect
- sufficient warning for the prudent
- sufficient warning for the skilled who can avoid injury
- instantaneous – no evasive action possible.

The preparation of an FMEA for each possible failure mode can be a lengthy process. It may present some ideas that are unusual to many engineers. Its aim is to show, in a logical form, the consequences of failure so that corrective action can be taken. It can open a previously undiscovered window to allow a new perspective to be obtained on product safety.

The safety profile

This technique was originally intended for small components, but it can be extended for application to equipment. The basis is a grid with ordinates of probability and criticality.

To prepare a product safety profile all potential injury-producing failure modes, their cause and their effect are identified.

For each mode, or event, two factors are established: the probability and the hazard index. These are put together graphically to provide the safety profile of the product. The more complete the input data the more accurate will be the profile, although this may mean testing to failure rather than the usual tendency to test for conformance to specification. The first step is to define all possible failures that could cause a safety hazard, and here an FMEA is valuable. The effect of each potential failure mode is ranked for probability and hazard: where statistical data are not available an estimate is made using, for instance, 1, 2, 3, 4 and 5 as ranking levels for very low, low, medium, high and very high.

For each failure mode the hazard index is entered on the grid along the x axis and the probability of failure is plotted on the y axis. The most serious failure modes will gather in the upper right-hand corner of the matrix and the least serious in the lower left-hand corner.

The size and shape of the profile demonstrates the degree of safety of the component or product under analysis. There are a number of variations that can be used in the construction of a safety profile; such as the inclusion of a hazard index as a function of time so that the hazard increases as the time available to avoid injury decreases. Figure 3.3 shows a simple example of a product safety profile.

The Delphi technique

In Greek mythology the earth was flat and circular, with Greece occupying the middle and Delphi at its centre. The great temple of Apollo in Delphi housed a sacred stone, which was believed to mark the actual centre of the world.

There were many oracles in Greece, but the Delphi oracle was the most famous. It exercised supreme control, and the phenomenal expansion of Greece was inspired and directed largely by its priestess, who pronounced her cryptic revelations or counsels. The members of elite Delphi families sat around a tripod occupied by the priestess and transmitted her utterances

Hazard letter	Hazards	Product Life Phase Risk Rankings									Product
		Acceptance testing	Transport	Storage	Installation	Normal operation	Misuse/Failure	Maintenance	Disposal	Other	Notes: Key to Rank No's Rank No's 2/5 indicate occurence risk 2 and criticality risk 5. Worst combination is underlined. *Causes & Comments*
A	Electric shock	2/5	-	-	2/5	1/5	3/5	2/5	-	-	With rear cover off
B	Fire	1/2	1/2	1/5	1/2	1/5	2/5	1/2	1/5	-	Organic materials in cabinet & components
C	Explosion	1/4	2/4	-	1/4	1/3	1/4	1/4	2/4	-	Damage to CRT
D	Toxic fumes	1/2	-	-	1/2	1/3	1/3	1/3	3/3	-	Overheating or burning of organic materials
E	Radiation	-	-	-	-	-	1/2	-	-	-	Not normally hazardous
F	Harmful substances	-	-	-	-	-	-	-	1/3	-	Contamination of environment due to careless disposal
G	Cutting/crushing	1/2	3/3	-	3/2	-	-	2/3	2/3	-	Handling into position
H	Surface temperature	1/2	-	-	1/2	1/3	1/3	1/3	-	-	With rear cover off
I	Psychological	-	-	-	-	5/5	-	-	-	-	Harmful programmes, eg incitement to violence

Analysis date

Recommended actions:

i)   Hazard warnings for letters A, B, C, D, F, G, H.

ii) All organic materials to have Oxygen Index greater than 27.

iii) Fit cut-outs activated by smoke-detector, overload current, excess temperature.

iv) MD to receive and initial a copy of this Safety Profile.

Harm occurrence / Higher risk

	1	2	3	4	5
5					I
4					
3			DG		A
2		E		C	B
1			FH		

Lower risk — Harm criticality

Figure 3.3   Product safety profile: mains-operated TV receiver
Source: Boswell, D. and Brewer, R., *Guide to The Management of Product Safety and Occupational Health and Safety*, (draft BSI publication).

to posterity. This interpretation was necessary because a Delphi utterance was one which had ambiguity associated with it.

Today, in business, decision-making under conditions of uncertainty is often based on a group judgement. The board will have to reach agreement on critical questions for which inadequate information is available. The most common way of obtaining these group judgements is by the members sitting around the same table and reaching a consensus by face-to-face interactions. This has the disadvantages of conflicting schedules, time constraints, geographical separation, dominance by individuals, irrelevant communication and the group pressure for conformity.

To overcome these disadvantages the Delphi technique was developed by the Rand Corporation in the United States to enable geographically dispersed warfare experts to forecast military developments. Because of its confidential application, it remained a classified technique until the 1960s. Since then its use has spread, with organizations adopting it for forecasting future events in the USA, Canada, Europe and Japan.

The primary objective of the Delphi technique is to determine whether a group of experts, through anonymous and carefully structured interactions, can arrive at consensus about an uncertain state. It is a technique which uses group synthesis in an attempt to reach a decision.

According to one of the Delphi originators two options are available when one is working on a problem under conditions of uncertainty with insufficient data, incomplete decision theory and a high order of complexity.

> . . . we can either wait indefinitely until we have an adequate theory enabling us to deal with sociometric and political problems as confidently as we do with problems in physics and chemistry, or we can make the most of an admittedly unsatisfactory situation and try to obtain the relevant intuitive insights of experts and then use their judgements as systematically as possible.

The Delphi technique is a method of eliciting and refining group judgements. The rationale for the procedure is primarily the age-old adage: two heads are better than one where exact knowledge is not available. The procedure has three features.

1 Opinions of members of the group are obtained by formal questionnaire.
2 Interaction is effected by a systematic exercise conducted in several iterations, with carefully controlled feedback between rounds.
3 The group opinion is defined as an appropriate aggregate of individual opinions of the final round.

The disadvantage of the Delphi technique is that it does not lend itself to all types of decisions: a single decision-maker can probably make the best decisions in routine matters. The success of the method depends on selecting a suitable panel of experts which can be difficult, and it can take several weeks to complete all the questionnaire rounds in some applications, although the use of data processing equipment can help.

The basic feature of the technique is the anonymous filling out of questionnaires by members of the selected group; responses can be grouped statistically according to the median score. With repeated measurement the range of response will decrease and converge towards the mid-range of distribution, and the total group response will successively move towards the 'correct' answer.

Feedback and iteration are important in developing the application of the technique, with respondents in the second and subsequent rounds being asked to justify extreme positions. The number of iterations will depend on the degree of group consensus required, but generally they range from one to six. Failure to reach consensus may be as informative as its attainment in some situations.

Published industrial applications of Delphi include forecasts on the market for new and existing products, technological and social events, evaluation of research and development projects, availability and cost of materials, labour and capital, and changes in government attitudes.

There are a number of versions of the Delphi technique, and it is important to use that which most closely matches the problem. For instance, a simplified Delphi method has been used to evaluate the risks presented by hazards associated with product failure. Here it is useful in revealing which are the perceived most serious exposures facing a company in an area where there are no hard data, or where resources are not available to obtain them. The occurrence of such situations will increase for companies concerned with liability-sensitive products. Where database (Chapter 2) failure rates are available one of the other techniques may be more applicable.

The risks can be scored for each hazard using a 1–5 scale for probability and severity, with interpretations of each level to give guidance to the degree involved for each score.

Probability	Score	Severity
Very high	5	Very high
(one in ten)		(£1 000 000)
High	4	High
Medium	3	Medium
Low	2	Low
Very Low	1	Very Low
(one in a million)		(£100)

In some cases it is sufficient to ask for a probability response, while in others a severity response is a valuable addition. By multiplying the probability by the severity a risk index is obtained, which can help in ranking the different hazards by the degree of risk they present to the company. Such an approach enables the company to tackle the most serious exposures first, always bearing in mind that particular attention should be paid to hazards which have very high probabilities or severities, even though their risk indexes may be low.

The Delphi technique was used during a product safety audit with the board of a company manufacturing a beverage dispenser. The questions covered a number of areas, but the one of interest is that which dealt with the hazards of electrocution and fire. It was agreed that the electrocution of an employee of a company in which a dispenser was installed was a hazard. Also, there had been occasions on which a dispenser had caught fire (due to a design defect) on a customer's premises, fortunately with comparatively little damage to property and none to people.

Individually, the board members were asked to assess the probability and severity of the risks of electrocution and fire due to a design defect or a manufacturing error. The one to five scoring table shown above was used. A wide range of scores was revealed, with the director responsible for design assessing the risk as very low and two of his colleagues assessing it as high. In the context of a product safety audit, the Delphi technique proved its value by demonstrating that a risk area had been identified which demanded the board's urgent attention to reach agreement on the degree of exposure that faced the company.

The technique can be applied in a very sophisticated manner to obtain a view from a large number of respondents using advanced computerized and statistical methods. An example is a study of systems and data security where the objective was to identify and rate factors that should be considered by managers with twin responsibilities: integrity for data and private information, and protection and fallback for computer systems and installations and online systems.

A total of 266 factors affecting systems and data security was identified in the preliminary research. At the first stage, initial ratings of these factors (in terms of their importance now and in four years' time) were obtained from an international panel of 100 specialists in the field.

At stage two, these ratings were then refined in the context of the consensus views that emerged at stage one. The panel's responses and comments were used as a basis for developing comprehensive checklists. Significant variations between sectors were also noted. From an appraisal of these variations, it was shown how the checklists should be modified and adjusted in different parts of the world and different sectors of activity.

Similar methods have been linked to group discussions and interviewing techniques to add perspective and depth to the information for decision-making. The methods have been used successfully in studies of technological markets as well as in studies conducted within large and dispersed organizations.

A word of caution is necessary. The Delphi technique does not produce scientific or optimal results; it is a heuristic device and, as such, is a valuable management tool. By itself the technique does not make decisions, but it can aid the decision-making process.

Hazard and Operability Study (HAZOP)

This is a systematic technique for identifying hazards and operability problems, originally developed in the 1960s for use in chemical plants. It can be applied to process plants already in operation or during the procedure for their design. Used during the initial phase of the procedure it can often lead to a safer detailed design.

The objective is to

- produce a full description of the plant and process including the intended design conditions
- review systematically every part of the process to discover how variations from the normal operating conditions and intended design can occur
- identify which consequences such deviations will have on the process and its output and decide whether these deviations can lead to hazards or operability problems.

A HAZOP is carried out by a risk assessment team who are expert in the process they are assessing. Most design errors occur because the team fail to apply the knowledge they already possess, not because they did not have the knowledge in the first place. The HAZOP provides an opportunity to go through a design line-by-line and deviation-by-deviation so that nothing is overlooked. The team could include, for example, the design engineer, process engineer, commissioning manager, instrument design engineer and research scientist with an independent chairman. By brainstorming on a 'What can go wrong?' basis, the team identify the potential hazards and operability problems and then establish a programme of action to eliminate them.

In practice, HAZOP exercises can become extremely complex as a plant expands and the risk landscape widens. At the same time quality systems and tougher safety legislation create a need for more thorough and copiously documented studies. The danger is that the team can spend too much time and energy wrestling with data and too little on the potential hazards and remedies. The appointment of an outside chairman and the use of a software package can ensure that the discussions are more focused by integrating worksheets, review documents and tracking sheets for ranking severity and frequency levels.

Hazard Analysis Critical Control Point (HACCP)

The principle here is to anticipate hazards in a production process that could make the product defective and identify the points at which they can be controlled. It received much attention following the Food Safety Act 1990 which introduced the requirement that a defendant in a food-related lawsuit should be able to prove that he or she took 'all reasonable precautions' and that 'he exercised all due diligence to avoid committing the offence'. The ability to prove these requirements may be met by HACCP. The principles can also have a wide application outside the food industry.

As in the HAZOP, a team is established from specialists with the relevant qualifications and experience. The initial step is formally to define the operation to be studied and then examine the stages at which hazards to the product could arise. The risks for each hazard are quantified and the associated control points established. These are for control and not just for the supply or recording of information. Criteria must be available to indicate whether the controls are functioning correctly, and regular checks and reviews are essential to prevent complacency setting in.

Summary

A hazard is a potential for harm, while risk is a measure of its probability and severity if it occurs. There are a number of hazard analysis and risk assessment techniques which are valuable aids to the management of design risks. Two of the more sophisticated ones are Fault Tree Analysis and Failure Mode and Effect Analysis. The safety profile is suitable for small components and the Delphi technique helps decision-making under conditions of uncertainty. HACCP and the HAZOP are ways of anticipating hazards and establishing methods of controlling them.

References

1 *Risk: Analysis, Perception and Management*, (1992), Report of a Royal Society Study Group, London.
2 Kletz, T.A. (1981), 'Hazard analysis – the manager and the expert, *Reliability Engineering* **2** (1).

4
Reducing Product Design Risks: Standards and Management Information for Design Safety

Introduction

This book is concerned specifically with design safety, rather than the overall management of design – important though that is. The two British Standards below give guidance to the general framework of design management. Earlier we examined some of the tools available to the designer to help ensure the safety of the product. They can be slotted into place according to the management system adopted for a particular project. This chapter concentrates on some critical factors that must be addressed if safety is to be achieved in the design process.

Standards for the management of design

There are two complementary standards which deal with the management of design: BS 7000 and BS EN ISO 9000. They are both general in their approach and do not address safety specifically, although it can be read into virtually every line. They are briefly reviewed here to provide background.

Guide to managing product design: BS 7000 (1989)

This is but a short, basic introduction comprising 18 pages of text. The Standard 'provides guidance'; 'it is not a specification' and 'is complementary to BS 5750 Part 1'. It sets out some general management principles and techniques (although it does not describe the techniques themselves) for senior management, project managers and designers. There is no intention to give comprehensive information on the procedures to meet the statutory requirements for health and safety or product liability.

The Standard sets out the following principles.

- Responsibility for product design should be in the hands of a member of the board of a manufacturing company.
- Corporate objectives should be communicated to all concerned, and design managers should be trained in general management techniques.
- The object of design management is to provide a product design that meets the design brief. The necessary resources must be made available, with the associated implementation and control for design and development, and evaluation in a formal design review.
- Guidance at project level begins by setting the objectives – namely, the product concept which has to be assessed before it is expanded into a project proposal, a feasibility study and a design brief. The latter is the definitive statement to the designer of what is required. Project plans follow, with project control and a final project evaluation.

The Standard is simple and so wide in its possible application that it is difficult to gain any concrete advice from it. To those who need a broad overview of what could be involved it will provide an introduction to the areas requiring attention.

Further Standards in the BS 7000 series are: Part 3 (1994) 'Guide to managing service design' and Part 10 (1995) 'Glossary of terms used in design management'.

BS EN ISO 9001 (1994)

Often referred to as ISO 9000, this Standard is based on a series of generic Standards issued as BS 5750 in 1987 for a quality management system and not for a product. They are:

- **BS EN ISO 9000** which defines the basic concept and method of operation of management systems
- **BS EN ISO 9001** which defines the management systems for organizations that both design and manufacture products
- **BS EN ISO 9002** which defines the management systems for organizations manufacturing to customer-defined designs
- **BS EN ISO 9003** which defines the management systems where simple quality control will control product conformity
- **BS EN ISO 9004** which provides guidance as to the use of the standard in specific areas of business and specific situations.

The main Standards have, where appropriate, identical clauses. Only BS EN ISO 9001 deals with management systems for design. It outlines the common, wide range of key management factors needed to ensure that product quality conforms to the agreed specification. It does not include the specification itself, but rather sets out how to make products that will conform to the one that has been chosen.

In BS EN ISO 9001 there is a requirement for a design/ development programme with assigned responsibilities and resources; the identification and control of the interfaces between organization and technical aspects; the preparation and maintenance of drawings; consideration of regulatory require- ments; and the establishment of a design review system. The Standard emphasizes the need for a design system to have docu- mented procedures for control and verification. This will identify and coordinate the means to achieve the design task. The design *input* specifies what the customer expects, including safety, which is considered below. The design *output* communicates what is to be achieved. The revision of the Standard in 1994 introduced a new clause making design *reviews* mandatory; these are con- sidered below. A design must be *verified* to ensure that it not only meets the design input but also is capable of being manufactured and satisfying the customer. The 1994 revision introduced a new clause for design *validation* 'to ensure that the product conforms to defined user needs and/or requirement'. Case Histories 2, 8 and 15 illustrate the importance of design in safety.

TickIT

This is a special scheme for software. Promoted by the Department of Trade and Industry, it provides guidance for the construction and formal assessment of software quality, using a quality management system of certification to BS EN ISO 9001. Under the product liability laws,

> . . . software producers might be held liable for any injury, death or damage to personal property resulting from faulty software. Mitigating circumstances may well be that accepted 'good practice' was used during the development process. Certification to ISO 9001 could be considered evidence of good practice.

TickIT promotes quality management systems within the context of Total Quality Management. It is principally a certification scheme but its primary purpose is to stimulate developers into achieving product quality.

Speaking at the British Association Meeting in 1995, Professor Bev Littlewood of the Centre for Software Reliability at the City University in London stated that checking software safety for failsafe operation is beyond modern technology. Many computer systems use hundreds of mathematical codes and their reliability depends on the skills of a software designer. Nevertheless bugs can emerge with catastrophic effects, and systems to check software reliability are incapable of spotting all the millions of circumstances in which a bug might cause a malfunction. Failures could be hidden by industry and companies which blame human error.[2]

Design input

According to the Standard, the product will be specified in engineering, scientific or technical terms in accordance with the design management system in force. A number of different disciplines will make a contribution including purchasing, production, reliability, service, marketing and perhaps a legal and a customer's representative. Here we examine some of the areas that can affect the safety of the design.

Hazard analysis and risk assessment

There can be a requirement to develop documentary evidence of the application of one of the hazard analysis and risk assessment techniques described in Chapter 3. These may be used during the design review process itself and/or on the final product design and will show that a positive attempt was made to tackle the question of safety in a logical and structured manner. Furthermore, in any subsequent product liability case it would help towards proving that all due diligence was exercised and all reasonable steps taken.

One of the major vehicle producers categorizes its bought-in components according to their safety-criticality. The manufacturers of the parts that present the greatest risks have to supply a Failure Mode Effects Analysis using the vehicle manufacturer's own version of the technique. A large supermarket chain has a significant proportion of own-label products which are manufactured to the supermarket's specifications by third parties. One of the requirements is that the manufacturers must have documentary evidence of an active Hazard Analysis Critical Control Point programme.

After the *Amoco Cadiz* disaster in 1982, the Surveyor-General of the Marine Division of the Department of Trade strongly recommended that the design of the steering gear of large tankers should undergo a Fault Tree Analysis (see Case History 19). This was because of the basic weakness of the single hydraulic circuit whose failure would cause loss of steering. A very large international conglomerate, with several hundred industrial companies worldwide, used a modified Delphi technique to classify them for risk. This enabled it to select, for product safety audits, companies which would concentrate on the management controls adopted for the hazards of design and manufacture.

It may be possible to nominate potential hazards and specify the acceptable risks that they can present. Electrical products can specify a minimum time for a safety cut-out to operate or for the event which would trigger its action. Food, drink or cosmetics can have maximum permitted levels of named micro-organisms. A mechanical toy can define the maximum size of permitted openings to prevent access by, and injury to, inquisitive fingers. A self-assembly DIY product can have a design requirement to make incorrect and dangerous assembly impossible. The maximum emergency stopping distance for a vehicle can be stipulated. Selected fail-to-safer modes can be specified.

The end-user and the environment

An analysis of who is going to use the product is essential, as this could influence the extent of the safeguards that have to be incorporated. If the end-user has limited powers of discrimination or awareness of danger the design must accommodate this. A child or a geriatric will need more protection than a young, healthy executive. The General Product Safety Directive makes specific reference in particular of the need to be aware of the risks to children (Article 2 (b)). If the end-user is to be trained in the application of the product, as happens in some industrial applications (see Case History 10, for example), then different assumptions can be made.

Ethnic considerations have to be taken into account, especially regarding language and the understanding of warning signs. If members of an ethnic minority are to use the product this should be included in the end-user analysis 3.

The environment of use is also important. It may be necessary to specify, where appropriate, extremes of temperature, humidity, sunlight, vibration, noise, pressure and so on. The proximity of children and animals may be significant as may be the length of time that the product will operate unattended.

The analysis of the end-user and the environment of use should help to reveal the potential consequences of failure. People do stupid things – and that includes the highly educated as well as the less bright. People have been known to use rotary mowers to trim hedges, to use knives to free bread jammed in the toaster and even to use petrol to urge on a recalcitrant fire.

In order to ensure the safety of the end-user, another requirement may be to design a product so that it cannot do certain things; in this way designing for product safety can be both positive and negative. In defining the end-user and the environment of use a method for including some creative thinking may be helpful. For example, consideration of the following checklist of human hazards may repay study and investigation.

Ignorance	Physical skills
Overqualification	Horseplay
Boredom	Improper or insufficient training
Loafing	Alcohol
Daydreaming	Drugs
Negligence	Physical limitation
Carelessness	Sickness
Indifference	Exhaustion
Supervisory direction	Emotional distress
Overproduction	Disorientation
Poor judgement	Personal conflicts
Short cuts	Vandalism

The manner and the circumstances of use can be approached in a similar way. The following modes of product usage show some of the ways in which a product can be treated by the end-user.

Intended operation or use	Industrial use
Unintended operation or use	Assembly
Expected operation or use	Set-up
Misuse	Installation
Emergency use	Certification
Abuse	Testing
Inspection	Storage

Maintenance	Shipping
Service	Modification
Repair	Starting, stopping
Cleaning	Changing modes of operation
Packaging	Isolation
Recreational use	Disposal
Commercial use	Salvaging

Promotional material

If a company wishes to make specific claims for the product regarding safety in, say, performance this should be made known right at the outset. In this way the design can be developed to accommodate the claim as an integral part of the process. If the public were led, by advertising and promotional material, to believe that a product was especially safe it could be disastrous if a user were injured because of a design defect (see Case History 4).

Some products – a chainsaw, for instance – are dangerous by their nature but the benefits to society outweight the risks, providing that the dangers are clearly made known to the end-user. With such products the provision of warnings can become critical to the overall safety of the product, and these sensitive areas should be identified in advance and included in the design input.

Product standards and codes of practice

All relevant standards, codes of practice and customarily accepted practices of a particular industry must be met. But these are minimal from a design point of view and should be thought of as floors rather than ceilings. The standards of other countries should be examined, even if the product will not be sold abroad. It is always an advantage to be able to influence the course of events and having representation on the standard-making body could be helpful in forecasting future trends.

Many standards are concerned with performance and measurement and have nothing to do with safety at all. The design input should include a review of relevant standards, but it should not be assumed that compliance will result in a safe product (see Case Histories 1 and 2).

Legal requirements

There are two sources of legally required standards: UK legislation and EU Directives. Unlike many standards and codes of practice these have to be followed. Sometimes UK legislation will adopt a British Standard and make it mandatory. For instance, no crash-helmet can be sold in the UK unless it conforms to the relevant British Standard. Similarly, EU Directives are increasingly adopting 'essential requirements' (see Chapter 8).

A legal requirement can come about in a different way. If a product is being designed for a customer the contract may say that certain standards must be met. The contract may incorporate a specification for the product and, here, product safety criteria will need to be examined with care.

Expressions such as 'presents no danger to the user' or 'safe for use in the home' have no finite meaning (see Chapter 1). It may be necessary to define the level of safety required and include this in the design input.

Litigation information

A review of relevant cases concerning the product and personal injury or damage can be rewarding, when the final design is being developed. This will give specific information on what has gone wrong in the past and whether a defect was attributable to a failure in design, manufacture or warnings. By far the majority of design defect claims are settled out of court, which means that case law is merely the tip of the iceberg (see Case Histories 1, 2, 4, 8, 9 and 12).

The company's insurer or broker may be able to present relevant information in support of the case law. Although insurers have remarkably few detailed data in this field readily available, a special survey may be of assistance, particularly if the insurer has its own risk management department.

In-house product information

Just as it is necessary to gather information about the product from outside the company, it is also necessary to carry out a similar exercise internally. The obvious is too often overlooked because of its everyday presence. It was said of one company, 'It did not have 20 years' experience in the production of a certain product line . . . it had two years' experience, ten different times'. The company continually repeated the same mistakes and failed to learn from its experiences (cf. also Case History 17).

In-house product information relating to safety will be available only if a determined attempt is made to collect it. Each function should maintain a file on product safety as a matter of course. An alternative, in a bigger organization, is to apply the services of an information scientist or the technical library to maintain such information.

A valuable source will be complaints received by the company. These should be regularly collated, analysed and circulated to top management. The analysis should be carried out in a manner that exposes the cause of the complaint. If the product is implicated the defect that caused the complaint should be ascribed to one of three possible sources: design, manufacturing, or failure ot instruct or warn. Another source of information is the reports of service engineers. These should be treated in a similar manner to complaints (see, further, Case History 9).

An in-house information review should be prepared by each function on the safety record of previous products and form part of the support data of the design input.

Reliability

Reliability is defined as 'the ability of an item to perform a required function under stated conditions for a stated period of time'. The reliability requirements of the new product have an important place in the design input for these may influence its safety. Some type of reliability specification will be needed if the trade-off with maintainability is to be achieved without affecting product safety. This can be a difficult area to chart and at the design input stage it may be an advantage to allow some flexibility.

At a later stage in development more specific information will become available from feasibility testing, evaluation testing and environmental testing. Safety-critical parts can be identified so that particular attention can be paid to them in the design process. These will be the parts that would lead to conditions hazardous to the user should they fail. In some products it may be possible to weight different parts according to their potential danger.

Scientific and technical knowledge

If a product has a design defect which causes damage, a court will want to discover whether the manufacturer ought to have seen that the dangerous nature of the product was the probable outcome of the design. One expert[3] says:

> In most European countries, the conduct of the manufacturer is to be judged by reference not only to his actual scientific knowledge but also his constructive knowledge, i.e. the means of knowledge available to him when the product was under development – commonly called the 'state of the art'. He will be taken to have constructive knowledge of facts which are public knowledge within the industry and of which he ought to have been aware, whether by consulting the relevant scientific literature or appropriate experts . . . However, if the producer does everything which can reasonably be expected of him, but still does not discover the existence of a defect, then under fault liability principles, the 'development risk' falls upon the consumer rather than the producer.

This defence is to be found in the Directive on Liability for Defective Products. Article 7(e) which says that a producer has a defence under the Directive if he can prove

> . . . that the state of scientific and technical knowledge at the time when he put the product into circulation was not such as to enable the existence of the defect to be discovered. . . .

If the design requires a scientific or technical breakthrough then uncertainty in incorporating it into the product has to exist.

In such a case, additional risk analysis techniques are required during the design process and should be specified in the design input.

Packaging, warehousing and distribution

With some products these factors can be important to their safety. The regulations that apply to particular products should be given in the design input; for example, there are 20 Directives concerned with food packaging. The design may also have to accommodate certain packaging constraints. One company had to ship catamaran hulls overseas by container, so the container size determined the hull dimensions to ensure safe distribution. Temperature-controlled warehousing and distribution may be specified for some products to prevent deterioration.

Other factors

Product safety apart, the design input should take the form of a comprehensive document. An idea of the factors that can be involved is gained from the following:

Peformance	Size and weight
Quantity and manufacture	Aesthetics, appearance
Maintenance	Materials
Environment	Product lifespan
Politics	Competition
Standards and specifications	Quality and reliability
Ergonomic aspects	Shelf life
Customer	Process
Timescale	Testing
Target product cost	Company constraints
Packaging	Marketing constraints
Shipping	Patents

The danger is that product safety will be swamped by the many important activities that are needed to develop a new product. Unfortunately, product safety is not glamorous; to most non-technical people it can be a negative concept. It must be established as an activity in its own right with its own rightful demands on resources.

Summary

The management of design is dealt with in a general way by two Standards: BS 7000 and BS EN ISO 9001. The 'design input' will specify the product in engineering, scientific or technical terms but should include, in addition, a number of other important factors. These include hazard analysis and risk assessment, analysis of the end-user and the environment of use, promotional material, product standards and codes of practice, legal requirements, litigation information, in-house product information, reliability data, scientific and technical knowledge and packaging, warehousing and distribution.

References

1 Department of Trade and Industry (1992), *Guide to Software Quality Management System Construction and Certification using EN 29 000*, London: HMSO.
2 *The Times*, 16 September 1995.
3 Hodges, C. J. S. (ed.) (1993), *Product Liability: European Laws and Practice*, London: Sweet & Maxwell.

5
Design Review Systems

Introduction

There must be a formal documented procedure to manage design, with built-in checks and balances. The Standards mentioned in Chapter 4 give some general guidance but, because they are applicable to every situation, little in the way of hard fact. For example, the BS EN ISO 9000 series has been approved for over 45 000 organizations worldwide; they include legal, dental, medical and architectural practices, a dating agency, insurance brokers, a university, risk management consultants, hotels and manufacturers of all types and sizes.

It would seem that companies organize design management in an individual manner to suit their own particular operation.

A core of good techniques

A report on product development in 18 companies showed the need to pay attention to the *process* of innovation, rather than just the product itself. A PA Consulting Group survey[1] found that only 15 per cent of the designer's time was spent adding value to a design; much of the remainder was spent searching for information, liaising with colleagues or reformating or extracting data from a variety of sources. Multidisciplinary teams can create a product design process which gives priority to the project and the company, rather than to the needs of individual functions. The principal conclusion, from the 18 case studies, of what actually happens in the field was that there is a core of good techniques and issues, despite widely differing products, markets and turnover. These can be summarized as:

1 *Market and consumer issues.* Understand the market; get feedback and take action on it; bring a regular flow of new products to the market.

2 *Product planning and design.* Develop detailed targets before starting on design; share elements of design between different product ranges; handle projects in two main stages: preplanning and implementation.

3 *New product processes.* Have a defined process widely accepted and followed, strive for faster response times to market changes; control the new product process through a multidisciplinary team structure.

4 *The chief executive.* He or she should sponsor the new product process and be involved in the management of process decisions, as well as creating the multidisciplinary team.

There is also a core of bad techniques. They cut right across product groups and demonstrate that there is a commonality of defective design safety. Part 3 of this book examines this in detail and draws lessons from the case histories.

The design review system

It is crucial to keep product safety at the forefront of the design process. The danger is that it may become lost in the drive to get the product into production and on to the market. Indeed, product safety to some will be perceived as an absence of danger rather than a positive contribution to the success of the product. Control should be obtained by ensuring that the events and decisions made during the design review are recorded in a design review log which will provide evidence that specific topics were discussed and document the reasons for the actions taken. Product safety should have a prime place in the process. This could be valuable evidence if the safety of the product was challenged subsequently. In addition, it provides useful background information when assessing the effect of later, proposed changes to the design. The design review is for decision-making and not for information transfer; those attending must therefore have the appropriate level of authority.

It can be an advantage to have fixed stages in the review at which the members of the team have to sign off that they are satisfied with the specified progress to date. If all the required signatures are not present the review does not proceed, unless the chief executive so authorizes. Hazard analysis and risk assessment can be part of this system which will make certain that it has been addressed.

Broadly speaking, the risks of an identified hazard can be reduced by

- designing out the hazard or
- designing in safety or
- by safety information.

It may be possible to design out a hazard by eliminating it altogether or reducing the frequency with which it occurs. Alternatively, safety can be designed in to prevent injury or damage – for example, by incorporating a safety device such as a thermal fuse or a magnetic brake to prevent overrun or a pressure relief valve to prevent injury or damage. Some products, such as nailguns, are inherently dangerous and these require adequate warnings, directions and instructions which should be generated as part of the design review and not added on as an afterthought to the final product.

Safety information should be permanently fixed to the product, catch the end-user's attention and be in a form which he or she can easily understand. A *warning* tells the user of any danger in the product – for example, 'Danger high voltage. A *direction* is a command concerning the use of the product – for example, 'Disconnect from the mains before removing this cover'. An *instruction* tells the user how to use the product most effectively – for example, 'To empty turn the valve anti-clockwise'. A direction should not be given in place of a warning nor should an instruction be a warning or direction in disguise (see Case History 22).

One of the pressures that can attack even the best design review system comes from the marketplace. When the customer is demanding the product immediately or the competition looks as though they will have their version on sale first, it is tempting to take short-cuts and thereby defeat the checks and balances of the system. An example illustrates the point. A certain company was professional in its approach to the safety of its products which were sold to the vehicle industry as original equipment. The development of a new product for a major customer had been delayed. The only way to meet the deadline was to postpone some of the actions of the design review process and complete them during the initial phase of production. To provide a safe-guard a 100 per cent check was introduced at the end of the line. Despite this, some defective products escaped to the cus-tomer and caused considerable problems. The post-mortem showed that a postponed hazard analysis and risk assessment would have revealed the fault. And no one seemed to remember that 100 per cent checks are not 100 per cent accurate: they have to be designed, maintained, calibrated and operated by human beings.

Examples of design reviews

The illustrations of design reviews that follow show that there can be no single way of applying a review. Each industry – each company even – will have its own specific design concepts which have been developed over a period of time. There are two great truths, however. The first is that there is no such thing as fail-safe in the true sense of the term. Totally fail-safe is an unattain-able absolute, because somewhere along the line those fallible human beings are involved. The aim should be fail-to-safer or fail-to-safest. The second is that complicated safety systems can introduce their own hazards and perhaps create a false sense of safety. Keep it simple.

An example of a design review from the electronics industry has six stages, at each of which the following points are con-sidered:

Reliability	Installation
Performance	Simplicity

Maintenance	Safety
Manufacture	Ergonomics
Product test	Appearance
Interchangeability	Cost and value

The first review is the design concept review, which is held before the development work commences and all the specifications and procedures have been established. The second review deals with the design approach and unit specification, the design verification test specification and the reliability test programme. The next four design reviews, accompanied by the appropriate checklist, will cover unit design, experimental data and value analysis, documentation and manufacturing planning and the final design review.

Another major company, much concerned with ensuring that the design of its products is as safe as possible, has adopted a special procedure for design review and design change. The following is an outline of the procedure used.

For new products the objectives are

1 to ensure that
  - they can demonstrably meet design criteria and functional requirements; they are safe to use
  - all documentation, including drawings, specifications, literature and so on are to the highest standard and accurately reflect the manufacturability and performance of the product
  - there is a smooth handover from development to manufacturing;
2 to provide a documented procedure for deciding whether changes to the design of existing products or extensions to existing product ranges should be submitted to a full design review;
3 to ensure that the company develops safe, reliable products, takes all reasonable steps to reduce anticipated product liability exposure to a minimum, and provide a sound documentary basis for defence in the event of any claim challenging the performance or safety of company products.

For new products at least two design reviews are held before the product is launched, which are

1 **Prototype reviews**. The purpose is to understand the extent to which the current design meets the defined design and performance criteria and to decide if the prototype design is acceptable for delivery to the customer for testing for a particular purpose. Prototypes which are accepted by the review as suitable for customer testing are released under a Development Product Release Certificate signed by the project leader. This states that the product has not been subject to qualification testing and that no warranty of performance is offered for any particular application; responsibility for experimental testing lies with the customer who undertakes to indemnify the company against any liability, claims or damages that might arise therefrom.

2 **Final Design Review**. The purpose is to decide whether
   - the product design is complete, meets all the applicable performance criteria, both internal and external, and is ready for market launch
   - any limitations of the product design are clearly understood and documented
   - all drawings, specifications, manufacturing and inspection procedures have been raised and approved to ensure manufacture of the product with consistent quality
   - all documentation and literature to ensure the correct and safe use of the product has been raised and approved.
   All new products must be approved at a Final Design Review, before they can be released for general sale. If normal production samples are not available before the Final Design Review, then full product qualification must be carried out on the first production run. If the production samples fail qualification a further design review must be convened.

For existing products all changes to established designs are processed through a document change system, which ensures that the impact of the change is reviewed. In certain specified cases the changes are submitted to a full design review.

A new design which is merely an extension of an existing

product range would probably not require a full design review, but the basis for such a decision has to be fully documented and filed.

For one company the design review procedure is only initiated when certain criteria are met; these are concerned with the estimated demands of implementation measured in terms of cost and time. The procedure has three major stages:

1 The feasibility of the concept with, where appropriate, an input from a customer and a senior representative of production.
2 The formal evaluation of the proposal by a committee of experts who examine all aspects in detail.
3 The project management phase which follows written procedures. It includes feedback from the field to prevent mistakes being repeated, a study for cost-effective manufacture, hazard analysis and risk assessment and pre-production trials leading to a full product run to confirm quality, performance and cost parameters.

There is a review after six months' production. The whole procedure is subject to sign-offs and the maintenance of a formal record.

Post-design

A design should be verified and validated to confirm that it meets the design input. But, as illustrated in Part 3 by Case History 9, a designer's responsibilities do not cease once a product moves to manufacturing and the market. As latent defects may only become known through use, surveillance of the product on the market is wise. Indeed, the General Product Safety Directive makes this mandatory for consumer products: Article 3.2 states that, within the limits of their respective activities, producers shall:

> ... provide consumers with the relevant information to enable them to assess the risks inherent in a product throughout the normal or reasonable period of its use, where such risks are not immediately

obvious without adequate warnings, and to take precautions against those risks.

. . . adopt measures commensurate with the characteristics of the products which they supply, to enable them to be informed of risks which these products might present and to take appropriate action including, if necessary, withdrawing the product in question from the market to avoid these risks.

The feedback from the market should reach the designer to close the loop. This should be a positive action and not one activated on an 'as-and-when' basis. Designers like to hear the good news too.

Summary

Design review systems provide a formal, documented procedure with built-in checks and balances. It is the *process* of innovation that is important rather than the product. Fixed sign-off stages can ensure that product safety is kept at the forefront of the process. A report on product development in 18 companies found a core of good techniques which concerned market and consumer issues, product planning and design and new product processes. The chief executive should be involved. Design reviews should be carried out and documented. Once a product is launched, feedback from the market should reach its designer to close the loop.

References

1 Department of Trade and Industry/Design Council (1994), *Successful Product Development. Managing in the 90s*, London: DTI and the Design Council.

6
Residual Risk Transfer: Insurance and Contract Conditions

Introduction

However good the risk reduction programme some residual risks will always remain. The perfectly safe product can never be made. As we saw in Chapter 1, a key element of the strategy for the management of design risks lies in arranging for the transfer of some of the residual risks to third parties. The chief mechanisms for this are insurance and contract conditions. However, these should be seen as a long-stop rather than as part of the up-front protection; they are to catch some – but not all – of the fall-out from a design defect. For example, insurance cannot cover the cost of fines or other criminal sanctions. It is simply prudent management to have in place such mechanisms, while realizing that they cannot be perfect.

Insurance

The danger here is the 'it's alright we're insured' syndrome. It is not uncommon for managers to assume that there will be an insurance policy to pick up the pieces if something goes wrong. This assumption is made in ignorance of the facts. Although insurance is valuable and important it is not a catch-all. It depends on which policies are in place and their conditions and exceptions. The following example illustrates the problem.

In an international engineering company the chief design

engineer and the group insurance manager scarcely knew each other, apart from chance meetings at company occasions. It was an old-established organization in which the senior managers took care not to intrude into each other's territory. During a product safety audit it became clear that the chief design engineer was woefully ill-informed about the insurance cover that he believed protected him. Equally, the group insurance manager had no appreciation of, what was to him, the mysterious world of design. A lunch was fixed at which each was introduced to the other's activities. The chief design engineer was disturbed by what he discovered. For example, the product liability policy in force at that time specifically excluded design risks from the cover, which caused him to review some of his controls. Moreover, he had thought that there would be a policy to meet the cost of a product recall but was taken aback to find there was no recall cover at all, as it had been considered to be too expensive. Equally the group insurance manager found that he had no understanding of a designer's problems and the trade-off between an ideal and commercial reality. He had based his views on the sales and marketing literature without appreciating its limitations.

Some insurance principles

In simple terms a risk is insurable if it can be properly identified, precisely defined, and quantified in words and figures for probability and severity. The insurer will put the risk alongside other similar ones and make a 'book' on the underwriting probabilities. The premium he charges, to accept the transfer of the risk, will reflect his assessment of it. The greater the probability and severity, and the more difficult the risk is to define, the higher will be the premium. Some risks are not insurable and some only at penal rates, while other high-risk areas, such as aviation or pharmaceuticals, can only be placed in limited specialist markets.

The insurer has a number of variables which he can employ to adjust his exposure, apart from the premium itself. A *deductible* (or excess) is an amount or percentage, specified in the policy, which is deducted from partial loss claims. The insured may have to pay the first £100 000 of any claim under a product liability policy, which means in fact that he, the insured, retains that part of the risk. An *aggregate* is the maximum amount that the underwriter will pay under the terms of a policy in a given period of time, whatever the claims made; for example, not more than £500 000 in a particular year.

Another method by which an underwriter seeks to protect himself from some of the management risks is by *percentage participation*. An example of this would be that when a claim was paid a proportion of the loss would remain uninsured (perhaps 10 per cent) and this amount would have to be met by the insured. Loosely, it is an across-the-board deductible.

One of the most important changes in the insurance market is an alteration in the terms of cover from 'claims occurring' to 'claims made'. This has considerable importance for the designer, especially when a design defect only comes to light after a period of use – for example, in claims arising from a disease caused by long-term exposure to a harmful substance, such as blue asbestos. If a company puts a product containing blue asbestos on the market the claim that injury had been caused may be made many years after the original supply. A product liability policy written on an '*occurrence form*' – one that was in force when the damage or injury originally happened – would respond to such a claim. When damage occurs over a period of time policies in force in different years may all be called upon to respond to these claims, possibly involving a number of different insurers.

The fundamental point for the designer is that a policy written on an occurrence form will respond to an occurrence happening during the period of insurance, without any reference to when the loss is discovered or when any claim is made by a third party. Most policies have a condition which ensures that the insured has to report any loss as soon as he becomes aware of it, but it is a feature of liability insurance that the injury or damage which results in a claim may be caused years before it becomes apparent. This is called the latent damage exposure.

The advantage of the claims occurring basis for the designer is that, should latent damage occur, the policy in force at the time will respond and provide cover in the future. A major disadvantage is that, if a claim is made 10 or 20 years after the occurrence, the limit of indemnity of the policy may not be adequate in relation to current court awards. Furthermore, in the interim it may be that no insurance was purchased, the insurer has gone out of business or records have been lost.

From the insurer's point of view the principal disadvantage of the occurrence form is that, once the policy is written, it is impossible to establish when the liabilities arising from it are extinguished. In the United States the combination of the occurrence form and latent damage, coupled with the legal system, produced nothing short of catastrophe for some sectors of the liability market.

The *claims made form* takes a fundamentally different approach to the occurrence form. The claims made form signifies that a liability policy will only respond to claims actually made during the period of the policy, regardless of when the event that gave rise to the damage occurred; usually there will be a retroactive date.

The advantage of the claims made form for the designer is that the limit of indemnity is more likely to be adequate for current conditions, without having to guess what would be required in 10 or 20 years' time. The disadvantage arises mainly when continuous cover cannot be maintained from year to year. If there is a break in cover, or the insurers will not renew, the designer will be at risk for incurred but not reported claims from previous years.

For the insurer the claims made form has the major advantage of shortening the uncertainty of liability business. It responds in the year that a claim is notified and cover ceases once the current policy is completed. The risk of aggregation of limits of indemnity is removed, because only the current limit of indemnity applies. At the end of any policy year the insurer can amend the terms of coverage to eliminate further claims for particular types of damage; indeed, it would be possible to cancel the coverage altogether.

With an occurrence form, even if the policy is cancelled, the insurer will still be liable if claims arise in the future for damage which occurred during the policy period. With the claims made form this problem is very largely eliminated.

The liability insurance market has no common approach to the move towards claims made covers. The designer should be well aware of this change in risk transfer. He should realize that once the liability moves to a claims made form it becomes difficult, if not impossible, to revert at some future date to an occurrence form, because, unless a future occurrence form insurer were prepared to give a retroactive cover, a gap in cover would be opened up. This gap would be in respect of future claims made relating to occurrences during the claims made policy period.

The principal way in which an insurer will control his exposure is in his *wordings* – his contract conditions. These are the statements in the policy which set out what is covered and what is not, including specific exclusions which may vary with individual risks. There are numerous different wordings, each dealing with defined areas of risk, such as life, motor, marine, aviation, property, fraud and so on (see Case History 21).

There is no one policy which deals with design, because the effect of a design defect can be revealed in a number of different ways depending on the risks it presents. For example, if a design defect resulted in the product causing injury to a user, product liability insurance would provide cover to meet such a legal liability. A design defect could cause a product to fail to do the job for which it was bought, without injuring anybody, and here product guarantee cover would be the appropriate transfer mechanism. A third party could suffer financial loss because of the design defect in a product and financial loss insurance would provide indemnity. An extensive product recall could be required if a design defect in a product made it sufficiently dangerous, and product recall insurance cover many respond. A design engineer who was guilty of professional negligence in the course of his work could find protection under professional indemnity cover.

For each type of cover it is necessary to examine the exact wording in order to be clear about precisely what is covered. It may be unwise to look at one particular cover in isolation, as one may interlock with another – public liability and product recall, for instance. Deductibles and aggregates will also affect the degree of cover provided.

Before a design defect can trigger a particular policy to respond, one has to be certain that a design defect *is* the cause. A manufacturing error may be traced to a poorly designed product, which did not give production a reasonable chance of replicating it without fault. Alternatively, an inadequate instruction or warning could be the cause of a fault which was wrongly blamed on a design error.

Insurance contracts are subject to the doctrine of utmost good faith – *uberrimae fides*. This is because they are different from other contracts in that only one party knows (or should know) all about the risk, and that is the proposer. The other party, the insurer, has to rely largely on the information given to him by the proposer. If one of the parties does not exercise the utmost good faith then the other can repudiate the contract.

It follows that it is the duty of the proposer to disclose all material facts relating to the proposed insurance. A material fact is one which would affect the judgement of a prudent under-writer and includes any communication made to, or information received by, the proposer (*Rivaz* v. *Gerussi* [1880]). The proposer consequently has a positive duty of disclosure. Failure to disclose all material facts renders the contract voidable, even if the failure was inadvertent or even if the proposer honestly considered the facts to be immaterial.

It is very difficult to say what insurance will *cost*. Each risk has to be assessed separately and the premium will be influenced by the company's claim record, the products it sells and the coun-tries in which it sells them. The capacity of the insurance market to underwrite risks will also be an important factor, and the availability of reinsurance will affect this.

International insurance

The insurance field is complex, and expert advice is needed to ensure that the right mix of covers is in place to give the best protection. In recent years there has been a change in the

European insurance market, as the restrictions on insurers are dismantled. In the EU, Member States have more freedom in writing certain types of insurance, which is important as the barriers to trade come down and products move more freely across borders.

This has been achieved by the First Non-Life Insurance Directive 1973, the Second Non-Life Insurance Directive 1988 and the Third Non-Life Insurance Directive 1992. The latter, which came into force in 1994, requires that an insurer authorized in one Member State can write product liability insurance for any risk in any other Member State, without the need for authority from it.

Insurance policies

A brief description of the relevant insurance policies is given below. They should be read in conjunction with Chapter 11, the Personal Liabilities of Designers.

Product liability insurance

This insurance is designed to protect the insured company against its legal liability for injury to third parties, caused by goods which the insured has sold, supplied, serviced or repaired. Liability can arise under statute or common law, and can be incurred outside the country where the goods are manufactured. Product liability insurance is usually offered in conjunction with public liability insurance. In these cases perhaps 90 per cent of the premium may be accounted for by the product risk, and only 10 per cent by the public liability for a manufacturer with no unusual exposures. Most general insurers provide product liability insurance which will give cover for the insured's legal liability for accidental bodily injury and/or accidental loss or damage to material property caused by a product.

Insurers have a fairly precise definition of what they mean by the product that gives rise to the loss, and some exclude liability where the goods are still under the insured's control. A claimant's costs and expenses will be met where the insured is legally liable and so will the insured's own legal fees if they have been approved by the insurer. Territorial limits will be specified, for even 'worldwide' cover will have important excluded areas. The policy will have clauses to limit the indemnity. The term 'insured' usually takes in the insured's personal representatives, and certain wordings include in the definition the names of principals for whom the insured is carrying out work. There will be a definition of what the insured's 'business' includes and what it excludes.

A standard policy will not provide indemnity for any damage to the goods themselves, nor for the cost of putting right such products, nor for recalling products. Some insurers may not accept liability for faulty design or instructions, nor will they provide cover where an insured has accepted liability by contract or agreement which would otherwise not have been incurred. High-risk products – for example, aircraft – may be excluded and many policies also exclude the results of deliberate acts. All wordings exclude claims associated with war or nuclear events.

Extensions or endorsements will be used to modify the range of cover provided by a standard policy. Most policies require the insured to exercise reasonable care in loss prevention and to give the insurer written notice of any impending prosecution or injury. A clause prevents the insured from admitting liability, or making a payment in connection with a claim, without the insurer's agreement and, if it so wishes, the insurer will conduct any proceedings on behalf of the insured.

Product guarantee insurance

Cover is provided for the liability for the replacement or repair of products which are defective or fail to do the job for which they are intended. This cover can be extended to protect against other risks, such as product recall and pure financial loss, not occasioned by death or injury to persons, or damage to property – the standard operative clause of the basic legal liability wording.

Financial loss insurance

An indemnity is provided against a legal liability to compensate for consequential or financial loss suffered by a third party purely because a product was defective, or did not function as intended. It does not depend on injury or damage. To a limited degree it is possible to extend a public and product liability policy to include financial loss.

Product recall insurance

Few underwriters or brokers are involved with this risk and, some would argue, even fewer have any conception of what the risk is all about. The object of recall insurance is to indemnify the policy-holder for payments for specified expenses incurred in the withdrawal of declared products.

Some areas that may not be protected are: improper, inadequate or faulty formulae or design; breach of warranties of fitness, quality, efficacy and efficiency; withdrawal of kindred products; the cost of destruction of the recalled product; and the redistribution or replacement of the recalled product.

Professional indemnity insurance

This cover protects a professional person (engineer, architect, accountant, designer, doctor, pharmacist, lawyer, insurance broker) against his or her legal liability to pay damages to persons who have sustained loss arising from his or her own professional negligence, or that of his or her employees. Any person who practises a profession and holds him or herself as competent to give advice or assistance, must exercise that degree of care which one is entitled to expect from any other competent practitioner in the same profession. If the degree of care falls below this standard an action for damages will lie, based on negligence. When a design or formulation defect is the cause of the failure of a product, it may be necessary to look to professional negligence insurance (a product liability policy may exclude design or formulation from its cover) or errors and omissions insurance.

Contract conditions

These contract conditions relate mainly to terms and conditions of purchase and are used to regulate price, quantity, method of payment, contingencies and so on. They may specify the remedies, such as arbitration, to be adopted if something goes wrong.

This book is not the place to review contract conditions but rather just to mention some of the elements of concern to design safety.

The designer can have an interest in the contract terms and conditions if he or she has required certain components or sub-assemblies to be used in the end-products and similarly, if he or she has formally specified certain items which the purchasing department has to obtain. It is possible that the legal contract could compromise his intentions by allowing concessions or variations to the goods without reference to the designer. Purchasing departments are commercial operations which cannot have a designer's depth of technical knowledge.

A defective incoming component could make the end-product, into which it is incorporated, unsafe and cause the producer serious problems. In such a case, the terms and conditions may determine where the liability will lie and who will pay what to whom. If the defect was due to the design of a component, formally accepted by the designer of the end-product, then there can be no recourse against the supplier. But if the supplier recommended his design as being suitable for the producer's purpose then some liability will arise on the part of the supplier.

In practice the circumstances may not always be so clear-cut. The design of the component may be the result of a dialogue between the designers on both sides, but the responsibility for the final specification will be that stated in the terms and conditions of purchase.

Component suppliers may limit their liability to a particular sum or a multiplier of the contract price or to the value of the component itself on the grounds that it is commercially unacceptable for them to incur liability for consequential losses. This is common practice among suppliers of high-volume, low-value products. To cover their liabilities manufacturers of complex equipment may take out insurance, which will have exclusion clauses. Where appropriate they may then pass on some of these exposures to suppliers by means of terms and conditions of purchase. The insurer may require the right of veto over contract terms.

Standard form contracts for purchase and sale are used by

parties with strong bargaining powers. The weaker party often cannot shop around for better terms, because the supplier may have a monopoly or because everyone in the same field uses the same form, as with professional and trade associations. The advantage with the standard form is that time and expense are saved in negotiating separate agreements. Difficult risks can be excluded and contingencies accommodated.

The Sale of Goods Act 1979 had its origins in the end of the last century and implied certain conditions into contracts. One of these was that goods had to be of 'merchantable quality'. The Sale and Supply of Goods Act 1994, which came into force on 3 January 1995, replaced this Victorian expression with 'satisfactory quality'. As well as fitness for purpose, aspects of quality include freedom from minor defects, appearance and finish, durability and – significantly from the designer's point of view – safety. For the supplier the implied condition of satisfactory quality is that the liability is strict. This means that if the goods are defective the supplier is liable, even if there was no way he or she could have known about it.

Summary

However good the risk reduction programme some risks will always remain. Specified parts of some of these residual risks can be transferred to third parties by the mechanisms of insurance and contract conditions. Arranging adequate insurance cover requires expert advice in what is a complex international market. Contract conditions are a specialized area of which the designer should be aware.

7
Residual Risk Retention

Introduction

The risk reduction programme will have minimized the design risks, and the risk transfer programme will have moved part of the residual risks to third parties, but some will always remain. These have to be retained within the company.

In risk management terms there are two types of risk suitable for retention: those that occur frequently and cause small losses and those that occur infrequently with catastrophic losses. The first are represented by the small everyday complaints which inevitably arise in products made by the million, and the second by major aircraft catastrophes and industrial accidents.

A design risk may have to be retained for a number of reasons. The cost of further risk reduction may not be commercially practicable; or the state of the art such that it is not possible, whatever the financial circumstances; or probability estimates may show that to attempt to do so would be unrealistic.

Relevant design risk transfer by the insurance mechanism may not be available because the company cannot afford the premiums involved, or an appropriate cover may not be available for the product concerned. An insurer may require such a large deductible before accepting cover that the company concerned feels that this is unacceptable, or the exclusion clauses in the wording may make the cover provided inadequate.

Design risks can accompany a bought-in component or subassembly, the failure of which can cause a dangerous defect in the end-product. The component supplier may be unwilling to accept, under the terms of the supply contract, full liability for the consequences of such a failure. The contract may limit the liability in a number of ways – for instance, to a maximum of a multiplier of the contract price or the value of the item supplied. Risk transfer in this case is of limited value so that risk retention has to be accepted for the major part of the residual risk.

The successful management of retained design risks depends on the establishment of an active programme in which they are dealt with in a positive manner. Some of the methods of doing this are discussed below.

Captive insurance company

This is a company created and owned by an organization to insure the risks of its parent. The advantage lies in the formalization of funding so that the reserves can be moved forward, year by year, with sufficient capitalization to ensure solvency. There are no acquisition costs, only one insured, and no special organization or offices required. In addition, profit is non-essential since investment income will discount premiums.

A company may find that a captive provides the answer if it cannot obtain the cover required on the insurance market, or if it cannot be obtained at an acceptable cost. A company that sets up its own captive demonstrates its confidence to carry part of its own risks, which could influence other insurers or reinsurers to take up a share.

A captive insurance company can be managed by its parent if it has the necessary experience, or specialists can be recruited for the purpose. The usual method is to use outside managers such as underwriters, insurers, insurance brokers, lawyers, bankers or accountants.

It is important to remember that the formation of a captive does not bring independence from the insurance market. The part played by reinsurance becomes critical for, without it, a captive would have considerable difficulty in spreading its risks.

Insuring in a captive is self-insurance, and the only real insurance is that part of the risk which the captive reinsures or co-insures. In effect it is a combination of risk retention and risk transfer.

Deductibles

An insurer can avoid its liability for some losses by including a deductible in a policy. A simple deductible is a lump sum deduction from each claim. This device is widely used to eliminate small claims with disproportionately high handling expenses and also makes the insured retain the first part of the risk himself or herself.

For example, in a product liability policy the insurer may require a deductible of, say, £50 000. In effect the insured has to pay the first £50 000 of the cost of each incident to which the policy will respond. In fact, he or she retains this part of the risk. The amount over the deductible will be paid by the insurer, according to the cover provided by the policy, up to the maximum provided by the premium. This is the part of the risk that has been transferred to the insurer, according to the cover provided by the policy. If the costs are greater than the maximum, the insured will have to pay them him or herself, and this once more is risk retention.

A first loss cover is the mirror image of a deductible. Here the insurer pays for the loss up to the first loss limit and the insured has to pay the balance. So the insured transfers the first part of the risk and retains the balance.

Special funds

By this method a fund is created by putting aside a sum each year and then drawing on it when a loss occurs. This spreads losses over a longer period. The fund must be readily converted into cash and carry sufficient reserve to absorb the wide fluctuations that might occur from year to year. The actuarial viability of a fund depends on the spread of risk which it is designed to retain. The sums put aside each year may not be tax deductible, and may not be accumulated, year on year, beyond a limited period; the losses themselves will be allowable tax expenses.

Another way to meet losses is by diverting funds from

alternative uses. This has a disadvantage of having to forego the opportunity for which the fund was established, of the possibility of having to turn assets into liquid form at a disadvantageous time or that insufficient capital will be available to cope with the loss and the demands of the business.

Revenue

A company may ignore the residual risks and do nothing to manage them positively. Following this negative approach implies a reliance on being able to meet the cost of these liabilities out of revenue. While this may well be satisfactory for small everyday claims it may not be adequate to deal with anything more significant – at least not without seriously damaging the bottom line. If the company is part of a large organization it may be possible to borrow from the centre, but this may involve some form of penalties.

Leaving the cost of residual risks to revenue is a matter of a judgement which all managers have to make at one time or another. Indeed, it is an element of running a business for there is no profit without risk – otherwise it would be just as effective to invest in a building society. But the decision should be taken after consideration and not arrived at by default, which can lead to unpleasant surprises.

Summary

The remaining residual risks are retained within the company by means of an active risk management programme. These design risks may have to be retained because further risk reduction is not commercially practicable, or the state of the art does not allow it, or probability estimates show that an attempt to do so would be unrealistic. The available methods include the creation of a captive insurance company, deductibles, first loss cover and special funds. Without a positive risk management programme the cost of residual risks has to be met out of revenue.

Part Two
THE LEGAL BACKGROUND

8
Legal Developments in Europe

Introduction

During the last 20 years or so the European Community has set about radically reshaping responsibilities for placing products on the European market. The result, for the UK in particular, is that the process of designing products and bringing them to the market is now probably more heavily regulated than ever before. At the same time, the principles upon which liability to pay compensation for defective products are based have altered significantly with the extension of strict liability under the Product Liability Directive. More recently, the Directive on General Product Safety has thrown into sharper focus the positive obligations on producers to ensure products are safe before they are placed on the market, and to reappraise the safety of products in the light of post-marketing surveillance.[1]

Expansion of consumer safety policy

Surprisingly, perhaps, consumer policy only became formally recognized as an end in itself after the 1992 Maastricht changes which incorporated a new Article 129(a) of the EC Treaty specifying that:

> The Community shall contribute to the attainment of a high level of consumer protection through:
>
> > (a) measures adopted pursuant to Article 100a in the context of the completion of the internal market;

(b) specific action which supports and supplements the policy pursued by the Member States to protect the health, safety and economic interests of consumers and to provide adequate information to consumers.

These cryptic words represent the culmination of some 20 years of consumer policy expansion within Europe.

Lord Denning, one of the century's most celebrated judges and a master of prose, once observed in one of his judgements that:

> ... when we come to matters with a European element, the Treaty is like an incoming tide. It flows into the estuaries and up the rivers. It cannot be held back, Parliament has decreed that the Treaty is henceforward to be part of our law. It is equal in force to any statute.[2]

Nowhere is this effect more evident than in relation to product safety, which is being subjected to detailed scrutiny by European Community institutions. As a result, fundamental legal changes have taken place during the last decade.

In the main, European Community policy has focused on the responsibilities of producers and others, such as importers, who actually bring goods to market within the Community. Designers could never be insulated from the effects of these changes since the design process is an integral part of product safety. Increasingly, however, legislation is emerging from Europe which demands the specific and direct attention of design departments, as the criteria for safety and basic product specifications are being enshrined in the legal process, harmonized standards and formal attestation procedures. In terms of Lord Denning's analogy, the tide is truly lapping at the designer's feet.

In 1975 the European Community took its first major step forward in promoting product safety as part of a preliminary programme for a consumer protection and information policy.[3] This specified protection of health and safety as one of a consumer's basic rights. The programme also enunciated a number of general principles including the following:

■ Goods and services offered to consumers should be such that under normal or foreseeable conditions of use they present no risk to the health or safety of consumers.

■ There should be quick and simple procedures for withdrawing products from the market in the event of their presenting such risks.

■ Consumers should be informed in an appropriate manner of any risk liable to result from a foreseeable use of goods, taking into account the nature of the goods and the persons with whom they are intended.

■ Consumers should be protected against the consequences for physical injury caused by defective products.

It was stated that priority would be given to harmonizing Member States' legislation in key areas which were defined as foodstuffs, cosmetics and detergents, utensils and consumer durables, cars, textiles, toys, dangerous substances, materials coming into contact with foodstuffs, medicines, fertilizers, pesticides and herbicides, veterinary products and animal feedstuffs.

The programme was effectively readopted and expanded in 1981, with a further programme following in 1985 for a 'new impetus' to consumer policy but this time, however, developments of deeper significance were taking place in different areas, affecting product liability and the implementation of the single market.

New liabilities for defective products

Product liability laws across Europe, by no means a straightforward field, were pinpointed by the European Council in the early 1970s as an area in need of attention. The European Convention on Product Liability emerged after several years of consideration by an expert committee. This criticized the absence in all countries of special rules governing the liability of producers, and in particular the need to prove fault before a person could succeed in claiming damages for injury caused by a defective product. The committee was in favour of jettisoning the 'fault' notion which was thought to be 'unsatisfactory in an era of mass production, where technical developments, advertising and sales methods had created special risks which the consumer could not be expected to accept'. Instead, liability would stem from the condition of the product itself and the fact that it had caused injury. In these terms, it was possible just to describe a product as having a defect when it was unsuitable for the purpose for which it was designed.

It was not considered possible simply to list categories of product which could be described as 'dangerous'. What was recommended was a compromise solution which retained the notion of defect as the basis of liability, described in terms of the absence of safety which a person is entitled to expect. Although – as will be seen below in relation to the later legislation – putting it this way is a considerable oversimplification of the concept of defectiveness, it threw into sharp focus the designer's responsibility to ensure the suitability of the product, as well as his or her need to have channels of communication with both those who would engineer the manufacturing of a product and those who would market it for particular purposes. The reason for this was that the basis of liability was homing in on the intrinsic qualities and application of the design.

The Product Liability Directive

The conceptual difficulties, as well as the commercial implications of this reformulation of product liability principles, meant that it was not until 1985 that the European Directive concerning liability for defective products (the Product Liability Directive) emerged.[4] Although this was implemented in the UK in 1987 by the Consumer Protection Act, the process took several more years elsewhere in Europe and France, at the time of writing, has still not formally introduced implementing legislation.

The Product Liability Directive is very similar to the 1975 Convention, but has an expanded definition of a defective product:

1. A product is defective when it does not provide the safety which a

person is entitled to expect, taking all circumstances into account, including:

(a) the presentation of the product;

(b) the use to which it could reasonably be expected that the product would be put;

(c) the time when the product was put into circulation.

2. A product shall not be considered defective for the sole reason that a better product is subsequently put into circulation.

This definition is helpful to a designer in that it may confine its liability to the 'state of the art' as it was at the time when the product was put into circulation; with hindsight, a product might admittedly be seen as defective as technology and standards move on, but this will not render the producer retrospectively liable.

Producers' defences

A number of defences are afforded to producers under the Product Liability Directive, the most significant among these for present purposes being:

- a probability that the defect which caused the damage did not exist at the time when the product was put into circulation or that this defect came into being afterwards. This is effectively a defence where the product has deteriorated or been damaged in the supply chain or in the hands of the consumer, which is not necessarily a straightforward matter where the product has not been designed adequately to resist damage in handling or use.

- that the defect is due to compliance of the product with mandatory regulations issued by public authorities; this is sometimes termed a 'pre-emption' defence – that is, that the mandatory requirements can pre-empt there being a duty to design a product differently or to give warnings that are inconsistent with any mandated wording in this respect.

- that the state of scientific and technical knowledge at the time when the product was put into circulation was not such as to enable the existence of the defect to be discovered; known as the 'development risk defence' this has aroused ongoing controversy and was seen by many as detracting from the principle of strict liability on producers. It is not concerned directly with the state of the art in terms of product design; rather it is to do with whether the defect itself could have been discovered.

- in the case of a manufacturer of a component, that the defect is attributable to the design of the product in which the component has been fitted or to the instructions given by the manufacturer of the product. This defence, available only to the manufacturer of the component itself, effectively places the onus on the designer of the final product to check the suitability of the components which are specified or incorporated. However, as Case History 8 shows, if the component itself, being suitable for the application, turns out to be faulty, the component manufacturer will be exposed to liability along with the producer of the finished product. (Note that there is a common misconception that the component manufacturer defence can work in reverse to exonerate the producer of the finished product; this is not correct.)

It was expected that the additional economic cost of meeting damages under strict liability would be treated as an expense of the business, in contrast to the perceived situation in which the consequences of defective products are borne entirely by the injured consumer unable to prove fault. In essence, this would be an additional insurance risk, with the cost of cover reflected in the price of products. Indications so far are that there has been no 'claims explosion' as some predicted as a consequence of strict liability in Europe, and this socioeconomic theorizing has not yet been put to the test.[5]

Avoiding trade barriers

In the mid-1980s Community policy underwent a radical change as measures were introduced to promote the completion of the internal market for 1992. As part of a wide-ranging process (including removal of physical customs barriers, free movement of labour, opening up the public procurement process to competitive tendering and approximation of VAT and other fiscal measures) the removal of 'technical barriers' to trade across the Community was made a priority.[6] The different standards for individual products adopted in different Member States for health and safety, environmental or consumer protection, would be subject to convergence. This meant a move away from the concept of an imposed harmonization of laws and administrative measures towards 'mutual recognition and equivalence'. The Community adopted the general principle that, if a product is lawfully manufactured and marketed in one Member State, there should be no reason why it should not be sold freely throughout the Community.

In order to prevent new technical barriers to trade being raised, Directive 83/189/EEC obliged Member States to notify the Commission in advance of all draft regulations concerning technical specifications that they intended to introduce on their own territory and provide a justification for them. Under this system a process follows in which the Commission first seeks comments from other Member States and may then object to the requirements as being barriers to trade, or decide to propose a new directive to cover the subject. Similar notification requirements and 'stand still' provisions apply to the adoption of standards by national standards institutions.

From the point of view of the producer, the avoidance of technical barriers to trade was a means of reducing costs both generally and per unit and rationalizing production patterns. The consequence has been the creation of a complex framework of laws and standards, which in turn has meant that product design has gained increased prominence in the legislation. In short, safety has become a design imperative.

The 'New Approach'

The practice of incorporating detailed design and technical specifications into the text of directives had given rise to long delays because of the unanimity required in Community decision-making and because of the perceived need to make the legislation as comprehensive on the technical detail as possible. There were also concerns that Member States did not actually implement the detailed measures, and even frustrated them by erecting other barriers – for example, by declining to recognize foreign tests and technical approvals.

Under the 'New Approach', legislative harmonization in the Community can be by a form of majority voting (where larger States have more votes than smaller ones, and no single country can operate a veto), and the basic features of all relevant directives are pre-ordained. The key legal obligations for safety are confined to core requirements, conformity with which entitles a product to free movement within the Community. The foundation for the New Approach is in the Council Resolution of 7 May 1995 which stated 'four fundamental principles':

1 Legislative harmonization of Member States' laws is limited to the adoption, by means of directives, of 'essential requirements' (or other requirements in the general interest) with which products put on the market must conform. Conforming products should therefore enjoy free movement throughout the Community.
2 The task of drawing up the technical specifications needed for the production and placing on the market of products conforming to the 'essential requirements' is entrusted to organizations recognized as competent in the standardization area – that is CEN (Comité Européen pour la Normalisation – the European Standards Organization), CENELEC (Comité Européen de Normalisation Électro-technique – the European Electrotechnical Standards Organization) and ETSI (the European Telecommunications Standards Institute).
3 These technical specifications are not mandatory and maintain the status of voluntary standards.
4 National authorities are obliged to recognize that products manufactured in conformity with harmonized standards (or, provisionally, with national standards) are presumed to conform to the 'essential requirements'. In other words, the producer need not manufacture in conformity with the stan-

dards, but if it so chooses there can be an obligation to prove that its products conform to the essential requirements – it does not benefit from the presumption in its favour which compliance with the harmonized standard would create.

The quality of harmonized standards is ensured by 'standardization mandates' which are confirmed by the European Commission on the European standards organizations. Where, on a provisional basis, national standards are used, their quality and acceptability must be verified by a procedure at Community level backed by the advice of a standing committee of officials from national administrations.

The goal of the New Approach, therefore, is to concretize in law only the essential requirements and to leave the official standards flexible and capable of revision through the technical committees of the standards organizations.

Outline of a New Approach directive

The Council Resolution defines the main elements which will be addressed in any New Approach directive:

- **Scope**. The definition of the range of products or the types of hazard covered.
- **General clause for placing on the market**. The products covered by the directive may only be placed on the market if they do not endanger the safety of persons, domestic animals or goods when properly installed and maintained and used for their intended purposes. The clause may extend further to the 'foreseeable use' of a product, which can conceivably include its misuse where this can be anticipated.
- **Essential safety requirements**. A description of the safety requirements which are essential for the application of the general clause.
- **Free movement clause**. Statement of the obligation on the Member States to accept, subject to proof of conformity, the free movement of the products concerned.
- **Means of proof of conformity and effects**. Member States are obliged to presume conformity of products which are

accompanied by one of the means of 'attestation' declaring they are in conformity with:

a) harmonized European standards (that is, those adopted by the European standardization bodies with competence in the particular area); or

b) (as a transitional measure) national standards insofar as harmonized standards do not exist in the area.

Member States should also accept that products for which the manufacturer has not applied any standard (because one does not exist) are considered to conform with the essential requirements when this is demonstrated by certificates and marks of conformity issued by a third party or by the results of tests carried out by a third party. Thus conformity is dependent upon attestation by an independent body.

■ **Management of the list of standards**. A standing committee of Member States' representatives and expert advisers is to consider complaints that the harmonized standards do not fully satisfy the essential requirements and advise the Commission on necessary changes or withdrawals of the standards.

■ **Safeguard clause**. National authorities are expected to exercise control of products on the market – for example, by means of 'spot checks'. The so-called safeguard clause provides for manufacturers claiming conformity with the essential requirements when the means of attestation of conformity are valid but the product is nevertheless found to compromise the safety of individuals, domestic animals or property. A Member State 'shall take all appropriate measures to withdraw or prohibit the placing on the market of the product in question or to restrict its free movement'. The Member State may also be required to notify the Commission of the action it has taken and the reasons for doing this. The Commission is then responsible for consulting the other Member States concerned and, on the advice of the standing committee, informing other Member States of the obligation to prevent the product being placed on the market. This may also entail a review of harmonized standards themselves where the safeguard clause has been exercised because of some shortcoming there. Action may also be taken against the person issuing the means of attestation – either the manufacturer or any independent body involved.

■ **Means of attestation of conformity**. The available means of attestation are:

a) certificates and marks of conformity issued by a third party;

b) results of tests carried out by a third party;

c) declaration of conformity issued by the manufacturer or his agent based in the Community (this may be coupled with the requirements for a surveillance system);

d) other means of attestation specified by a directive.

The choice between these different means or the options open to a manufacturer may be determined by the directive itself – see the description of the 'Global Approach' below.

■ **Notified bodies**. National bodies authorized to issue marks or certificates of conformity shall be 'notified' by each Member State to the Commission and to the other Member States. Such bodies will be notified for the purposes of the particular directives; they may be laboratories, certification bodies or inspection bodies, depending on the circumstances. It is irrelevant whether they are privately owned or state owned, but they come under the jurisdiction of national authorities and must meet competence criteria so that their attestations can be relied upon. The notified bodies themselves are subject to accreditation under the EN 45000 series of Standards.

The 'Global Approach' to conformity assessment

At its inception the New Approach left the method of attestation to be specified in the individual directives that emerged, but within a few years there were still problems with the mutual recognition of test results and certificates issued in other Member States and the whole process of mutual recognition. The New Approach needed to be firmer about the assessment of conformity being on an equal footing in all Member States. At the end of 1990 the Council Resolution on a Global Approach to conformity assessment emerged stating five 'guiding principles':[7]

1 A consistent approach in Community legislation should be ensured by devising *modules for the various phases of conformity assessment procedures* and by laying down criteria for the use of those procedures, for the designation and notification of bodies under those procedures, and for the use of the CE mark (or CE marking as it became known).

2 Generalized use of the European Standards relating to quality assurance (the EN 29000 series which has in the UK since become BS EN ISO 9000) and to the requirements to be fulfilled by the above-mentioned bodies concerned (EN 45000), the setting up of accreditation systems and the use of techniques of intercomparison should be promoted in all Member States as well as at Community level.

3 Mutual recognition agreements on certification and testing between the bodies operating in a non-regulatory sphere should be promoted; a European-level, flexible, unbureaucratic testing and certification organization promoting such agreements should be set up.

4 Possible differences in levels of development in the Community and in industrial sectors with regard to quality infrastructure (especially calibration and metrology systems, testing laboratories, certification and inspection bodies and accreditation systems) likely to have an adverse effect on the internal market should be studied.

5 In its relations with countries outside the Community, the Community would endeavour to promote international trade in regulated products and promote mutual recognition agreements while ensuring that the other countries' bodies are of equivalent capability etc.

The most important of these principles for the purposes of product design is the first, and this has been addressed by further Council decisions concerning the 'modules' for the various phases of the conformity assessment procedures to be used in technical harmonization directives. Details of the modular approach were published in 1990, and after substantial amendment and consolidation with other developments the key document is now Council Decision of 22 July 1993 concerning the modules for the various phases of the conformity assessment procedure and the rules for affixing and use of the CE conformity marking which are intended to be used in the technical harmonization directives. The full text can be found in Appendix I.

Modules for conformity assessment

Under a number of 'general guidelines' conformity assessment is divided into the design phase and production phase of products. As a rule, a product should go through both phases before being placed on the market. The choice of modules applicable to a particular directive will depend on various circumstances, including the nature of the risks involved: higher risk products are subject to more extensive assessment – for example, module H, full quality assurance, requires the manufacturer to operate quality systems for design, production and testing which are approved by a notified body. It is intended that the designation of modules should leave manufacturers with as wide a choice as possible as to how to deal with compliance whilst at the same time minimizing the economic burden. The individual directives will specify circumstances in which the manufacturer can choose between those modules which are applied in the particular directive.

There are nine modules for assessment. The main differences between them lie in whether the manufacturer or a notified body is responsible for testing and certification, and the stage at which testing must occur. Individual directives may use certain models, in combination, or with additional provisions for supplementary requirements. Module B (design) will normally be used in conjunction with modules C, D, E and F (production), but the latter may be used on their own without B (see Appendix I). The modules are:

Module A   Internal production control. (Also Module Aa consisting of Module A plus supplementary requirements)
Module B   EC type-examination
Module C   Conformity to type

Module D Production Quality Assurance

Module E Product Quality Assurance

Module F Product verification

Module G Unit verification

Module H Full Quality Assurance (with possible supplementary requirements for design examination)

All the modules (except B which is confined to the design stage) contain a requirement for the manufacturer to fix the CE marking to each product and to draw up a written 'declaration of conformity'. Under each module the manufacturer (or in some cases the 'authorized representative' in the Community) is required to keep a copy of the declaration of conformity and of any specified documentation for a prescribed period normally of at least ten years from the date of last production. EN 45014 sets out the general criteria for declarations of conformity, but the precise requirements are laid out in the individual directives. Although the phrase is not used here, the declaration of conformity is effectively a form of self-certification, as certification is usually taken to imply the involvement of an independent third party.

CE marking

CE marking acts as a final declaration of conformity by the manufacturer. It is not a 'quality mark', or a badge of safety or an independent approval/certification. Its meaning is circumscribed by the Council Decision of 22 July 1993 and the individual directives, and symbolizes the fact that the person who was responsible for affixing it has verified that the product conforms to all the Community total harmonization provisions which apply to it (that is, one or possibly more applicable directives) and has been the subject of the appropriate conformity evaluation procedures. Under the individual New Approach directives Member States are required to consider products so marked as meeting the relevant conditions for being marketed in their territory, unless they can be shown actually to be non-compliant (see the 'safeguard clause', page 90 above). For this reason, the

CE marking has been described as acting like a 'passport' under which a product is allowed free movement within the Community market.

Products may well have to meet the requirements of more than one directive (for example both the Low Voltage and Electromagnetic Compatibility Directives). Affixing CE marking on such a product will imply that the products are presumed to conform to the provisions of *all* those requirements. If one or more of these directives is not yet mandatory (because – as is common – there is a transitional period during which new European requirements are phased in) CE marking can be applied to a product where conformity with the new directive has not been established, as long as the marking is accompanied by formal particulars of the directive(s) which *have* been applied.

Prior to 1993 a number of inconsistencies emerged in the way directives specified the use of CE marking and accompanying information, and even the terminology was variable (terms 'EC mark' and 'CE mark' had been used). A single set of CE marking principles has now been adopted and the configuration standardized as shown in the form in Figure 8.1.

Figure 8.1   The CE marking

The proportions (which are deliberately set so as not to be exactly circular in their dimensions) must be adhered to – the directives give a grid for the precise design. Where a directive does not impose specific dimensions, the CE marking must have a height of at least 5mm. It must be affixed to a product or to its data plate but, where this is not possible or is not warranted on account of the nature of the product, it must be affixed to the packaging, if any, and to the accompanying documents, where the directive concerned provides for such documents. The CE marking must be affixed visibly, legibly and indelibly. The fixing must be done at the end of the production control phase – that is, after the attestation procedures have been dealt with.

Where a notified body is involved in production control the identification number assigned to it by the Commission must accompany the CE marking.

Various provisions are laid down preventing Member States from introducing rival conformity marking, other than CE marking, for the purposes of the directives concerned, and requiring them to police any abuse of CE marking that may occur. In particular, affixing marks that are liable to deceive or confuse third parties is not permitted, although a product can still bear different marks – for example, marks indicating conformity to national or European Standards (or other directives where these are provided for) – as long as they are not liable to cause confusion with the CE marking.

Designing compliant products

Any new product being introduced to the market must have undergone a process of technical and legal review for safety and compliance with legislative requirements (see Chapter 5). If a New Approach directive applies, the process is to an extent predetermined.

Taking as an example Directive 90/396/EEC on appliances burning gaseous fuels (implemented in the UK by The Gas Appliances (Safety) Regulations 1992), Figure 8.2 summarizes the route for the manufacturer applying CE marking.

Other directives which require this approach with varying attestation requirements are those which apply to:

- Machinery (89/392/EEC)
- Low Voltage Electrical Equipment (73/23/EEC)
- Electromagnetic Compatibility (89/336/EEC)
- Construction Products (89/106/EEC)
- Toys (88/378/EEC)
- Simple Pressure Vessels (87/404/EEC)

1.   *Define products in scope*
Gas burning appliances used for cooking, heating, water heating, refrigeration, lighting and washing at normal water temperatures not exceeding 105°C; also fittings (safety, control or regulating devices).

2.   *Identify 'essential requirements'*
In summary, appliances must operate safely, present no danger to people, domestic animals or property when used normally; must be accompanied by installation, use and service instructions and warnings; there are further detailed requirements on materials, design and construction, ignition and gas release, temperatures, sanitation.

3.   *Conformity assessment*
Either: Specified European Standards*:

EN 297 –   Gas-fired central heating boilers
EN 549 –   Rubber materials for seals and diaphragms for gas appliances and equipment
EN 126 –   Multifunctional controls for gas burning appliances
EN 203–2 – Gas headed catering equipment (Pt 2, rational use of energy)

Or: Examinations and checks for conformity with the essential requirements.

4.   *Attestation choices*
For series manufacture:

1.   EC type-examination (Module B) *and* either
2a   EC Declaration of conformity to type (with random checks by Notified Body) (Module C) or
2b   EC Declaration of Conformity to type (guarantee of production quality (Notified Body approves quality system) (Module D) or
2c   EC Declaration of Conformity to type (guarantee of product quality) (Notified Body approves quality system) (Module E) or
2d   EC verification procedure (Module F)

For fittings/small quantities/single units there are slight variations on these options.

CE marking:
■   affixed by manufacturer under 1, 2a, 2b and 2c; otherwise by the Notified Body. Fittings have a 'fitting certificate' instead.
■   CE marking not be applied unless product also complies with other applicable directives, eg EMC and low voltage electrical equipment.

Figure 8.2   Gas appliances: conformity procedures

* as at July 1995, gazetted in the *Official Journal*, no, C 187, 21 July 1995, p. 9.

- New Hot Water Boilers (efficiency requirements) (92/42/EEC)
- Personal Protective Equipment (89/686/EEC)
- Non-automatic Weighing Instruments (90/384/EEC)
- Medical Devices (93/42/EEC)
- Active Implantable Medical Devices (90/385/EEC)
- Telecommunication Terminal Equipment (91/263/EEC)
- Explosives for Civil Uses (93/15/EEC)
- Equipment and Protective Systems for Use in Potentially Explosive Atmospheres (94/9/EC)
- Recreational Craft (94/25/EC)

More New Approach directives are planned, and the list will continue to grow. However, the body of existing product specific legislation existing outside the New Approach remains extensive and also needs to be researched by designers; the scope is very large indeed, from food and food packaging to tractors, cosmetics, industrial chemicals and lawnmowers. In addition, there continues to be a host of national requirements notwithstanding the ongoing harmonization of legislation.

The General Product Safety Directive

The approaches described so far all assume that specific products (or product-related hazards) are identified for the purposes of being addressed by specific Community rules and recognized standards. The limitations of this approach are obvious in terms of products which are left wholly or partly unregulated for safety purposes. Certain Member States (among them the United Kingdom) therefore imposed what was known as a 'general safety requirement' representing a legal standard of safety applicable to all consumer products. The same concept of a general safety requirement has now been recognized at Community level in the General Product Safety (GPS) Directive.

The GPS Directive is not a New Approach directive; there is, for instance, no CE marking provision, but its overall structure is closely related and there are provisions specifying how the

general safety requirement in the GPS Directive and requirements of other directives (in particular, New Approach directives)
interact. In outline, the GPS Directive imposes obligations on
both producers and others in the chain of supply '*to place only
safe products on the market*'. There are two dimensions to this
duty: first, the safety characteristics of the product itself; and,
second, the systems operated by the producer or other person
supplying the product by virtue of which safety is assessed.
Without imposing formal procedures for attestation of conformity, the GPS Directive describes generally the legislative and
technical standards for assessing conformity with the general
safety requirement. Separate obligations are imposed on the
Member States to exercise various enforcement powers to ensure
that only safe products remain in circulation, and a Community
procedure is laid down to avoid conflicting approaches to
enforcement.

For these purposes it was necessary for the first time to define
in European law the concept of a 'safe product', and Article 2(b)
describes this as follows:

Safe product shall mean any product which, under normal or reasonably foreseeable conditions of use, including duration, does not
present any risk or only the minimum risks compatible with the
product's use, considered as acceptable and consistent with a high
level of protection for the safety and health of persons, taking into
account the following points in particular:

- the characteristics of the product, including its composition, packaging, instructions for assembly and maintenance;
- the effect on other products, where it is reasonably foreseeable
  that it will be used with other products;
- the presentation of the product, the labelling, any instructions for
  its use and disposal and any other indication or information provided by the producer;
- the categories of consumers at serious risk when using the product,
  in particular children.

The feasibility of obtaining higher levels of safety or the availability of
other products presenting a lesser degree of risk shall not constitute
grounds for considering the product to be 'unsafe' or 'dangerous'.

Article 2(c) then goes on to define 'dangerous product' as any product which does not meet this definition of safe product.

Although this definition correlates quite closely with that of a defective product for the purposes of the Product Liability Directive, it nevertheless has shortcomings when viewed from the designer's perspective. The critical component to the safety test is the notion of risk/minimum acceptable risk. The absence of any definition of risk or an explanation of the threshold of what is deemed as acceptable and consistent with high levels of protection necessitates turning this lawyer's definition into an engineering reality and requires a fresh approach to the design function in the terms described in Chapter 1. Furthermore, it is stressed that, whilst the product's characteristics are an essential feature of assessing its safety, there are broader considerations in terms of the instructions for use. This requires designers to consider not just the presentation of the product, protection features and servicing and repair regimes, it takes them into the more difficult areas of foreseeing and anticipating possible misuse and also into categories of vulnerable consumers (not just children but also the elderly and those with specific impairments). One significant difference, however, between this definition of safety and that in the Product Liability Directive is that the feasibility or means of making the products safer is specifically excluded as a reason for treating a product as being unsafe.

The duties of producers and distributors under the GPS Directive are considered again in Chapter 9, along with the way in which conformity of the general safety requirement is assessed in the context of regulations and standards. In concluding the description here, there are two notable aspects of the GPS Directive – the safeguard clause and the role of the Commission – which demonstrate its pedigree as the latest in a line of measures seeking to harmonize the approach to product safety across the Community:

The safeguard clause

As has already been noted, the principle behind the directive is that, once conformity with the general safety requirement has been established, the product may circulate freely. Initially, it may therefore come as some surprise that Article 4(3) specifies that a product's conformity with the tests of safety:

> ... shall not bar the competent authorities of the Member States from taking appropriate measures to impose restrictions on its being placed on the market or to require its withdrawal from the market where there is evidence that, despite such conformity, it is dangerous to the health and safety of consumers.

At face value, this provision is contradictory, and it attracted some criticism during the development of the GPS Directive. It is, however, essentially the manifestation of a residual degree of national sovereignty reflecting matters of national interest set out in the original Article 36 of the EC Treaty. These justify restrictions on trade between Member States and the Article fulfils the same function as safeguard clauses in New Approach directives of enabling action to be taken where, for example, a harmonized standard turns out to have shortcomings or where a Member State's product specific laws are insufficiently stringent in authorizing the supply of safe products. Whilst the provision may prove to be valuable (for example, in enabling action to be taken against improper use of an intrinsically safe product) there is undoubtedly scope for the unscrupulous imposition of restrictions on exports into other Member States, and the clause gives rise to a degree of uncertainty as to how effective the GPS Directive will ultimately be in one of its stated aims of eliminating barriers to trade and distortions of competition.

The role of the Commission

The GPS Directive reflects similar provisions found in New Approach directives requiring notification and exchange of information about restrictions on products or their withdrawal between Member States and the Commission (see Chapter 2). The Commission may ultimately take the view that action taken by a Member State was unjustified, although no mechanism or legal instrument is specifically provided for in the GPS Directive to give effect to the Commission's opinion, except where the distinct 'emergency situation' provisions apply.

The Commission's powers to take direct action against products were watered down considerably from earlier proposals. Nevertheless, it still has a role of pivotal importance involving coordination, initiation and decision-making on Community-wide action. As mentioned earlier, the Commission must be informed of any measures taken by a Member State (other than those which are local in effect and limited to the Member State's territory) which restrict the placing of a product on the market or require withdrawal from the market: the Commission is also to be informed of any 'emergency measures' taken by a Member State to deal with any 'serious and immediate risks' and coordinates the informing and response of other Member States. In certain limited circumstances (where Member States disagree about appropriate measures), the Commission may itself initiate action in a case of a serious and immediate risk from a product. After consultation, and at the request of at least one Member State, the Commission may issue a (binding) decision – effective for up to three months in the first instance – requiring Member States to take urgent temporary measures to restrict sales or withdraw products. The Commission is responsible for the initial draft of proposed measures and has ultimate power of adoption if its measures are accepted by the requisite majority of a Committee on Product Safety Emergencies established under the directive and comprising representatives of Member States. (Otherwise the measures must be referred to the Council for approval.) At the very least, therefore, the Commission will be highly influential.

Community priorities for policy 1996–98

On 9 November 1995 the Commission adopted its Third Consumer Policy Action Plan with a list of priorities for the following three years' Commission Work Programmes. These include efforts to improve information for consumers, reviewing and updating the internal market legislation (including proposals on easier 'access to justice' and greater enforceability of consumer guarantees and after-sales services), and concentrating particularly on food safety/purity control systems. Another goal is to strengthen representation of consumers' interests in various influential forums, including CEN and CENELEC, and to implement streamlined consultation procedures.

Summary

Community policy on safety of products has travelled a long way in two decades, gaining considerable momentum through the legislative mechanisms promoting the single market. All the developments described above affect the design function. Some sectors have had their own legislative frameworks for many years – motor vehicles, pharmaceuticals, chemicals and food products being the prime examples. Businesses in these sectors are generally well informed about these requirements and are familiar with the rules they lay down – for example, on testing or type examinations. (That said, as the case histories in Part 3 show, these businesses still encounter serious defects with products in circulation that have escaped notice during design; recall notices in newspapers are an increasingly familiar sight.) Consumer organizations argue strongly that reliance on standards alone has not resulted in safer products, and they point to examples such as the Candy washing machines fires (see Case History 2) as evidence of a wider pattern of design defects emerging with new products.

The trend is towards identification of new sectors for product safety legislation, with the focus being on the 'essential requirements' for their acceptability throughout the whole Community market. The safety of users (consumers and workplace operators) is often paramount in the essential requirements laid down by the directives, and requires a reappraisal of established design considerations.

On the whole, designers will probably feel comfortable with the Community's general approach to defining these essential requirements, which revolves around approved European and

National Standards and the quality systems. None of the legislation, however, actually dictates that compliance with standards conclusively demonstrates compliance with 'essential requirements' or any other specific legal duty. Indeed, the regime of 'approved' British Standards under UK product legislation, compliance with which did in fact pre-empt any further discussion of whether products were safe or not, has had to be withdrawn to fit with the new European approach. It is not the role of notified bodies approving products under the rules to perform risk assessments or give guarantees of safety; this remains the ultimate responsibility of the designer.

At the same time, the rules of liability have been changing – and changing almost wholly in consumers' favour. The onus is on producers to justify the safety of their products, the methods they use for monitoring them and reacting to any safety issues that arise, and to pay compensation whenever injury is caused by a product defect unless very circumscribed statutory defences apply. As illustrated by Case Histories 1, 14 and 19, a design department cannot therefore content itself with merely consulting a published standard and assuming that the absence of any complaints by customers or enforcement authorities implies that the level of safety in its products is adequate. In the modern world of Community-based product safety legislation the challenge is to integrate design into a combination of related legal considerations, including:

- identifying relevant European directives and national regulations
- monitoring European standards for those which create a presumption of conformity with safety requirements
- ensuring conformity with other national standards – standards which may not be directly applicable but which indicate the existence of hazards which may need to be addressed in order to reduce the overall risk of products in the marketplace
- liaison with testing and certification bodies, in particular notified bodies for whom there is a separate agenda in terms of meeting their own quality standards and who therefore may

have a strong interest (even a duty) to check or audit the designer's work

- undertaking comprehensive risk assessments on products which cover their full range of uses and take into account their lifespans

- establishing internal systems for monitoring the changing state of scientific and technical knowledge about the products, as well as the products with which they may be used, the circumstances of use (and possible misuse that may become apparent) and any other factors which could impinge on the state of the art defence or criteria which affect whether or not a product can be described as safe.

As has been seen, it can no longer be assumed that problems with product safety can be contained as a local or even a national issue. Action taken by the authorities in one state, or even a recall by the producer, can rapidly escalate into a crisis for a producer across the whole of the Community market. The liability implications and the practical considerations for designers are the subject of the following chapters.

References

1 See Hodges, C. J. S., Tyler. M. L., and Abbott, H. (1996), *Product Safety*, London: Sweet & Maxwell.

2 *H. P. Bulmer Ltd and Another* v. *J. Bollinger SA* [1974] 2 All ER 1226.

3 Council Resolution of 14 April 1975, on preliminary programme for consumer protection and information policy (OJ No. C 92, 25. April 1975).

4 Council Directive 85/374/EEC of 25 July 1985, on the approximation of the laws, regulations and administrative provisions of the Member States concerning liability for defective products (OJ L 210, 7 August 1985, p. 29).

5 See *First Report on the application of Council Directive on the approximation of laws, regulations and administrative provisions of the Member States concerning liability for defective products*, COM(95) 617 final, Office for Official Publications of the European Communities.

6 See *Completing the Internal Market: White Paper from the Commission to the European Council*, COM(85) Final – 14 June 1985, Office for Official Publications of the European Communities.

7 *A Global Approach to Certification and Testing* (Commission communication to the Council submitted on 15 June 1989) OJ No. C 267, 19.10.89, p. 3.

9
Product Liability in the United Kingdom

Introduction

The term 'product liability' tends to be used in a variety of contexts. It can include many forms of liability for loss caused by a product. Moreover, for many companies product liability issues overlap substantially with regulatory controls, product safety requirements and even environmental protection issues. However, it is most usually thought of as having connotations of physical injury and, more specifically, as the obligation a producer may have to compensate the victim of a defective product. The principles of liability are summarized in this chapter, along with the framework for consumer protection administered by governmental agencies and a number of related legislative provisions.

Liability for defective products

Product defects are commonly divided into the three main categories of manufacturing defects, design defects, marketing defects and warnings, although, in particular cases, the boundaries between them often overlap.

Manufacturing defects

Where a product is defective because there has been some irregularity or breakdown in the production process, with the result that it fails to meet the manufacturers' own specification for the product, it may be said to have a manufacturing defect (see Case History 10). Cases of contamination and mistakes in assembly sometimes occur even with the highest standards of quality control. These cases are not uncommon, as can be seen from the warning and recall notices published in the national press from time to time.

Example 9.1: Poor workmanship in packing cases
A workman was injured when wooden packing cases on which he was standing collapsed. The manufacturers were liable because the boards had not been properly nailed and the weakness in the packing cases should have been foreseen.

Hill v. *James Crowe (Cases) Ltd* [1978] 1 All ER 812

Design defects

Clearly any product could contain a design defect which makes it intrinsically unsafe, regardless of whether it is manufactured correctly. This could arise, for example, from errors in calculations, inadequate specifications or a poor choice of materials, components or sub-assemblies (see Case History 8). Much of the major litigation in the UK has involved medicinal products and, in such cases, it is routinely alleged that insufficient research and testing was carried out into the composition and properties of the compound or device concerned. In the USA some of the most celebrated product liability cases have involved allegations of design defects in vehicles.

Where the design of a product is sufficiently safe for general purposes but may be hazardous in some conditions of use (or for certain categories of users), liability could still arise for a defect of this type (see Case History 1). In such circumstances, however, instructions and warnings may, in effect, render the product safe; if this is so the focus may be more upon the third category of defect.

Example 9.2: Defective trailer coupling

A trailer became detached from the vehicle towing it and veered across the road killing two people in an oncoming car. The manufacturers were held negligent for the coupling design which did not provide an adequate locking mechanism.

Lambert v. *Lewis* [1978] 1 Lloyd's Rep. 610

Marketing defects and warnings

A common type of allegation is that a product was defective because the user received no warnings, or inadequate warnings, from the manufacturer about the need to take necessary precautions to avoid injury by the intrinsic characteristics of the product. Clearly, as Case History 18 demonstrates, the absence of an appropriate warning can make a product unsafe to use.

Example 9.3: Absence of directions for correct usage

A manufacturer did not warn of the known propensity of a chemical substance to react violently with water. He was found liable for death and injury caused by the explosion of an ampoule containing the chemical which occurred when the labels had been washed off.

Vacwell Engineering Co Ltd v. *BDH Chemicals Ltd* [1971] 1 QB 111

If, on the other hand, proper warnings – in the form of packaging labels, data sheets or brochures – are provided and the user ignores these warnings, then the causal link between the product on the one hand and the injury on the other is not made and no liability should result.

In some circumstances the duty to supply adequate information may in fact be discharged by supplying details to a responsible (or 'learned') intermediary, as is the case with pre-scription drugs where the medical practitioner is responsible for advising the patient. More often, though, warnings have to be available in terms comprehensible to the ordinary person. In today's legal environment if the producer can foresee scope for incorrect use or misunderstanding the prudent course is to counter this danger with explicit warnings.

Positive statements made in promotional material and representations by dealers or others prompted by the manufacturer might also affect the legal position by inadvertently creating in the consumer expectations of suitability and safety, as might inferences drawn from the wording or design of a mark applied to the product (as early as 1936 registration of the trademark VITASAFE for vitamins was refused because it implied an assurance of safety). Promoting an established product for use in a new way can also create risks. 'Overselling' may detract from, or be inconsistent with, printed product information and may lead to liability on the part of not only the manufacturer but also others involved in the development of the marketing strategy, including advertising agents, dealers and even trade associations.

Basic principles of liability

A liability claim succeeds by establishing that one or more 'theories' of liability apply to his or her case. In essence, these are principles governing the existence of a legally recognized duty between citizens. The claimant can try to rely on all the theories, but some may ultimately fail – for example, because the plaintiff fails to meet all the requisite criteria or because the theory incorporates a defence applicable to the defendant (for example, that the claimant voluntarily accepted the risk). The claimant only needs to 'score a hit' with one theory to win the case, and normally legal advisers will look at the circumstances early on to choose which principles hold the best chances of success.

Contract

This is potentially the most potent basis for a claim. The nature of the duties in contractual situations are usually well defined and specific to the transaction between the parties. Transactions under which goods are purchased are normally governed by the law of contract, and such contracts embody express terms or certain conditions and warranties implied by law (see Chapter 6).

Express terms

A contract (which need not necessarily be in writing) may, by its 'express terms' (those aspects which are actually stated), lay down the precise quality or safety requirements for the products to which it applies. A manufacturer might, for example, be required to meet a performance specification or certain key criteria such as those demanded by a British Standard. This means that the manufacturer will be liable if there is a design defect or a fault in production, *whether or not* this is due to any carelessness on his part. Even if the blame lies elsewhere entirely – a bought-in defective component, for example – the contract will have been broken. It does not help the manufacturer to argue in defence that he took all reasonable care. Unless the contract has terms which lay down how the consequences of such a breach will be dealt with between the parties, the manufacturer is strictly liable for all losses to his customer caused by the breach.

Implied terms

The effect of the terms implied by statute as part of a contract for sale of goods is that the seller will be liable for injuries or damage suffered if the product is defective or otherwise unfit for use. In this context liability is also strict, and it does not avail sellers to argue in the defence that they took reasonable care.

In the UK this type of liability is governed by The Sale of Goods Act 1979 (as amended with effect from January 1995) which has various provisions, such as those concerned with delivery and transfer of title. The Act makes it a term of supply contracts that the goods will be of *satisfactory quality*, a new expression replacing the previous archaic 'merchantable quality' requirement. The practical distinction is that instead of the focus of quality being on the saleability of a product it is now centred on the consumer's expectation.

Section 14 of the Act says that:

> . . . goods are of satisfactory quality if they meet the standard that a reasonable person would regard as satisfactory, taking account of any description of the goods, the price (if relevant) and all the other relevant circumstances.

The quality factors to be assessed are not defined in any set way, but the Act requires the state and condition of goods to be considered and, if appropriate, the following specific aspects:

- fitness for all purposes for which goods of the kind in question are commonly supplied
- appearance and finish
- freedom from minor defects
- safety, and
- durability.

Example 9.4: Sale of an unsafe motor car

A new car was supplied with a minor defect in the lubrication system but one which caused the engine to seize up on a motorway. The sellers were liable to pay damages as the car was dangerous and the implied terms of quality were breached.

Bernstein v. *Pamson Motors (Golders Green) Ltd* [1987] 2 All ER 220

Consumers therefore have strong contractual claims against the immediate seller of the goods – normally the retailer. Moreover, the UK legislation invalidates exclusion clauses which seek to eliminate the implied terms as to quality and so on from consumer contracts (see page 120).

If the retailer or other seller is sued all is not lost for him. He may in turn bring a claim for reimbursement of his loss against the manufacturer, or an intermediate distributor if that is the person from whom the goods were purchased. A distributor can, in turn, bring a similar claim up the chain of supply, ultimately reaching the manufacturer, with each party in the chain relying on the implied conditions relating to quality and fitness for purpose which exist by virtue of the 1979 Act. It is possible, though, that the manufacturer or a distributor higher up the chain than the retailer may have taken the opportunity to insert exclusion clauses into their supply contracts; because these are not contracts directly with the consumers they are permissible under the legislation, although the court may strike out the exclusions if they are regarded as 'unreasonable'.

Contractual remedies are potent, but they are not universally applicable in product liability claims because this type of liability is personal to the contracting parties ('privity of contract') and it ignores any of those involved with the use of the product who were not purchasers, such as the purchaser's friends, family or employees who may be the ones actually injured. These parties will need to pursue liability through a different route.

Tort

The second way in which a person injured by a product can recover damages is by the tort of negligence. The law of contract is concerned with the rights and liabilities established by agreement between two or more parties, whereas the law of tort is concerned with the rights that one person has against other persons generally. Tort is concerned with civil wrongs rather than criminal wrongs; the remedy for the former being compensation and for the latter imprisonment or a fine, although this distinction is no longer firm.

Under the tort of negligence a person harmed by a product can bring an action against anyone who was responsible for the defect in the product, but must prove negligence and causation. Indeed, the plaintiff has to prove that:

1 the law imposes a duty of care in a given situation – a straight-forward matter between producer and consumer;
2 there is a breach of that duty of care – that is, conduct falling below a standard which the law considers to be reasonable;
3 this breach of duty actually caused the injury.

The duty of care was established in the famous 'snail in the gingerbeer bottle' case, *Donoghue* v. *Stevenson* [1932] AC 562. In a frequently quoted judgement Lord Atkin said:

> A manufacturer of products, which he sells in such a form as to show that he intends them to reach the ultimate consumer in the form in which they left him with no reasonable possibility of intermediate examination, and with the knowledge that the absence of reasonable care in the preparation or putting up of the products will result in an injury to the consumer's life or property, owes a duty to the consumer to take that reasonable care.

This case established the famous 'neighbour principle': a person must take care to avoid acts (or omissions) which it can reasonably be foreseen would be likely to affect his neighbours – in other words, someone who is so closely and directly affected that the safety of the person ought to be in contemplation. This means the duty of care applies not just to the consumer but anyone else who may be affected – a distributor, a storage provider, people providing disposal services and so on (see Case History 10).

Negligence is based on an assessment not of the intrinsic qualities or defectiveness of a product but on the *reasonableness of the conduct* of the defendant. This feature is most clearly shown in situations where a producer fails to recall a product. He may not have been *negligent* in the original design or manufacture if the defect only becomes apparent later; but his obligations to conduct his business with reasonable care can sometimes extend to a duty to recall, or at least warn, the product's current owners (see Case History 7). British Leyland, who were sued over a car accident after they did not act to recall its cars for a fault in the wheel bearings (Case History 9), prompted the judge to say:

> In my view, the duty of care owed by Leyland to the public was to

make a clean breast of the problem and recall all cars which they could, in order that the safety washers could be fitted. I accept, of course, that manufacturers have to steer a course between alarming the public unnecessarily and so damaging the reputation of their products, and observing their duty of care towards those whom they are in a position to protect from dangers of which they and they alone are aware. The duty seems to me to be the higher when they can palliate the worst effects of a failure which, if Leyland's view is right, they could never decisively guard against. They knew the full facts; they saw to it that no one else did. They seriously considered recall and made an estimate of the cost at a figure which seems to me to have been in no way out of proportion to the risks involved. It was decided not to follow this course for commercial reasons. I think this involved a failure to observe their duty to care for the safety of the many who were bound to remain at risk. . . .

The concept of reasonableness has considerable advantages, particularly relating to its flexible application. In contrast with the restrictive nature of a contractual claim, negligence claims also allow for the possibility of a number of defendants being included in an action all of whom may have breached distinct duties of care to the ultimate consumer. Normally the claim for product liability would be against the producer, but it may also be against an independent designer or another person who has been involved in the development and marketing of the product.

Example 9.5: Negligent failure to remove residual chemicals
A purchaser of woollen underpants contracted dermatitis because of excess sulphites left over from processing the fabric. The removal process required the exercise of care by the operators. Although the process was designed adequately and the manner of manufacture was correct, if excess sulphites were present it must have been because someone had made a mistake; negligence was found as a matter of inference from the existence of the defect.

Grant v. *Australian Knitting Mills* [1936] AC 85

It is sometimes possible for claims to be brought for breach of a statutory duty, which may alleviate a claimant from the burden of proving negligence. In particular, contravention of product safety regulations may – depending on certain rules applied by the courts – sometimes be relied upon as the basis for a civil claim even though criminal penalties are the only direct sanction against the producer.

Strict liability

The different European Member State jurisdictions have developed broadly similar liability principles (see Chapter 10) but, as a means of providing fair compensation, there were limitations. Where the burden of proof is on the plaintiff (as it is in the UK) to establish negligence a highly technical and complex analysis of all the surrounding circumstances may be required to assess whether there has been negligent conduct. Even if this can be established, the plaintiff will normally still have to prove that it was the defendant's conduct that actually caused the injury as opposed to some other factor, including the plaintiff's own contributory negligence.

Under the Product Liability Directive the enquiry is not as to the reasonableness of the defendant's conduct but whether, on an objective determination, a given product was *defective*: liability is therefore strict rather than fault-based as it is under contract law.

The advantage to claimants that this has over contract claims is, however, that the class of potential defendants is much wider than the immediate seller.

The Consumer Protection Act 1987

The Product Liability Directive is implemented in the UK by Part I of the Consumer Protection Act 1987. For designers this was a significant watershed as it brought strict liability to the statute book. In a sentence it means that the manufacturer or importer of a product with a design defect will be liable to compensate a person who suffers damage, because of the defect, without the sufferer having to prove negligence or a contractual relationship.

The Act received the Royal Assent on 15 May 1987. A summary of Part I is given below and the full text is in Appendix II. The principal provision is that any person who supplies a defective product will be liable for any damage that it causes. It will not be necessary to prove negligence to recover compensation. The remedy is in addition to all existing remedies in contract and tort.

A product is defined as any goods, electricity, components that are part of a finished product and raw materials; game and agricultural produce (from the soil, stockfarming or fisheries) are excluded unless they have undergone an industrial process.

The Act places liability on four groups of people:

1 the producer of the product – 'producer' being defined to include the manufacturer of the product and/or its defective components;
2 the person who 'won or abstracted' a non-manufactured product;
3 the person who held himself out to be the producer – for example, by using an own brand label or trademark on the product (an 'own-brander');
4 the importer of the product into the European Community.

Own-branders are defined as those who have held themselves out to be the producer of a product, by putting their name on the product, or using a trademark or other distinguishing mark in relation to a product.

Apart from manufacturers, importers and own-branders, a person who *supplies* a product can also be liable if he fails to identify the person who supplied him with it.

The four groups above are not mutually exclusive and it may be possible to have two or more products for legal purposes[1]. Also, a product is held to be defective if its safety is not such as people generally are entitled to expect. This includes the safety of components or raw materials comprised in another product. Safety is considered in the context of the risks of death, personal injury or damage to private property – although, for a claim for damage to property the amount must be in excess of £275.

A court will consider all the circumstances in determining the degree of safety that people are generally entitled to expect, but the Act refers specifically to the relevance of:

- the manner in which, and purpose for which, the product has been marketed, its presentation and the use of any mark in relation to it
- instructions for, or warnings with respect to, doing or refraining from doing anything in relation to the product
- what might reasonably be expected to be done with, or in relation to, the product
- the time when the product was supplied by its producer to another.

The producers of goods will not be prejudiced if they (or others) later improve on the safety of the product in question. The Act provides that later improvements in the safety of a product or its successors will not of themselves be sufficient cause to infer that the original product was defective.

There are six defences available to the producer. He would have to prove:

1 that compliance with a requirement imposed by any Community obligation caused the defect;
2 that he did not supply the product;
3 that the product was not supplied in the course of his business or for profit;
4 that the defect did not exist in the product when he supplied it;
5 that the state of scientific and technical knowledge at the time he supplied the product was such that no producer of such a product could have been expected to have discovered the defect;
6 for a component or raw material, that the defect was wholly attributable to the design of the product in which it was comprised, or was due to compliance with the instructions given by the producer of the subsequent product.

Where two or more persons are liable for the same damage –

because under the Act there can be two or more producers as broadly defined – their liability is 'joint and several', which means both are equally liable to the plaintiff for the full amount of the claim (although the court may apportion shares between them). If the damage was caused partly by a defect in the product, and partly by the fault of the person suffering the damage, then the claimant's contributory negligence will be taken into account.

Employers' Liability (Defective Equipment) Act 1969

This Act is a strict liability provision, specific to the UK, that predates the Product Liability Directive. If an employee suffers death or personal injury through a defect in equipment supplied, his or her employer is deemed to have been negligent. This liability is strict as it is not possible to exclude or limit any liability imposed by the Act. It is not enough, however, for the employee to suffer injury at work and plant or equipment to be involved. To come under the umbrella of the 1969 Act the employee must show that the defect in the equipment caused the accident.

The word 'equipment' includes any plant and machinery, vehicles, aircraft and clothing. The courts have taken an expansive view of the word as applying not just to tools and other means of production but also the actual product being worked on (a flagstone) and even the overall structure worked on (a ship).

The Employers' Liability (Compulsory Insurance) Act 1969 ensures that employers, other than governmental and local authority employers, must have insurance that will compensate employees injured by defective equipment, and that the insurance must be in the terms of an 'approved policy' as defined in the Act.

Exclusion clauses

Exclusion clauses play a limited role in eliminating liability to the ultimate consumer, mainly because of the 'privity of contract' doctrine referred to earlier – the contractual relationship with the manufacturer is not normally a direct one because the retailer is the party supplying the consumer. Nevertheless, the scope for excluding, capping or imposing conditions on liability, or for escaping by notices 'disclaiming' liability (either to consumers or others in the supply chain) is now strongly curtailed by legislation.

Unfair Contract Terms Act 1977

The principal aim of the Unfair Contract Terms Act (UCTA) is to invalidate or restrict attempts, by means of contractual terms or notices, to exclude liability for negligence arising in the course of business. Under UCTA liability for death or personal injury resulting from negligence cannot be excluded. Contractual terms or notices that try to do this are void; neither can they be used as a basis for saying an injured person knew of, and therefore accepted, the risk.

Attempts to disclaim liability in a contract with a consumer for breach of the implied undertakings of satisfactory quality or fitness for purpose are also ineffective. Moreover, it is an offence under separate provisions even to include this form of disclaimer in a consumer contract document.

Further restrictions apply to contracts which are made with a consumer, or made between two businesses on one of the other's written standard terms. Here liability for loss or damage can only be excluded insofar as the contract term or notice satisfies, in the view of the court, a reasonableness test. The general 'reasonableness' test is whether the term is a fair and reasonable one having regard to the circumstances which were, or ought reasonably to have been, known to or in the contemplation of the parties when the contract was made. In the case of an exclusion notice the test is whether it is fair and reasonable to allow reliance on it in view of all the circumstances obtaining when the liability would arise.

In all applications of the reasonableness test, the burden of showing reasonableness is on the person who is asserting that the clause should be upheld as reasonable. The provisions are very wide-reaching, covering sellers and hirers of goods, providers of services and some less obviously commercial activities.

Example 9.6: An unfair limit on damages recoverable for breach of contract

A software error in a database supplied to a local authority for a community charge register led to losses of £1.3 million. In the computer company's standard terms it had limited its liability to only £100 000. The judge held the restriction on liability to be unreasonable on account of unequal bargaining power and absence of an opportunity to negotiate the contract, the unrealistically low limit given the potential losses in the event of breach of contract, and the fact that a major international company was better placed than a local authority to foot the bill, especially as it was insured in an aggregate sum of £50 million worldwide.

St Albans City & District Council v. *International Computers Ltd, The Times,* 11 November 1994

The bar on excluding liability for death or injury in UCTA does not apply to strict liability, but the Consumer Protection Act 1987 (s.7) prohibits exclusion clauses or notices against this form of liability, as does the Employers' Liability (Defective Equipment) Act 1969.

The Unfair Terms in Consumer Contracts Regulations 1994

The European Directive on Unfair Terms in Consumer Contracts (93/13/EEC) was implemented by these 1994 Regulations which came into force on 1 July 1995. UCTA remains in force: the two sets of controls exist in parallel – the 1977 Act being concerned with exclusion clauses and reasonableness for both business and consumer transactions (as well as some warning notices), and the 1994 Regulations with fairness of terms generally in consumer contracts.

The Regulations apply to:

a) contracts made between a consumer and a seller of goods or a supplier of services acting for business purposes;

b) any term in a contract concluded with a consumer where the term has not been individually negotiated (a term is treated as not having been individually negotiated if it is drafted in advance and where the consumer has not been able to influence the substance of the term) and terms which define the main subject matter of the contract or the price are not subject to the Regulations, as long as the term in question is in 'plain, intelligible language'.

A term which is not individually negotiated must not be 'unfair'. Here, unfair refers to a term which '*contrary to the requirement of good faith, causes a significant imbalance in the parties' rights and obligations under the contract to the detriment of the consumer*'. All the circumstances of the relationship are relevant to this test, but the Regulations emphasize four particular factors:

- the strength of the parties' bargaining positions
- whether the consumer had an inducement to agree to the term
- whether the goods or services were supplied to the special order of the consumer
- the extent to which the seller or supplier has dealt fairly with the consumer.

The Regulations also contain an '*indicative and non-exhaustive list*' of terms which *may* (but not necessarily *must*) be regarded as unfair – for example, any provision excluding or limiting liability in the event of death or personal injury to a consumer caused by the seller to the supplier. If a term is deemed to be unfair, it will not be binding on the consumer. The contract as a whole will continue to bind the parties if it is capable of continuing in existence without the unfair term.

The Regulations also contain a requirement that the seller or supplier ensures that terms are expressed in plain, intelligible language. If there is doubt an interpretation favourable to the consumer is to prevail.

Enforcement of the Regulations is limited; like UCTA, the main sanction is the risk of a term being unenforceable. However, an important new feature is power given to the Office of Fair Trading (OFT) under the 1994 Regulations to obtain injunctions to prevent the use of an unfair term (or even similar terms, or the recommendation to others of such terms, which is a measure designed to allow the OFT to tackle trade association or professional bodies recommending unacceptable standard terms).

Indemnities

The courts recognize the distinction between exclusion of liability on one hand and indemnity on the other. The latter is concerned not with preventing the recovery of damages where there is a breach of duty, but rather transferring or allocating the risk, so identifying who is to bear the consequences of the particular act or omission. The courts have upheld indemnities dealing with accidents. For example in *Thompson* v. *T Lohan (Plant Hire) Ltd*[2] it was a condition in a plant hire contract for the hirer to 'fully and completely indemnify the owner in respect of all claims by any person whatsoever for injury to person or property caused by or in connection with or arising out of use of the plant' whether arising under statute or common law. Because the negligence of the driver supplied with the plant caused a fatal accident the hire company was found liable and sought to claim against the hirer under the indemnity. It was held that liability for negligence had been successfully transferred to the hirer and that UCTA did not affect this term since it was not excluding or restricting liability in relation to the victim of the negligence.

Civil Liability (Contribution) Act 1978

This Act represented a considerable change in the position of those liable for an award for damages. Before the Act was passed a person held liable for damages could not directly recover any contribution towards the overall loss from another whose actions had contributed. The Act makes provision for contribution by two or more persons held to be liable for the same award for damages.

Section 1 of the Act states:

(1) Subject to the following provisions of this section, any person liable in respect of any damage suffered by another person may recover contribution from any other person liable in respect of the same damage (whether jointly with him or otherwise).

(2) A person shall be entitled to recover contribution by virtue of sub-section (1) above notwithstanding that he has ceased to be liable in respect of the damage in question since the time when the damage occurred, provided that he was so liable immediately before he made or was ordered or agreed to make payment in respect of 'which the contribution is sought'.

A person cannot, by way of contribution proceedings, be required to pay more than he or she would have been liable to pay if he or she had been sued directly by the plaintiff. A defendant's right to contribution is subject to a period of limitation of two years from the date on which it arose.

Limitation Act 1980

To bring or defend an action successfully a party has to call evidence. The cogency of evidence, particularly eye-witness evidence, obviously diminishes with the passage of time. Parties cannot be expected to keep documents which might be evidential for an indefinite period. Expert witnesses find difficulty in explaining, for example, what the state of knowledge of the art was years ago. It is inequitable for a potential claim to be hanging over the head of a defendant for an unconscionable period.

The law, recognizing such problems, has developed periods of limitation so that, even if all the essential elements of a successful claim are present, an action will fail if it is not brought within the requisite time. It will be barred by reason of limitation.

The provisions of the Limitation Act 1980 include those whereby an action in tort or one founded on simple contract, or one to enforce an award must be brought within six years of the cause of the action accruing.

There are also provisions for actions for personal injuries or death when the period is three years from the date the claimant knew or should have known of the injury, that the injury was significant, that the defect in the product caused it, and the identity of the person to whom this is attributable. These are abstract notions of what amounts to a person's knowledge which are hard to apply in practice, and they can result in complex issues requiring a trial by the court separately to determine whether the main issues of the claim need to be dealt with at all if limitation is a complete defence.

An important provision is to be found in section 33, which is concerned with the discretionary exclusion of the time limit for actions in respect of personal injuries or death. If the court considers that it would be equitable to allow an action to proceed, the time limits provided for in the Act may be disregarded. It is difficult to predict the findings of the court as to its discretion, but the interests of individual consumers are often treated as outweighing the inconvenience to large companies having to face actions which have been initiated outside the normal three-year period.

Special rules apply to strict liability actions brought under the Consumer Protection Act 1987. There is, in addition, a 'long-stop' for any liability: the claimant must bring his claim within ten years of the 'relevant time', which is defined as the time that the defendant supplied the product unless he is not the producer, own-brander or importer into the European Union. For persons not in one of these categories – for example, intermediate suppliers – the relevant time is when the product was last supplied by a person who does fall within these categories. In practice, these dates will be very difficult to identify and use against claimants unless careful records are kept.

Other relevant legislation

There can be no one Act that governs design. The government formulates laws and regulations to deal with a product in the hands of the user; frequently legislation appears after a disaster has drawn attention to a defect. Design criteria are usually the province of standards bodies, professional societies and trade associations. In certain cases, safety regulations may be imposed on specific products by a Secretary of State under a relevant Act. A review of some of the Acts that can affect design must, therefore, be selective.

The General Product Safety Regulations 1994

These Regulations, which implement the General Product Safety Directive (92/59/EEC) require a basic level of safety, termed the 'general safety requirement', for products intended for, or likely to be used by, consumers (see also Chapter 8). Various categories of products are excluded from their scope – secondhand products which are 'antiques' or products supplied before being repaired or reconditioned prior to use. More importantly, the GPS Regulations do not affect a product insofar as there are either specific safety provisions for a product type in Community law, or a product is already subject to total harmonization rules which lay down safety requirements governing it. Consequently, the provisions of the Regulations continue to apply where they have not been ousted by other product-specific rules: the provisions have been described as 'filling the gap' for situations where an aspect of product safety is otherwise unregulated.

This approach contrasts sharply with the provisions of Part II of the Consumer Protection Act 1987 which formerly represented the principal legislation in this area; there, named categories of products (for example food) were wholly excluded from their requirements and were left to be dealt with under their own legislation. Under the GPS Regulations a more substantive analysis must be undertaken to compare the safety provisions in, for example, a New Approach Directive with the GPS Regulations. This gives rise to many uncertainties; for example, the Toys Directive does not include essential requirements on noise, and the Cosmetics Directives do not deal with a number of safety aspects, such as flammability.

Regulation 7 provides that a product may not be placed on the market unless it is safe, and contravention is an offence unless 'due diligence' can be proved by the producer. The definition of safe products have, with a few minor alterations, been adopted straight from the GPS Directive (see page 98) and stress the need for both sound design and forethought in terms of the recommended use of a product and proper instructions to the consumer. This obligation falls principally on the producer who will normally be the manufacturer, but there is an extended definition which includes any person presenting himself as a manufacturer by use of his name or trademark, a person who reconditions the product, an importer or the representative of a manufacturer outside the Community. A person can also be classed as a producer if he is in the supply chain and his activities may affect the safety properties of a product. This is a new concept and, whilst it is likely to be clear in some circumstances that, for example, a product's reprocessing causes this provision to apply, there are a number of grey areas, such as storage of a product or even its retail, where conceivably the person concerned could have a duty to ensure the product remains safe.

Example 9.7: Exploding eggs

An importer of microwave egg boiler devices did not supply instructions to break the eggs before cooking them. Retailers were later sent information by the importers, but it was not acted on and there was evidence of the danger of eggs exploding. The general safety requirement was contravened and the subsequent information to retailers had not given sufficient prominence to the danger.

Coventry City Council v. *Ackerman Group* (unreported case in the Divisional Court, 13 July 1994)

In addition to these obligations there are separate requirements on producers to provide, and also obtain, information about their products. Consumers must be given relevant information to assess the product's risks throughout its normal or reasonably foreseeable period of use where those dangers are not obvious without adequate warnings. Producers are required to exercise vigilance through measures such as the marking up of batches so the products can be identified, sample testing, complaints investigations and keeping the supply chain informed of monitoring. This is reinforced by the further requirement 'to take appropriate action, including, if necessary, withdrawing the product in question from the market' in order to avoid risks to consumers. There is debate about whether this is a statutory obligation to recall products. The UK government position is that it could require the cessation of sale but not the actual recall of products in the hands of consumers.

Supplementary duties are placed on 'distributors'. These are persons in the supply chain (including retailers) who do not affect the safety properties of products themselves but who are required to participate in the post-marketing surveillance under-taken by producers, and specifically not to supply products which they know – or should presume – are dangerous.

Supplementing the definition of safe products are further pro-visions in the Regulations which provide guidance on what is an acceptable level of safety. Where a product conforms to specific rules in UK law laying down health and safety requirements which must be fulfilled for the product to be supplied, there is a presum-ption that the product is safe for the purposes of the GPS Regu-lations. As with the safeguard clause in the New Approach Directives, the producer could still be prosecuted if it is shown that, despite such compliance, the product is still actually dangerous.

Example 9.8: Cooker hoods compliant with the regulations but fail to meet the 'general safety requirement'

Cooker hoods supplied with gas hobs were found to catch fire. They complied with the Low Voltage Electrical Equip-ment Regulations and the relevant British Standard. The court held the general safety requirement was nevertheless contravened because the hoods (while intrinsically safe) were dangerous in combination with the hobs, and com-pliance with the other product-specific regulations and standards was not relevant to this particular danger.

Whirlpool (UK) Ltd and Magnet Ltd v. *Gloucestershire County Council* (unreported case in the Divisional Court, 13 December 1993 – see also Case History 1)

In the absence of specific regulatory requirements the following criteria have to be taken into account to assess the general safety requirement:

1 voluntary national standards of the UK which give effect to a European Standard; or
2 Community technical specifications; or
3 in the absence of these:
   ■ standards drawn up in the UK
   ■ codes of good practice in the product sector concerned (for example, government guidelines, trade association codes or other procedures adopted by producers) or
   ■ the state of the art and technology.

The safety which consumers may reasonably expect is a further consideration which is to be taken into account alongside these various standards and codes. As a result, the courts are liable to disregard compliance with standards, even if they are well recognized and treated as a benchmark within the sector of industry, if there is evidence that the products which actually reached the consumer did not meet what is termed 'a high level of protection' that consumers are entitled to expect. Increasingly, courts are pointing to the need for more sophisticated risk assessment techniques to be applied than has hitherto been treated as the norm in product design.

The penalties for failure to comply with these Regulations are fines up to £5000 and/or up to three months' imprisonment (for convicted individuals – see Chapter 11). In addition, there are various enforcement powers that can be exercised, details of which are set out in the Consumer Protection Act 1987 Part II. They consist of:

■ Department of Trade and Industry powers to prohibit sales or require mandatory publication of warning notices
■ local authority powers to carry out investigations and prevent sales by temporary 'suspension notices'
■ powers of the court to forfeit dangerous goods and order their destruction.

The GPS Regulations are not meant to affect products for use in the workplace, and production equipment, capital goods and materials for trade use are not covered. The absence of precise definition in this area gives rise to a number of uncertainties for 'border-line' products, such as transport vehicles and lifts made available to consumers incidentally to the provision of the commercial services, and goods such as those available through DIY outlets which are available for both business and domestic use. Much will depend on the way in which the products are marketed, but designers need to anticipate that products may be covered by the alternative provisions which regulate the supply of products used in business.

Health and Safety at Work Act 1974

Producers of products used in business are governed by this Act which provides a legislative framework for the protection of people at work and others affected by work processes. Every employer has the duty to ensure, so far as is reasonably practicable, the health, safety and welfare at work of all his employees. He or she must, so far as is reasonably practicable make sure that

- the plant and systems are safe and without risks to health
- the use, handling, storage and transport of articles and substances are safe and without risk
- the necessary information, instruction, training and supervision are provided
- there are no risks involved with access to or exit from the working environment.

One of the principles of the Act is that industry should take responsibility for the health and safety of those people likely to be affected by its activities. The critical link in this chain is section 6 governing products for use at work, which aims to ensure that acceptable levels of health and safety are incorporated at the design and manufacturing stage. Section 6 provides that it is the duty of any person who designs, manufactures, imports or supplies any article or substance for use at work, or any article of fairground equipment, to ensure, so far as is reasonably practicable, that it is so designed and produced that it will be safe and without risk to health at all times when it is used by people at work.

The responsible person has to arrange for the necessary testing and examination to be carried out to ensure that the duty is met. There is also a specific duty to take the necessary steps to ensure that adequate information is supplied with the article so that it will be safe and without risk to health when used and when disposed of. He or she has to provide revisions of information, if that becomes necessary, because a serious risk to health or safety is discovered after the products are supplied.

In conjunction with section 6, the Regulations implementing New Approach Directives – for example, the Supply of Machinery (Safety) Regulations and the Personal Protective Equipment (EC Directive) Regulations 1992 – contain enforcement provisions relating specifically to the effects of specific product risks in the workplace (see Chapter 8). Enforcement is carried out by Health and Safety Executive inspectors who can serve Improvement and Prohibition Notices to require alterations to products or prevent their supply as appropriate. They can also bring prosecutions for the supply of unsafe products, for which the courts can impose fines with no financial limit.

Designers of structures that are part of a building are subject to special rules contained in the Construction (Design and Management) Regulations 1994 ('CDM') which are part of health and safety, rather than product, safety legislation. They are required to minimize risks to workmen on the project and to provide information about safe construction methods. Reference should be made to the relevant Health and Safety Commission literature.[3]

Summary

In simple terms, a company must design and supply only safe products. Not only must the design be safe for the intended use, but it also should accommodate foreseeable misuse, and the designer needs to give consideration to all the necessary instructions and warnings for the protection of people using the product. Reliance on contractual exclusions of liability later in the chain of supply will be of limited effect and will not give reliable protection.

The designer must also take into account all those who may be affected by the product – that is, people other than the eventual user, such as distributors, installers, service engineers and even bystanders. The duty to take reasonable care extends to the duty to warn the end-user when the risk in a product may be hidden.

Under modern law, strict liability will arise if a product has a defect in it and someone is injured regardless of any issue of carelessness. The defences available to the producer are quite limited; if defendants are to succeed in proving them the product's design will have to have been carried out to the highest standard of safety currently available.

Even if a product has caused no actual harm, government agencies with power to enforce consumer and workplace legislation are empowered to prevent supply if the goods are considered unsafe; under the statutory tests, compliance with product Regulations and recognized standards are key considerations. Nevertheless, this legislation places on the designer a duty to exercise his or her judgement beyond such prescribed criteria to determine that products are objectively safe.

References

1 *Ralph* v. *Yamaha Motor Corporation, USA* unreported 24 July 1996, High Court, London.
2 1987 2 A11.E.R 631.
3 See *Management Construction for Health and Safety* (1995) – CDM Regulations Approved Code of Practice L54 (1995), HSE Books. See also Peters, R. and Gill, T, *Health and Safety – Liability and Litigation*, London: FT Law & Tax, para. I3.34 *et seq.*

10
Liabilities outside the UK

Introduction

This chapter looks at the way different countries apply product liability laws and product safety requirements to protect their consumers. It is not intended as a complete survey, neither in terms of the countries mentioned nor the contents of their laws. Reference should be made to the works listed at the end of the chapter for more detailed sources of information. The examples taken for these purposes are from Europe (France, Germany and Italy) and, looking further afield, the United States, Australia and Japan.

France

The French legal system is different from that of the UK, other Commonwealth countries and the USA in that it is based on entirely distinct tenets of civil law and it is largely codified in the French Civil Code. Nevertheless, on analysis, the consequences for producers are broadly equivalent to contractual and fault-based liability, supplemented by remedies for breach of statutory duty, as in the UK. France is currently the only country not to have formally implemented the European Product Liability Directive, although it is felt that French law can be construed in a manner consistent with the operation of the Directive anyway.

Draft implementing legislation for the Product Liability Directive in France has been pending since 1990, consisting in part of a transcription of the main provisions of the Directive itself, which would comprise an additional Title in the Civil Code, but which could also render void certain aspects of the existing

French product liability law. This is controversial, because the Directive provides that its measures should not affect pre-existing rules of contractual or non-contractual liability. The particular difficulty insofar as the simultaneous application of the pre-existing French liability laws is that (as will be seen below) this could, for instance, render the development risk defence ineffective. This has been one of the points of debate on implementation, and it remains to be seen how far French claimants will still be able to rely on existing product liability principles. There are further departures from the framework of the Directive in the draft-implementing measure, in that the producer could be liable for not recalling a defective product; there would be liability placed on all sellers, lessors and suppliers as if they were producers (and no 'exoneration' of a supplier who names the producer or other prior supplier). There are various other differences in the finer details.

Even prior to implementation of the Directive, there are indications that the French courts are aligning national law with strict liability when it comes to dealing with individual cases (although it has to be noted that the concept of binding precedent following previous decisions is not a feature of the French system).

Under the law as it stands, without formal implementation of the Directive, claims can be brought under express or implied contractual obligations, including an implied obligation against latent defects making a product improper for the intended use. (For these purposes the French courts do not apply a rigid privity of contract rule so a consumer can have a direct cause of action against the manufacturer despite having obtained a product from a retailer.) In some circumstances there has been held to be an implied duty to provide warnings and instructions about dangerous products. The distinction between strict and fault-based liability for the purposes of these provisions is somewhat blurred, but on the whole a claimant does not have to demonstrate negligence if the product is actually defective; however, manufacturers will not generally be liable for 'apparent' defects which the purchaser could have discovered. In addition to implied warranties about hidden defects there is also a concept of a general *obligation de sécurité*, which is a duty to deliver products that do not create hazards for persons or property.

Tortious liability is also included in the Civil Code, although due to the way the courts have interpreted this, it is generally not now necessary for a claimant to prove negligence; generally, negligence is inferred from the fact that a defective product has found its way on to the market. A development risks or state of the art defence is not available in the face of this approach. However, on this basis, liability can also arise for failure to recall a product from the market. A variant on these principles is the concept of *garde de la structure*, whereby a manufacturer is deemed to be in a position to control the 'structure' of the product even after it has been supplied, although cases on this basis are rare and have been confined to a limited class of products which have exploded, for example, because of a build-up of pressure.

In criminal cases French courts are able to award sums representing civil damages, and may do so on a provisional basis pending fuller investigation of the full entitlement to a civil claim.

By the end of 1995 France had not implemented the European General Product Safety Directive, but under the law of 21 July 1983 there is a provision equivalent to a general safety requirement:

> Products and services must, under conditions of normal use or in conditions which are reasonably foreseeable by the professional, offer the safety which one may legitimately expect and not be harmful to persons.

As well as being a criminal offence, there are extensive other enforcement mechanisms including forfeiture and destruction, and sequestration of profits arising out of the sale of the defective products. In cases of serious and immediate danger the government has various powers to impose temporary measures suspending manufacture, importation or distribution. It also has the power to order the products on the market to be checked by an authorized body, and to require the application of warnings. Under these provisions the full recall of products can also be ordered by a government minister (although it is unclear as to how vigorously a direction to retrieve products from consumers can be enforced; the authorities have recognized in the past the serious practical difficulties this can entail). Parliament can also decree the permanent withdrawal of products from the market on the advice of the National Consumer Safety Commission, and French courts can, in certain circumstances, grant injunctions to restrain the sale of products where proceedings have been launched for product safety offences.

Industrial products are dealt with under the French Labour Code – for example, there is a general obligation that any machine, apparatus, tools, engines, materials and other equipment defined as work machinery must be designed and constructed for safety in installation, use and maintenance – and the Code forbids importation into France of non-compliant machinery.

A particular characteristic of the French product safety system is the involvement (to a more significant degree) of the general criminal law. Until recently it had been the practice in France for prosecutions for involuntary homicide or the infliction of involuntary bodily injury to be brought against individual managers. Under the new 1994 French Criminal Code companies as well as individuals can now be subject to criminal proceedings. In 1995 the President of Reckitt & Coleman was convicted of criminal negligence after an explosion, the cause of which was alleged to be inadequate instructions involving a serious fire and serious injury to an individual, for use supplied with an aerosol insecticide spray.

Germany

Germany has implemented the European Product Liability Directive but, at the time of writing, not the General Product Safety Directive. Notably, however, the General Product Liability Act implementing the former excludes all pharmaceutical products which are covered separately under a pre-existing strict liability regime, and that legislation includes lower financial limits on damages which would not otherwise apply under the Directive itself.

Even before the Product Liability Act 1990 the German Civil Code provided for a form of strict liability. Contractual warranties that products are reasonably fit for their intended purpose exist as implied terms under the German Civil Code but, as in the UK, these are available only against the seller, and German law provides only limited remedies for the consumer in such cases. Fault-based liability developed gradually in Germany for product liability, emerging from general principles of liability for culpably causing injury to others in relation to matters under a producer's control. For these purposes, negligence is an element of liability but the German courts effectively reverse the onus of proof in this respect where a defect can be established. (The plaintiff still bears the burden of proof of proving causation between the breach and his injury.) The producer would have to bring evidence to show that the defect occurred notwithstanding compliance with proper safety controls. Fault-based liability under the German Civil Code may be taken to imply a duty to recall products where this is necessary to meet the basic obligation to protect the health and safety of consumers.

As with the UK, the Product Liability Act (*Produkthaftungsgesetz*) supplements, rather than replaces, these existing remedies. It includes the development risk defence and generally follows the pattern of the Product Liability Directive. As a consequence of specific provisions describing the compensation that shall be paid (which includes medical treatment, pecuniary loss experienced during illness and loss of financial support suffered by third parties dependent on an injured deceased) damages for non-pecuniary losses – specifically pain and suffering as they would be recognized in the UK – are not recoverable unless negligence can be proved.

Germany is notable for having a number of reported decisions made under the new strict liability provisions (the only other judgment published at the time of writing being an Italian one – see page 139). One case for damage caused by the emission of oily particles from the burning of advent candles concerned the owner of an apartment; the compensation included a sum for the inconvenience to the plaintiff of being unable to use the apartment for a substantial period afterwards. The court found that causation was obvious in this case:

> ... The first impression of the situation speaks for the Plaintiff. As there was no other source of soot in the apartment apart from the Advent candles, common sense indicates that these are the cause of the damage. The fact that the candles actually produced soot was shown during the burn experiment during the oral Court hearing. The Plaintiff was also not in a position to give any other cause for the damage.

Here it was in fact the retailer who was found liable, on account of being unable to name the previous suppliers pursuant to the provisions of the German law mirroring the Directive.

Another case is a more questionable application of the strict liability rules. The plaintiff was successful in his claim that the resulting colour of a timber protection product when painted on his car port was darker than the 'pine' description. Although the framework was held to be contributorily negligent to the extent of 50 per cent of the claim the case indicates that, whatever was the draftsman's ambition for the Directive, the term 'defect' is capable of being construed very broadly. Certainly it is questionable whether UK courts would regard this as anything other than non-performance or misdescription of a product. The absence of any safety indication in this case makes that judgment questionable.

The German government challenged the validity of the General Product Safety Directive in the European Court, arguing (unsuccessfully) that there was no legal basis for introducing the Directive under Article 100A of the Treaty. Following the Bundesrat's rejection of earlier proposals, a draft law for implementing the General Product Safety Regulations was published in 1995 which, without implementing the GPS Directive word-for-word, followed the basic principles. (The proposals also incorporated a general prohibition against use of CE marking except where permitted by law.) In contrast to the UK implementation, the German proposals would list product categories – for example, medicines and building products – which are not covered by the general safety requirement. Various other categories of products (for example, food and explosives) would only be covered by those provisions concerning warnings and withdrawal from the market. The responsible authority would be able to order recall or arrange for a product's destruction, unless a manufacturer or distributor took measures to avert the danger.

There are various product safety requirements in German domestic law. Under the Safety of Equipment Act 1968 which lays down the safety requirements for all technical equipment displayed or marketed by a manufacturer or importer in the course of business, including household equipment and equipment for sports, hobbies and toys, there is a specific requirement to supply appropriate instructions for using, assembling or maintaining technical equipment. The law of Foodstuffs, Tobacco, Cosmetics and Commodities 1974 has as its main objective the protection of health and safety of consumers, including various general prohibitions on commodities not satisfying the legal requirements and powers to ban sales of products considered by the government to be dangerous.

Italy

The European Product Liability Directive was implemented in Italy by Presidential Decree No. 224 of 24 May 1988, and this incorporates the development risk defence. There are restrictions on the recovery of damages for non-economic loss (pain and suffering), effectively for situations where the conduct of the defendant is in breach of the criminal law. The secondary liability of suppliers who cannot name the producer is more circumscribed by virtue of certain procedural requirements and time-limits to which the claimant must adhere in making a request for the information. (The suppliers' release from liability upon giving such information is, however, more limited than in the UK legislation in that it mainly enables the producer to be brought into any action rather than exempts the supplier from strict liability under the Decree.)

Liability has been determined under the Directive in Italy in a case involving an accident in which the frame of a two-year-old mountain bike collapsed, and the producer was identifiable by his name, trademark and from the sales receipts. Expert evidence was produced to show that part of the frame was made of defective steel tubing of insufficient strength and, on this basis, the court concluded that there was a defect for the purposes of strict liability.

In addition to Presidential Decree No. 224, fault-based liability exists in Italy under section 2043 of the Civil Code for negligent acts causing injury, and, in a number of cases, Italian courts have developed this effectively to reverse the burden of proof so that negligence may be inferred from a defect.

The General Product Safety Directive was implemented by Presidential Decree No. 115 of 17 March 1995 which includes a number of administrative provisions to supplement what had previously been quite a fragmented system of product safety legislation. Food and food supplements are excluded from the scope of this Decree and are covered by a separate Decree of 3 March 1993. Other product safety provisions include Law 547 of 1955 (as subsequently amended in respect of the European Machinery Directive) which is of broad application to mechanical equipment and lays down highly detailed minimum safety standards, and Law 791 of 1977 which deals with electrical equipment.

The United States

The US legal system is often seen as having a seminal influence on product liability litigation and practice. The US courts (and the attornies who practise there) have shown themselves more inventive than most in both refining existing principles of law and expounding new theories upon which product liability claims can be developed. To most, however, the system of justice in this particular field of litigation seems to be characterized by voluminous litigation – attorneys generating claims by virtue of providing their services on a no-win-no-fee basis, cases being decided by juries who also determine the amount of damages, and laws which enable claimants to receive massive 'punitive damages' going beyond what would normally be regarded as compensation for injury suffered. In one case the jury awarded $62.4 million (including $58 million in punitive damages) for a claim for a vehicle accident, the punitive damages apparently being calculated simply by the jury multiplying the $83 estimated cost per vehicle to redesign the stability features by the number of vehicles sold by the defendant.

There is little to be gained in recounting the many stories circulating about extraordinary product liability cases in the United States which undoubtedly displays many cultural differences between it and other jurisdiction. However, many of the excesses are corrected through appeal hearings. In some instances – for example tobacco litigation – juries have in fact acted as a brake on claims that are seen as unjustified against the background of claimants' acceptance of products' alleged inherent risks. Indeed, claimants in the United States have been singularly unsuccessful in this particular area and have never recovered any damages at all from the tobacco companies.

There are a number of additional features which make product liability litigation in the United States a considerably more sophisticated process than elsewhere. In particular, some states apply 'market share' theories where individual manufacturer's products cannot be distinguished as the cause of injury, 'successor corporation' liability and extended liability for group companies. The concurrent jurisdiction of federal and state courts can lead to plaintiffs 'forum shopping' for a jurisdiction with the law most favourable to them. There may be uncertainty about state laws as to their enforceability under the Constitution or, for instance, because any finding a state court might make in relation to instructions and warnings might be of no effect because federal law governing the product in question lays down specific requirements which 'pre-empt' findings that different information should have been given to consumers.

Product liability claims may be brought on a variety of bases which broadly equate to those found in UK and the other European jurisdictions: fault-based liability (negligence); breach of express or implied warranties (contract); and strict liability (see below). In addition, claims are also commonly framed in terms of misrepresentations being made about the product, violation of consumer protection statutes, and even fraud, conspiracy and other criminal behaviour under state or federal statutes might be alleged.

Strict liability has its roots in the 1963 case of *Greenman* v. *Yuba Power Products Inc.* (see Case History no. 4) where the court held that a 'manufacturer is strictly liable in tort when an article he places on the market, knowing that it is to be used without inspection for defects, proves to have a defect that causes an injury to a human being'. In 1977 the American Law Institute sought to encapsulate this principle as developed in subsequent cases in what became known as section 402A of the Restatement (Second) of the Law of Torts. This principle is adhered to today by most state courts as a principle of state legislation of common law:

> One who sells any product in a defective condition unreasonably dangerous to the user or consumer is subject to liability for physical harm thereby caused to the ultimate user or consumer, or to his property, if:
> (a) the seller is engaged in the business of selling such a product; and
> (b) the product is expected to and does reach the user or consumer without substantial change in the condition in which it is sold.'

A substantial body of case law has developed on what amounts to 'unreasonable dangerousness'. Under the Rule, it is not a defence to show the exercise of all possible care or that there was no contractual relationship between the defendant and the consumer or user. The main defences to US strict liability claims are that the product was being misused or had undergone change. Development risks defences may also be available. Usually termed the state of the art defence in the United States, these concepts have only been loosely developed by most courts and have not yet evolved into a clear defence.

In the 1970s the popularity of product liability litigation led the White House to set up a special body to investigate the problem. The Federal Interagency Task Force of Product Liability reported in January 1977 that there was no widespread difficulty in obtaining product liability insurance, but that certain industries with high-risk product lines found difficulty in obtaining suitable cover while, for others, premiums appeared to be unaffordable. Nevertheless, pressure for changes continued, and more recently federal product liability reform legislation progressed through Congress until vetoed by President Clinton in April 1996. Among the measures proposed are financial limits on the amount that can be awarded as punitive damages.

The US Consumer Products Safety Commission is empowered to make product safety standards and to regulate consumer safety under the Consumer Product Safety Act 1972 and various other provisions. It enables the Consumer Product Safety Commission (CPSC) to ban products containing hazards which cannot be reduced to reasonable level, or to order other action. In contrast to the position in most other countries the Consumer Product Safety Act requires manufacturers and others in the supply chain to notify the CPSC of certain product defects or contraventions of product safety standards, whereupon the CPSC takes an active role in investigating the defects, the distribution of the product and the level of risk to consumers. If the CPSC's criteria are met then it may require the mandatory recall of products and they may specify actual measures the manufacturer is required to take. The US Food and Drug Administration (FDA) also has its own recall procedures including a classification system for determining the severity of risk. A number of other federal agencies have a role in product safety regulation including the Occupational Safety and Health Administration (OSHA) and the Environmental Protection Agency (EPA).

Below federal level, state legislators and administrative agencies (sometimes even municipal governments) are involved in the regulation of safety; these requirements tend to be diverse and have been criticized as 'a hodgepodge of tragedy-inspired responses', being difficult to operate through their 'narrow scope, defuse jurisdiction, minuscule budgets, absence of enforcement, mild sanctions, and casual administration'. The CPSA was created to give a more coherent approach.

Australia

The Australian legal system retains many features deriving from its ancestry in English law. Its product liability regime in particular resembles closely that of England, and strict liability now exists on a basis very similar to the European Product Liability Directive. If Government policy initiations put forward in 1995 are adopted there will probably be a general safety requirement underpinning product safety laws which are already well developed. The Australian states have their own product laws supplementing the federal requirements; the federal rules are summarized here, and reference to specialist works should be made for the state rules.

In many respects, the law on product liability is the same as that in England, comprising a combination of the law of tort, contract and now strict liability under Part VA of the Trade Practices Act 1974 (as amended in June 1992). Actions may be brought under the law of negligence, based on the same duty of care and neighbour principle delineated originally in *Donoghue* v. *Stevenson* (see Chapter 9). Claims may also be brought for breach of contract – that is, for a failure to conform with terms implied by law that products are of merchantable quality and fit for their purpose. The principles here are essentially the same as the UK Sale of Goods Act prior to its 1994 amendments, although the Federal Bureau of Consumer Affairs has proposed introducing a guarantee of 'acceptable quality' similar to 'satisfactory quality' in the UK. Australian common law imposes the same restrictions on contractual claims, subject to the doctrine of privity of contract. Changes made to the Trade Practices Act in 1978 relaxed the privity rules so that actions could be brought direct against manufacturers in a range of circumstances that would (under sale of goods law) be breaches of warranty, such as goods not being of merchantable quality, not corresponding with their descriptions or not fit for a stated purpose.

For essentially the same reasons as Europe – inadequate consumer protection being afforded by tort and contract law – Australia introduced a strict liability regime in June 1992. The

Australian legislature took the European Product Liability Directive as its model and, unsurprisingly, the Trade Practices Act provisions are very similar in their approach. Strict liability is placed on *corporations*[1] supplying goods they have manufactured, which are defective and where the defect has caused an individual to suffer injury. Liability may also arise where land or other goods are damaged, provided they are for private and not commercial use. The definition of defect is broadly the same as that in the European Product Liability Directive. However, unlike the European Directive, the Australian legislation provides for the Trade Practices Commission to be able to bring a representative action on behalf of named individuals who have suffered loss as a result of a defective product.

There is an extended definition of manufacturers to include own-branders, and others who hold themselves out as a manufacturer, and importers. As in Europe, intermediate suppliers can be liable where they fail to name the manufacturer or the person who previously supplied the goods.

The defences under the Act are again broadly the same as those under the European Product Liability Directive, including the development risks defence. Limitation periods for the commencement of actions are three years after the time the person became aware, or ought to have become aware, of the loss or injury suffered and the identity of the manufacturer. Actions must, in any event, be commenced within a ten-year long-stop period.

There is an additional basis of liability under the Act where there is a right to compensation for loss resulting from contravention of product safety requirements (see below). This is another form of strict liability where the defences described above will not generally be available but, as under mainstream strict liability, it remains a requirement for the claimant to prove the breach of the rules which actually caused the alleged injuries.

Product safety requirements are also covered by the Trade Practices Act the various powers of which are administered by the Federal Bureau of Consumer Affairs on behalf of the Federal Minister. Under the Act the government can use regulations to prescribe consumer product safety standards relating to performance, composition and contents, manufacture and packaging, testing of products and the form of warnings and instructions. Standards prepared or approved by the Standards Association of Australia or other recognized bodies can also be designated as having legal effects. Under separate powers, product information standards can be laid down specifying appropriate instructions to be provided.

The Minister is also able to publish warnings to the public declaring that the possibility of certain goods causing injury is under investigation, and also notices declaring goods to be unsafe. These powers extend further to imposing permanent bans on products and ordering product recalls from consumers in certain circumstances, particularly where the Minister considers that the supplier has not voluntarily taken satisfactory action to prevent injury being caused. Where product recalls are carried out voluntarily, the legislation includes further requirements for the Minister to be notified, and also for the supplier to notify persons who have been supplied with any recalled goods outside Australia.

The supply of products which breach a standard or failure to comply with other requirements under the legislation is a criminal offence punishable by fines. In some instances a defence of due diligence applies.

In June 1995 the Federal Bureau of Consumer Affairs issued proposals under the title 'Culture of Safety'. This acknowledged that the Australian system lacked some of the beneficial features of the European legislation, particularly in its failure to promote high safety standards on a systematic basis and by having mandatory standards which acted as technical barriers to trade. The four principal proposals are as follows:

1 A general safety requirement should be introduced based on the EC General Product Safety Directive.
2 Current vertical or individual 'product-focused' standards should be supplemented with more responsive 'horizontal' standards which concentrate on hazards rather than individual product types.
3 A certification mark – along the lines of CE marking – should

be introduced so that compliant products may be recognized by consumers.

4 A Consumer Product Safety Institute, acting as a 'think tank' on product safety issues, advising on policy and providing guidelines to industry, should be established.

Japan

The Product Liability Law (*Seizobutsu sekinin ho*) (Law No. 85, 1994) came into force on 1 July 1995 and applies only to products delivered after this date. For products supplied earlier, liability is determined on the basis of negligence being proven (proof here often being regarded as difficult to establish) or on the basis of breach of contract under Article 415 of the Civil Code of Japan. Based on the EC Product Liability Directive, the Japanese Product Liability Law represents a major shift away from fault-based liability contained in the Japanese Civil Code. Liability is established where there is damage and causation between the damage and a defect.

The Product Liability Law covers all manufactured, or processed, movable property but does not cover services, information, software or electricity nor does it cover immovables such as forests. Manufacturers, importers, anyone selling original equipment manufacturer (OEM) products using his own brand name and anyone who may be recognized as its 'manufacturer in fact' may be sued and liable for any damage caused by defects in products.

'Defect' does not mean mere lack of product quality but more specifically a lack of product safety which may cause injury to life, body or property. Defect is defined as 'lack of safety that the product ordinarily should provide taking into account the nature of the product, the ordinarily foreseeable manner of the use of the product and the time when the manufacturer delivered the product'.

The Product Liability Law also contains two defences: the development risk defence; and the component or raw material manufacturer's defence. If the manufacturer of a component or raw material proves that the defect is substantially attributable to compliance with the instructions given by the assembling manufacturer who incorporated the component or raw material into another product, and the component manufacturer has not been negligent, the manufacturer of the component or raw material will not be liable.

Actions under the provisions of the Product Liability Law must be brought within three years from the time when the injured person, or his legal representative, becomes aware of the damage and the liable party for the damage ('short-term negative prescription') or after a period of ten years from the time when the manufacturer delivered the product ('long-term liability period').

Product safety issues are hardly covered at all by central legislation; instead, a form of self-regulation is carried out by the various industry associations. The unfamiliarity of the Japanese with mandatory safety requirements is evidenced by a statement in the afterword to the Electronic Industry Association of Japan's (EIAJ) guidelines (see below) that the Committee which drew up the guidelines found it very difficult to devise good warning labels because of their previous lack of detailed experience in that area. The electronics industry provides an example of the rules and regulations pertaining to product safety which are administered in this informal manner.

Against a background of increasingly sophisticated consumer electronic equipment and an increasing, international and older consumer market there have been increasing calls for higher levels of safety, resulting in the setting up of the Safety Research Committee by the EIAJ. In 1973 the Committee undertook a complete overhaul of the warning labelling in instruction manuals and this is now published as the 'Unified Recommendations on Warnings on Usage'.

Subsequently, in December 1994, the Consumer Electronics Products Association (CEPA) published '*Guidelines relating to labelling to ensure the safety of consumer electronic products*' which crystallized thinking on the labelling of consumer electronic products. They also recommended that each industry association should produce its own guidelines and periodically update them to reflect the increase in variety of consumer electronic products and advances in safety technology. To this end, the EIAJ put together the '*Labelling guidelines in order to ensure the safety of electronic equipment (television and video)*' which came into force on 1 October 1994 and are intended to be applicable to all companies.

The preamble of the guidelines states that they aim to set out the views of the association pertaining to warning labelling for preventing injury to people and damage to property and, in the case of long-term use, the labelling relating to safety inspection. The guidelines apply to warnings on products made for the Japanese market – to labelling the products themselves, instruction manuals, catalogues and related materials used by manufacturers (including sales agents) to explain the products or their use to consumers.

The guidelines then go on to outline some of their basic tenets. These include the fact that the abilities, habits and level of knowledge of the product's potential user should be taken into account and that this does not apply only to the person making the purchase but also to their family, visitors and any third party who may purchase the product at some future date. To make labelling work effectively the guidelines draw a distinction between the terms 'danger', 'warning' and 'caution' in order to prevent injury to persons or damage to property and also recommend that information be divided into four categories: warning symbols; signal words; picture labels; instructions. This information should apply to each stage of a product's life from purchase to destruction.

The current set of guidelines is to be reviewed every three years but, if necessary, will be reviewed before that. In addition, the EIAJ and the CEPA undertake to discuss, as necessary, anything about the guidelines' content or operation that is unclear or becomes dubious.

Summary

In practice the similarities in product laws around the world are considerably greater than the differences in the actual legislation might imply. Particularly since the recent convergence of strict liability principles, marketing products in Europe, Australia, Japan and the United States entails essentially the same product liability issues. Nevertheless, there remain important differences in local practices, which are apparent in the different approaches to how damages are awarded, precautions for product safety, the varying extent of reliance on mandated standards with statutory force and governments' abilities to require recalls, compulsory warnings and other measures to protect their nationals. Even in Europe, where the GPS and New Approach Directives should have harmonized the legislation, a country-by-country analysis will be required to appreciate fully the legislative context in which product design will be viewed and to understand how a company should later respond to the discovery of any defects.

Note

1 Manufacturers who are individuals or partnerships are not covered, because the federal authorities only have constitutional power to cover corporations; individual states are able to cover manufacturers who are not corporations in their own local Fair Trading Acts.

Further reading

Campbell, D. and Campbell, C. (1993), *International Product Liability*, London: Lloyds of London Press.
Hodges C. J. S. (1993), *Product Liability: European Laws and Practice*, London: Sweet & Maxwell.
Kellam J. (1995), *Product Liability in the Asia-Pacific*, Sydney: Legal Books.

11
Designers' Personal Liabilities

Introduction

Behind every faulty design there must be an individual, or group of individuals, at fault. The personal liability of designers for products that reach the market in a state that do not conform with legal requirements has not so far been explored to any significant degree by the courts. Nevertheless the principles of law whereby employees (and directors and other officers) can be held personally to account are reasonably well developed and could readily be applied in the design context. This chapter considers the responsibilities of designers to the ultimate users of a product, and also the responsibility they have to their employers. There are further specific provisions contained in the principal statutes and various product safety regulations which enable prosecutions to be brought against culpable individuals. These provisions, and the limited defences available, are also considered below.

Liability of the employed designer

Claims for compensation, based on principles of civil liability, are almost always brought against companies producing and selling products as opposed to the individuals whose inadvertence in design, production or marketing may, along the way, have led to a consumer being injured by an unsafe product. The reason for this is largely pragmatism; the doctrine of 'vicarious liability' makes a company or another employer wholly responsible for the fault of an individual employee, and in turn the company is likely to be covered by insurance. The pursuit of liability claims against individual designers would usually turn out to be wholly fruitless, given the limited personal resources the ordinary person has available to pay any compensation awarded. Nevertheless, there is no obstacle in terms of legal principle to such claims being brought. The *Opren* litigation of the 1980s, where an executive was named as one of a number of defendants, is indicative of greater attention being given by claimants' advisers to the tactical benefits of trying to pin the blame on individuals. (The case was settled before any findings on liability had to be made.)

Vicarious liability

Put simply, under the doctrine of vicarious liability the courts are prepared to accept the employer's liability for the acts or omissions of the employee. This doctrine has evolved through the courts' willingness to hold an employer responsible for the consequences of the conduct of its employees in carrying on the business. The rationale lies more in pragmatic social policy considerations of making sure that a party with a 'deep pocket' is responsible for paying compensation rather than in any clearly definable legal principle.

Although vicarious liability can be difficult to apply to cases where an employee's conduct is not wholly related to undertaking the employer's business (or, as the courts have frequently put it, where an employee is, to some extent, on a 'frolic of his own'), when it comes to designers there will rarely, if ever, be any doubt that they have been acting in the course of their employers' business. Consequently, it is appropriate for the designer's negligence to rest at the door of the company. It is well established that an employee's careless or unauthorized manner of performing a set task will be deemed the responsibility of the employer; in this respect, an unsafe design would therefore fall within the company's overall liability.

Why then should a designer have any particular concerns about his or her personal position in relation to claims? There are two reasons. First, vicarious liability on the part of the company does not mean that the employee is, as a corollary, exempt from a duty of care under the neighbourhood principle for the law of negligence originating from the case of *Donoghue* v. *Stevenson* (see Chapter 9). The plaintiff may choose to sue an employer company *and* an individual if he or she believes that there is a strong enough basis for alleging liability against both, or even to sue the individual alone as sometimes occurs when a company is insolvent and uninsured. In some cases, a plaintiff may be uncertain as to what defence the employer might deploy to defend a claim and suspect that attempts may be made to disown a negligent employee's conduct as being 'a frolic of his own'. In such circumstances a personal action might be initiated as a means of ensuring that all possible parties are drawn into the proceedings before the rules of limitation prevent new claims being brought.

The second principal reason why personal liability remains a live issue despite the fact that the employer is vicariously liable is due to a distinct liability which the employee can owe to his or her employer. There is an implied duty under the contract of employment to exercise reasonable skill and care, and an employer has a right to sue a negligent employee to recover any losses which the employee has caused in breach of this duty. These losses may include sums that the employer has had to pay to someone else who has been injured. The leading case in this area is *Lister* v. *Romford Ice and Cold Storage Co. Ltd.*[1] In this case one company employee (A) driving a lorry ran over and injured another employee (B). Employee B recovered damages from the company (because it was vicariously liable) but the insurers of the company (who in these respects by law stepped into the company's shoes and were able to enforce whatever rights it would have had itself) took the unusual step of pursuing a claim against employee A for his negligence in driving which had caused the company to have to pay compensation to employee B. In this case it was a key finding that not only was employee A personally liable to his employers, but he could not assert that, as an employee, there should be an implied term in his contract that he was entitled personally to whatever insurance cover the employers had taken out. The same principle applies to a claim by a consumer who is injured through an employee's default. (The standard of skill and care is discussed below.)

In practice insurers rarely take this approach – at least in the absence of evidence that an employee has deliberately inflicted harm or acted with a view to personal gain – and it is not a course of action that would appeal to most companies. However, there may be cases in which the adverse staff relations implications or other factors are deemed to be outweighed by the advantages of pursuing individuals – for example, if a company passes into the hands of liquidators or where gaps exist in insurance coverage or the company finds itself in financial difficulties. Similarly, joinder of individuals in actions, as occurred in the English *Opren* litigation, remains very much the exception in personal injury cases, but with US litigation practices beginning to make their presence felt in the UK it is possible that more consideration will be given to the tactical advantages of alleging personal liability, such as those of embarrassing company managements, driving a wedge between those responsible for design and the rest of the company, increasing the scope for discovery of documents and (particularly with ex-employees) using the threat of trial as a lever to persuade company employees to give evidence to a plaintiff. Very few such cases become public or reach trial, but in 1989 a company director who wrongly stated to architects that a particular design flooring system would meet their client's specifications was held liable for £93 000 in damages for remedial costs. The outcome would probably have been the same had his incorrect advice led to an injury claim.

Insurance

Insurance has been examined in more detail in Chapter 6. Individual employees are not generally party to their company's insurance contracts (unless they are board members holding specific directors' and officers' policies). How, then, can they expect to be covered by insurance? The answer in practice is that the wording of product liability policies commonly extends the insurers' indemnity for 'any director, partner or employee' (or similar terms) for which the insured company would have been liable had the claim been made against it instead. However, there may be a proviso that this cover is not automatic but given only if the company requests the insurers to protect the employee. The protection afforded is therefore not watertight, and an employee cannot always be sure that cover is in place or, if it is, that it will be renewed. Also, a product liability policy will generally not apply to claims made in respect of advice given for a fee – for examples, design consultancy. This has to be covered separately under a professional indemnity policy.

The freelance designer

A distinction is made for the purposes of vicarious liability between responsibility for the acts and omissions of employees and for those of independent contractors. Generally under tort law, where design has been contracted out to another company or to someone acting personally in a freelance capacity, with due care taken to verify their expertise, the employer will not be liable for that person's negligence. Even so, under the strict liability regime under the Product Liability Directive the 'producer' is now primarily liable if a product turns out to be defective and where one of the statutory defences does not succeed. Thus, for practical purposes, liability for contracted-out specialist design work or advice, or for faults in bought-in components, will lie with the manufacturer of the finished product (see Case Histories 3 and 8); in such cases, it will (subject to any enforceable exclusion clauses) have a contractual right of indemnity if it can be shown that a freelance designer has not brought reasonable skill and care to bear in his or her work. (If the designer is also supplying materials or components the courts will probably imply a contractual term that both the goods *and* the design will be reasonably fit for the purpose for which the designer knows it is intended to be used.)[2]

However, in a product liability case revolving round a design defect it is very likely that both the producer and a freelance designer would be sued jointly. Undertaking purely design work does not fall within the scope of the Product Liability Directive and the designer's liability would be determined by reference to common law negligence principles: as well as exercising a reasonable care, there may well be a duty on the designer under the law of negligence to make sure the product is 'safe' in precisely the same sense as the definitions in applicable consumer protection and workplace regulatory requirements (which could, for example, include making proper enquiries as to the suitability of materials or components). For insurance purposes, professional indemnity cover will be needed, and it must extend to claims in respect of death and bodily injury to be effective for present purposes (some policies exclude this).

Although there is scant authority on the liabilities that are incurred by the designer of a product it appears that, particularly where novel designs represent a safety hazard, the courts will impose a very high standard of care, and it has even been suggested that the duty may even extend to abandoning a design which cannot be brought within acceptable safety standards. In the case of *Eckersley* v. *Binnie*,[3] which arose out of the Abbeystead pumping station explosion, the court was required to undertake a massive enquiry into the potential liabilities of three separate parties: the water company owning the tunnel, the contractors and the designers. Ultimately the whole liability was placed on the designers by the Court of Appeal because it was held that, even though this was a developing area of engineering expertise, there was nevertheless a foreseeable risk of an explosion being caused by methane gas after the completion of the project for which insufficient precautions had been allowed in the design of the ventilation systems.

The standard of skill and care that is applied is '*the standard of the ordinary skilled man exercising and professing to have that special skill*'. The following detailed description has been given of the duties of engineers, and this probably applies equally to designers:

> ... a professional man should command the corpus of knowledge which forms part of the professional equipment of the ordinary

member of his profession. He should not lag behind other ordinarily assiduous and intelligent members of his profession in knowledge of new advances, discoveries and developments in his field. He should be alert to the hazards and risks inherent in any professional task he undertakes to the extent that other ordinarily competent members of the profession would be alert. He must bring to any professional task he undertakes no less expertise, skill and care than other ordinarily competent members would bring but need bring no more. The standard is that of the reasonable average. The law does not require of a professional man that he be a paragon combining the qualities of polymath and prophet.[4]

In any case involving the liability of a designer the critical issues will revolve round expert evidence and whether or not the court is persuaded that another competent designer would regard the work as having been properly carried out. In this context the whole body of scientific and technical knowledge comprised in specialist books, journals and professional courses will be highly relevant both in deciding whether a designer should have known about certain problems or risks and as to particular types of hazard or the means of dealing with them. Compliance with industry standards and guidelines, codes of practice and so on will be very important, but the court may nevertheless hold that a degree of skill and care must be exercised in applying such guidelines, or in recognizing where their limitations lie and properly identifying when extra testing or other design-related work is needed[5] (see, further, Case Histories 11 and 14).

Criminal liability

The potential criminal liabilities of designers are more complex and present a more substantial risk than that of being drawn into civil proceedings. This is because the general criminal law, particularly relating to manslaughter, is increasingly seen as an appropriate way of dealing with the most culpable acts of negligence but, at the same time, the incremental effect of New Approach directives and other introductions to the regulatory regime for product safety have meant that individuals, particularly those in senior positions, can be accused of failing to deal with not just product safety generally but specifically with various compliance procedures which are within the scope of their line management responsibilities.

Historically, one of the most vexing issues in this area was the basis on which it could be said that a corporation, having no physical existence or ability to act or form criminal intentions except through its directors and employees, could actually be said to commit a criminal offence. In cases of serious accidents prosecution of directors and other responsible company officers used to be seen as the norm on the basis that criminal liability was essentially personal. Vicarious liability principles have, however, been applied to the criminal/regulatory field, and Lord Denning has given the following description of the modern position:

> . . . a company may in many ways be likened to a human body. It has a brain and nerve centre which controls what it does. It also has hands which hold the tools and act in accordance with the directions from the centre. Some of the people in the company . . . are nothing more than the hands to do work, others are directors and managers who represent the directory mind of the company and control what it does. The state of mind of these managers is the state of mind of the company and is treated by the law as such.[6]

Only in limited circumstances, such as where a due diligence defence applies and a company's offence is due to the default of a junior employee who can be viewed as 'another person' distinct from the company's management, will a company cease to be vicariously liable. Generally, the company will be guilty of offences caused by its employees.[7]

Nowadays we have come to take the doctrine of corporations as separate legal entities almost for granted, and managers who, on the whole, operate as players in a corporate team often see the risk of finding themselves in the dock for an offence as a very remote prospect. Personal prosecutions are low in number, but they do occur on a regular basis and the risk should not be underestimated since inspectors now routinely seek information after incidents as to where management responsibilities lie.

Manslaughter

As many offences under the criminal law depend on a defendant forming a guilty intent, it still rules out corporations from most criminal proceedings. Nevertheless the law of manslaughter has recently come under close scrutiny as an appropriate medium through which to deal with cases where the public is exposed to danger and where, although no intent is present, there is culpable neglect. As well as the Zeebrugge case (which is discussed in more detail below) there have been manslaughter prosecutions in the health and safety field for work accidents and, for example, in relation to the medical negligence cases and provision of leisure services (for example, the Lyme Bay canoeing accident).

Conceptual difficulties with how the reckless conduct of individual managers can be identified with the company itself have now begun to be overcome following rulings in the Zeebrugge litigation where it was held that, where a company through the controlling mind of one or more of its agents commits an act or omission which fulfils the prerequisites of the crime of manslaughter, it is properly indictable for that offence.

It is unlikely that a corporate manslaughter prosecution will be brought, however, without there also being prosecutions brought against senior management at the same time. The reason for this is that, under the common law as it stands, an individual controlling officer has to be guilty in order for the company itself to be liable. (It is now clear that the company itself cannot be liable on the basis of an 'aggregation' of the faults of a number of different individuals, none of whose faults taken in isolation would have amounted to manslaughter.) To succeed, the prosecution has to prove (beyond reasonable doubt) that:

a) a person has been killed in circumstances where he or she was subject to an *obvious and serious risk* of some injury prior to the death;

b) the directors or senior officers who were the *controlling mind* of the company were responsible for an act or omission which was at least a substantial cause of the death; and

c) the directors or other managers behaved in this way either because they had given no thought to the possibility that the person would be endangered or because, if the risk was recognized, they nevertheless allowed it to continue regardless. For these purposes, a simple lack of care or ordinary negligence is not enough to constitute manslaughter; a higher degree of negligence (or *recklessness*) has to be established.

In the Zeebrugge case (case History 20), along with the company, seven individuals who had been involved in various senior positions with the running of the vessel and the practice of leaving port with the bow doors open were prosecuted. All the defendants were eventually acquitted because the prosecution encountered evidential problems in proving that the danger of capsize should have been obvious and serious to them, rather than as a result of the defence case establishing any particular 'benchmark' for future reference whereby company managers are able to demonstrate the exercise of reasonable care. Consequently this case provides little practical guidance on how a board of directors should properly delegate safety responsibilities. What is clear from the case is that, if actual knowledge of a serious hazard can be demonstrated, the outcome of future cases is likely to be different. It is also notable that, whereas the findings in the immediate aftermath of the Zeebrugge disaster highlighted widespread management failures ('from top to bottom the body corporate was infected with the disease of sloppiness' said Mr Justice Sheen, the Wreck Commissioner), in the longer term it has been the future design considerations and the need to improve safety in the event of the ingress of water that has been the subject of research and widespread debate. Design liabilities could well feature more prominently in future transport and other major public 'disaster cases', as for example they did following the Abbeystead explosion.

The law of corporate manslaughter remains unsettled and has been subject to proposals for reform by the Law Commission.

The Commission's recommendations (made in 1996)[8] are for a simplification which would in practice make it easier to prosecute both companies and individual managers by concentrating on whether a particular risk was significant and whether the defendant's conduct fell far below what could reasonably be expected.

Regulatory Offences

In contrast with the somewhat vague and abstract principles of manslaughter, personal responsibilities in relation to regulatory requirements are clearer in that they are specifically defined. Many statutes and regulations – including the Health and Safety at Work Act, Consumer Protection Act, GPS Regulations and regulations implementing New Approach directives – contain the common provision concerning directors and senior managers in a form similar to the following:

> Where an offence under any of the relevant statutory provisions committed by a body corporate is proved to have been committed with the consent or connivance of, or to have been attributable to any neglect on the part of, any director, manager, secretary or other similar officer of the body corporate or a person who was purporting to act in any such capacity, he as well as the body corporate shall be guilty of that offence and shall be liable to be proceeded against and punished accordingly.

There are two key questions in determining whether a person will be liable here: these are whether the person is sufficiently senior to be accountable, and whether there has been a causal link between some fault on his or her part and the commission of an offence by the company. (It should be noted for these purposes that conviction of the company is a prerequisite for liability to arise on the part of the individual.)

The question of the degree of seniority required for a person to fall within the scope of this provision was considered in the case of *R.* v. *Boal*[9] which concerned the prosecution of the assistant general manager of a bookshop for an offence in relation to fire precautions. It was held by the Court of Appeal that the provision was meant to catch those responsible for putting proper procedures in place, and was not meant to strike at 'underlings'. The intended scope is 'to fix with criminal liability only those who are in a position of real authority, the decision-makers within the company who have both the power and responsibility to decide corporate policy and strategy'. Thus a person ultimately responsible for design issues at company board level (or possibly even the whole board if each member can be shown to have been responsible in some material way) might be liable to prosecution. It is likely also, although not confirmed by the case law, that any other person in a company with a senior line management responsibility could be classified as sufficiently senior for these purposes, as it is a question of where actual responsibility is exercised.[10] For example, in another case the 'director of roads' for a local authority was convicted even though his status was essentially that of a council employee.[11]

The same case illustrates issues that arise with the second question relating to liability under this provision, which is the relationship between the fault on the part of the individual and the commission of the offence by the company. Here the director of roads was designated with responsibility under the local authority's safety policy for making appropriate provisions for safety, including devising a safe way of carrying out the job. Although this was not a statutory duty imposed upon him personally it was a duty on him that was delegated under his employment contract; consequently the court was able to say that there was a duty on his part which he had not properly performed, and this was sufficient to provide the necessary element of 'neglect' on his part which in turn led to the employer committing an offence under the Health and Safety at Work Act.

An example of this principle in operation would be liability of individuals who wrongly make a declaration of conformity for the purpose of one of the New Approach measures; these (and EN 45014 on General Criteria for Suppliers' Declarations of Conformity) provide for a signature and note of title or equivalent marking of the authorized person who gives final approval. In fact it is not the act of signing that makes an individual potentially liable for errors in the declaration; rather, it will be because that person has the requisite responsibility in line management. In effect, it is a risk that goes with the job of being, for example, Head of Quality rather than a risk created by putting one's name on the document. If the person is not at all at fault personally, notwithstanding the authorization (or even duty) to sign, he will most likely have a strong defence of due diligence (see below).

Most cases brought under this provision are based on allegations of 'neglect' rather than of consent or connivance. For example, a director has been convicted in relation to the importation by his company of brake lights which were marked (falsely) as conforming to a type approval. Although the director had made various enquiries, including asking a fellow director to check the products' legality for supply in the UK, it was held that the director should have done more to check that the co-director had consulted authoritative sources. There have, however, been cases brought on the consent and connivance basis – for example, directors being responsible for a misleading advertisement relating to a product, and for knowingly undertaking certain business activities without appropriate licences from the authorities.

A further provision commonly found in consumer protection statutes and other regulations is as follows:

> Where the commission by any person of an offence . . . is due to an act or default committed by some other person in the course of any business of his, the other person shall be guilty of the offence and may be proceeded against and punished by virtue of this subsection whether or not proceedings are taken against the first-mentioned person.

Again, the prerequisite for the liability of an individual under this provision is that the principal offender must be convicted. The scope, however, is broader than the provision previously described in that it can apply not just to company personnel but also to individuals outside the employment or service of the company itself (such as a director of a supplier of components or the company providing design services). Nevertheless, as with the previous provision, it does not catch designers who are junior employees, the reason being that the guilty individual has to be acting in the course of a business *of his or hers*, and it has been held that this means any business of which the defendant is either the owner or in which he or she has a controlling interest.

This 'own business' qualification effectively protects junior designers in relation to most consumer protection provisions and regulations implementing the New Approach directives. The result is slightly anomalous in that, in such situations, the person actually responsible for what has happened is immune from conviction. Only in exceptional cases where there has been some wider offence committed involving serious criminal intent – such as a conspiracy or deliberately aiding and abetting the commission of an offence where the provisions of the general criminal law can come into play against such an individual – will a prosecution be possible.

There is, however, one further anomaly, which is that not all statutory provisions contain the qualifying words about the individual's own business. One of the most important exceptions, for our present purposes, is in the Health and Safety at Work Act in which section 36 enables a prosecution to be brought simply where the commission of an offence by one person is 'due to the act or default of some other person'. Thus any designers of articles and substances for use at work are potentially more vulnerable to personal prosecution than those involved with purely consumer products and may be prosecuted personally in respect of offences under section 6 of the HSWA (see Chapter 9). It is therefore important to look at all relevant regulatory 'offences' provisions separately to find out whether a designer who lacks seniority under the test in *R.* v. *Boal* can be prosecuted under this separate provision.

Penalties

The sentence an individual can receive will depend on the penalties provided for in the particular Act or regulations contravened. In practice, fines are the normal punishment imposed. (Under Health and Safety at Work provisions imprisonment is only an option for certain very specific offences – in particular, contravention of an enforcement notice.) However, there is no limit on the level of fine. Under the CPA Part II, the GPS Regulations and most New Approach measures a fine of up to £5000 and/or up to three months' imprisonment can be imposed.

More stringent penalties may apply abroad: in 1995, it was reported that a French court had sentenced the chairman of a well known multinational household products group to a one-year suspended prison term after a consumer was injured by an exploding aerosol product. (The sentence was reduced to six months on appeal.)

Defence of due diligence

As mentioned earlier, there has commonly been a due diligence defence relating to regulatory requirements. The following wording, taken from the GPS Regulations, is typical:

(1) Subject to the following paragraphs of this regulation, in proceedings against any person for any offence under these Regulations it shall be a defence for that person to show that he took all reasonable steps and exercised all due diligence to avoid committing the offence.

(2) Where in any proceedings against any person for such an offence the defence provided by paragraph (1) above involves an allegation that the commission of the offence was due:

(a) to the act or default of another; or

(b) to reliance on information given by another, that person shall not, without leave of the Court, be entitled to rely on the defence unless, not less than seven days before, in England, Wales and Northern Ireland, the hearing of the proceedings or, in Scotland, the trial diet, he has served a notice under paragraph (3) below on the person bringing the proceedings.

(3) A notice under this paragraph shall give such information identifying or assisting in the identification of the person who committed the act or default or gave the information as is in the possession of the person serving the notice at the time he serves it.

(4) It is hereby declared that a person shall not be entitled to rely on the defence provided in paragraph (1) above by reason of his reliance on information supplied by another, unless he shows

that it was reasonable in all the circumstances for him to have relied on the information, having regard in particular:

(a) to the steps which he took and those which might reasonably have been taken, for the purpose of verifying the information; and

(b) to whether he had any reason to disbelieve the information . . .

The concept of due diligence is sometimes treated as being the same as showing the absence of negligence, but it is rather different in that it requires the positive proof by the defendant of a high standard of care, both in devising appropriate precautions and systems for dealing with safety as well as in actually implementing and observing them. In the prosecution of individuals the due diligence defence will very often be unsustainable, since if it is shown the basic offence has been committed on account of the person's act or omission a degree of negligence will be readily inferred anyway. However, there may be cases where there is little actual blame to be attached to the individual because someone else has caused him to make a mistake – for example, through providing incorrect information or erroneously indicating that a product or component meets certain criteria. Although the operation of the due diligence defence has not been tested in these circumstances, it appears that an individual designer could take advantage of the defence if he or she complies properly with the procedures of identifying and giving notice of the identity of the third party whose failure is the real cause of the offence, and can demonstrate that his or her default was caused by his or her employer, a colleague or some outside adviser.

Summary

The topic of personal liabilities is characterized by its unpredictability and uncertainty. The case law is sparse and much has to be inferred from decisions in other types of cases. There are no hard and fast rules as to exactly where responsibility lies; nevertheless it appears from the case law that the internal allocation of responsibility inside a company creates duties which go far beyond the employer–employee relationship under which members of a design department owe a contractual duty to their company to perform their work with proper skill and care. Such duties are taken as being at least a partial delegation of the employers' statutory responsibilities and, where there is evidence to show that an offence has occurred which is to some extent attributable to an individual, the legal mechanisms are in place for a prosecution to be brought.

The fact that such prosecutions are relatively uncommon is more an indication of the wide discretion that prosecuting authorities (in particular local authorities and the HSE) are able to exercise under the existing legislative regimes. In practice, a subjective decision is made by inspectors, based essentially on a moral judgement, as to whether an individual's behaviour has been so bad as to merit a prosecution. Whether it is desirable to vest so much decision-making power in unaccountable officers is debatable, especially when there are no clear guidelines from which an individual can discern the limits of the responsibilities which a court might decide he holds.

In terms of civil liability, the doctrine of vicarious liability on the part of the employer does not give immunity from claims against any individual designer whose work may have led to the production of an unsafe product, but the practicalities of litigation are such that nearly all claims are brought against the company under the doctrine, not least because it will be likely to have the necessary insurance cover to meet any award. There is, however, no reason why claims should not be brought against designers where they can be shown to have been negligent in a personal capacity, and some examples of lawsuits against individuals have been mentioned. There are therefore distinct advantages in clarifying a company's insurance arrangements and the extent to which cover extends to any such claims to individuals, and the circumstances and types of loss for which claims can be anticipated.

References

1 [1957] AC 555.

2 *IBA* v. *EMI and BICC* [1980] 14 Build LR 1 and *George Hawkins* v. *Chrysler (UK) and Burne Associates* [1987] 38 Build LR 40.

3 [1988] 18 Con LR 1.

4 Bingham LJ in *Eckersley* v. *Binnie & Partners.*

5 See Hodges, Tyler, M., Abbott, H., (1996), *Product Safety*, London: Sweet & Maxwell, pp. 128–30 and 158.

6 *H. L. Bolton (Engineering) Co Ltd* v. *T. J. Graham & Sons Ltd* [1956] 3 All ER 624.

7 *Tesco Supermarkets* v. *Nattrass* [1971] 2 All ER 127 and *R.* v. *British Steel* [1995] ICR 586.

8 *Legislating the Criminal Code: Involuntary Manslaughter,* Law Com. No. 237, (HMSO).

9 [1992] 2 WLR 890.

10 *El Ajou* v. *Dollar Land Holidays* [1994] 2 All ER 685.

11 *Armour* v. *Skeen* [1977] SLT 71.

Part Three
CASE HISTORIES

The Lessons from History

Introduction

With the inestimable advantage of hindsight, it is easy to see what should have been done to prevent many of the mistakes and disasters of the past. It is from these 'should haves' that valuable lessons can be learned. They may not be applicable to every product and every circumstance but there is something here for every designer. No one is exempt from getting it wrong, if they do not take calculated actions to prevent accidents happening.

The case histories which follow are grouped according to the products concerned: consumer products, motor cars, industrial products, aerospace and ships to provide a wide range of examples. But first we look at a different classification of the same cases according to their cause: design management, product standards, validation, third-party approvals, and product information. It will be seen that these cut right across the product groups demonstrating the commonality in defective design safety, whatever the product. Often the defect had a simple cause waiting to be found. The figures in brackets refer to the relevant case history numbers.

Design management

In virtually every case blame can be directed at a management failure somewhere along the line. This failure usually originates away from the scientific or engineering error in the product itself that was the immediate cause of the accident. The real origin is frequently to be found in the higher management levels, rather than with the technical people on the front line, but a direct link between the two may be attenuated as blame is scattered around.

The Apollo 1 space tragedy (17) in 1967 was a 'disaster waiting to happen'. The three crew members in a command module on a NASA Saturn rocket died when a training exercise went wrong. The investigation revealed many deficiencies in design and engineering, manufacturing and quality control. Then, nearly ten years later, there was a sense of *déjà vu* when the *Challenger* space shuttle exploded killing the crew of seven. It was an 'accident rooted in history'. The inquiry found that safety, reliability and quality assurance programmes were grossly inadequate. This dreadful parallel shows that, despite all the high-tech personnel and resources, the essential contribution of management was again seriously flawed. *Challenger* was a rerun of Apollo 1 because the lesson had not been learned.

A world away from space flight, the deep-fat frier case in Belgium (3) had the same underlying management flaws. The company relied on its management systems which were a byword for their quality function and approach to product safety. Yet the case occurred because, in the event, management did not prevent it with the methods that lay at their disposal. The rules were ignored.

The Flixborough chemical plant exploded and killed 28 people in 1974 (15). The Court of Inquiry found that there had been no proper design study, no safety testing, no reference to the design guide nor reference to the relevant British Standard. The Inquiry emphasized the need for a conscious and constant effort from everyone to identify risk. It was this management lack which caused the disaster.

The Persil Power washing powder case (5) caused no harm to anyone but certainly damaged the image of Unilever, its producer. In 1994 the new washing powder was launched amid a blaze of publicity. It was soon under severe attack by Procter & Gamble, Unilever's arch competitor, because it damaged clothes. The two companies fought a ferocious media battle and, eventually, Persil Power was withdrawn. As the design defect could be detected by a washing machine, there must have been some grave management shortcomings which allowed the product to be launched in the first place.

The *Herald of Free Enterprise* ro-ro ferry capsized and sank in 1987 with the loss of 188 lives (20). The immediate reason was that the bow doors were left open, which let the sea enter the car deck as the ship left Zebrugge. The inquiry found that 'From top to bottom the corporate body was infected with the disease of sloppiness'.

These cases all concern large organizations: NASA, ITT, Dutch State Mines and the National Coal Board, Unilever and Townsend Thoresen. Their mistakes attract media attention, while smaller companies escape publicity. Nevertheless, they, too, are vulnerable to similar mistakes in design management. Part 1 explored some of the ways in which this vulnerability can be reduced by being proactive to risk. It is not sufficient merely to be reactive to design problems. A proactive design management programme will help prevent the risks arising. This is illustrated by the management approach to reduce the fire risk in electric cabling in potential hazardous situations (11). In today's terminology, the Tay Bridge disaster of 1879 would be described as a failure in the management of design (16). The danger lies in allowing complacency to seep in and assuming that everything must be all right because nothing has gone wrong – yet.

Product standards

These can be a dangerous trap for the unwary in that they do not necessarily provide the protection that it is sometimes thought. The Magnet cooker hood (1), which suffered damage when it was installed according to the instructions, complied with the Standard of the European Committee for Electrotechnical Standardization. Even so, the divisional court of High Court found that it was still defective because the instructions supplied with it were inadequate.

When the *Amoco Cadiz* ran aground off Brest in 1978 (19) part of the cause was the design of the steering-gear, although the supertanker complied with all the international standards and regulations existing at that time. The Unilever washing powder, Persil Power, met 'all industry standards' yet still damaged clothes (5) and had to be withdrawn at a cost of £57 million in 1994.

It has to be recognized that a Standard itself may be defective. A Standard should be seen as a rebuttable presumption of non-defectiveness. In other words, evidence of its inadequacy can defeat an assumption that a Standard gives protection to a product that follows its specification. If a Standard has a legal standing, or is a mandatory obligation, it will only give protection if a product is defective due to the *inevitable* compliance with its provisions – that is, conformance with the Standard itself was responsible for the defect.

Validation

This is the process by which a product is subjected to formal procedures to make certain that it conforms to the design input. An addition to BS EN ISO 9001 in 1994 says that validation is 'to ensure that product conforms to defined user needs and/or requirements'. It is the final check before the product goes onto the market.

The case histories give ample evidence that rigorous validation could have prevented many of them happening. The 1974 Flixborough chemical plant explosion (15) was caused by the design defect in temporary pipework which was not tested before it was put into service. Validation of a design change in a deep-fat frier would have prevented Belgium's first product recall (3). Practical fail-to-safer challenges would have exposed the danger in the washer/drier that caused a death before it was revealed (2). A validation procedure would have given advance warning of failure of a crane which was not manufactured according to the design (10).

Sometimes validation cannot uncover a defect. Examples are pharmaceuticals and software which may need extended use before a latent defect is found. The development risks defence in the EC Directive on Liability for Defective Products (see Part 2) was included for this reason. With certain drugs the severity of their side-effects only becomes apparent when considerable clinical evidence is available; likewise software bugs, as we saw in Chapter 4, can wreak serious problems after deployment.

Third-party approvals

Many companies rely on third parties to help contribute to the safety of their products by formally recognizing them. The imprimatur of a well known organization can be important to would-be purchasers, as it apparently presents disinterested confirmation that all is well. However, producers should be careful to appreciate just how far such approval goes. Ultimately a producer cannot delegate responsibility for safety in this regard. The buck stops at the name on the product.

The washer/drier with a fundamental safety defect (2) was approved by a certification body, which was required for any appliance sold by the Electricity Boards. The defective cooker hood that ended up in the divisional court (1) was certified by the Istituto Italiano del Marchio di Qualita of Milan as complying with the safety Standard of the European Committee for Electrotechnical Standardization. The deep-fat frier recalled in Belgium because of a potential design defect (3) had been tested and approved by approval authorities in a number of countries. The office chairs which exploded had been authenticated for safety by the German test centre and given the Geprüfte Sicherheit-Zeichen mark (14).

Buying in components from reputable third parties does not exempt a purchaser from making sure that they are safe. The TVR car manufacturer bought Ford engines fitted with Weber carburettors for its cars. A design defect in a carburettor caused a fire in a TVR car for which TVR were held liable (8). It was not enough for TVR merely to 'cast an engineering eye' over the engine, they should have assessed the risk and minimized it.

Product information

Information about a product can be in the form of instructions, warnings, directions and claims, all of which can be part of the product. If they are wrong the product may not be safe, as the case histories demonstrate. Also, in-house company product information can be very revealing when brought to court.

The failure to supply information on the correct assembly of a mobile crane (10) contributed to its collapse and the death of seven people in a passing coach. The manufacturer of the cooker hood which suffered damage when positioned over a gas cooker (1) overcame its problems by providing information restricting its application. The advertising claims for a power tool were not justified and resulted in a US landmark case (4). An important factor in the Allegro case (9), in which a passenger was seriously injured when a wheel fell off on the motorway, was the internal documents of BL, the car manufacturer. Indeed, the product information they contained was damaging to BL's case.

When a user deliberately ignores product information containing a specific warning, as did Icarus (22), he or she voluntarily takes on those risks, and the design is not liable for the consequent lack of safety.

Defects have simple causes

A producer is not liable for a defective product if, at the time of supply, the state of science and technology was such that the defect could not have been discovered. As we saw above, under 'Validation', this is covered by legislation. The whole subject of development risks and state of the art has received a prominence that is not justified for many products. With a few high-tech exceptions, defects arise from simple causes which do not require an advanced technical knowledge to discover.

A glance at the case histories will show that most of the defects were there waiting to be found: by the application of hazard analysis and risk assessment, diligent management action or a contribution from a pragmatic engineer. Even the worst disasters which killed hundreds often had a simple reason. The DC-10 crash (18) was caused by a faulty mechanical linkage in the cargo door that gave a false indication of safety. The Flixborough explosion (15) had its roots in some fairly elementary physics, which also was a contributory cause to the Brent Cross crane tragedy (10).

The ro-ro ferry disasters (20), in which over 1000 people perished, resulted from the sea getting onto the car decks due to the bow doors being left open, or not ensuring that the bow was secure in a heavy sea, both of which seem to be pretty obvious precautions. The list of car faults (7) shows that many could be easily corrected by an ordinary garage mechanic. Similarly, the problems with the bunk beds (6) could be put right by the purchaser with a repair kit, without recourse to expert assistance.

Perhaps the best advice is also simple. Apart from the management actions we have already discussed in Part 1, design safety is concerned with doing the little things right every day.

Case History 1
The Cooker Hood That Went to Appeal

Whirlpool (UK) Limited & Magnet Limited v. Gloucestershire County Council
Court of Appeal: 13 December 1993

There are three strong messages in this case, the first two being especially significant for designers.

1 It is not enough to rely solely on certificates of conformance to international Standards when working on consumer products. All due diligence must be exercised and all reasonable steps taken.
2 A consumer product must be more than just inherently safe. It must be safe in the circumstances in which it is to be used.
3 Importers have a duty to exercise all due diligence in respect of safety, even if they do not actually handle the product themselves. It is not enough to rely on paperwork.

South of Cheltenham, in Charlton Lane, Leckhampton, Mr and Mrs Graham-Jones had a New World gas cooker in their kitchen. They bought a Magnet cooker hood from the local shop and, using the instructions supplied, Mr Graham-Jones fitted it just above the minimum recommended height over the gas burners.

The Graham-Joneses found that, in use, the hood could not be turned off, the switches distorted and became too hot to touch and the plastic casing warped, exposing the wires and bulb. Mr Mountford, the manager of the Magnet branch which sold the hood, inspected the damage in Charlton Lane and decided that the hood must have had a manufacturing defect. He replaced it free of charge. Exactly the same sequence of events was repeated.

Although the hoods bore the name 'Magnet', they were imported by Whirlpool (UK) via Whirlpool BV in Holland who obtained them from the Italian manufacturer, ELICA. The local Trading Standards Officer became involved with the result that Magnet and Whirlpool (UK) were prosecuted for failing to comply with the general safety requirement, in that the hoods were not reasonably safe, having regard to all the circumstances, contrary to section 10 of the Consumer Protection Act 1987. Whirlpool, in addition, were alleged to have offended under section 40(1) of the Act which is concerned with the liability of persons other than the principal offender. The hearing took six days at Cheltenham magistrates' court. On 29 January 1993 the defendants were found guilty. The appeal was heard on 11 December 1993 before Lord Justice Russell and Mr Justice Blofeld at the Royal Courts of Justice in the Strand.

The Consumer Protection Act is well known for implementing, through Part I, the provisions of the Directive on Liability for Defective Products. Section 10 comes under Part II, which starts by saying that a person is guilty of an offence if he or she supplies consumer goods which fail to comply with the general safety requirement. Under section 10(2) all the circumstances have to be taken into account in determining whether they are not reasonably safe, including 'the manner in which, and purposes for which the goods are being or would be marketed . . .'.

Counsel for Magnet and Whirlpool maintained that the hood was not caught by these provisions and that there was nothing unsafe about the hood as supplied. It was the New World cooker which was not reasonably safe. Lord Justice Russell found this a 'startling proposition' and even counsel acknowledged that it was a 'somewhat unattractive argument'. It was submitted that if the hood conformed with domestic or Community obligations then this demonstrated compliance with the general safety requirement of section 10.

This argument relied on section 10(3) which states that consumer goods shall not be regarded as failing to comply with the general safety requirement in respect of:

(a) anything which is shown to be attributable to compliance with any requirement imposed by or under any enactment or with any Community obligation;

(b) any failure to do more in relation to any matter than is required by

> (i) any safety regulations imposing requirements with respect to that matter;

Counsel submitted that the hood complied with the Low Voltage Directive (73/23/EEC) and the safety standard for domestic electrical appliances, BS 3456 1987. These requirements did not stipulate that suppliers had to warn of the danger if the hoods were used over gas cookers, and section 3(b) excludes from consideration any requirement beyond the terms contained in these regulations.

In his judgment Lord Justice Russell made a distinction which is very important to any designer concerned with the safety of consumer products. He said that 'all the circumstances' had to be taken into account when contemplating whether goods complied with the general safety requirement. This meant 'not the goods themselves viewed in isolation but the use to which they were put; in this case the use which must have been contemplated by all concerned, namely use over a gas cooker'. Section 10(3) concerned the goods themselves taken in isolation. They must not be inherently unsafe and regard must be paid to any enactment or any Community obligation. The hood was not reasonably safe because it became dangerous in the circumstances which prevailed. The hood could be made safe without falling foul of any directive or domestic regulation. 'Indeed we are told that this is now the position. The fact that there are now warning notices placed on these hoods to the effect that they are unsuitable for use with certain gas cookers . . .'.

Magnet claimed that they had available to them a defence under section 10(4) of the Act, that applies to retailers and says:

> In any proceedings against any person for an offence under this section in respect of any goods it shall be a defence for that person to show . . .
>
> > (b) (ii) that at the time he supplied the goods or offered or agreed

to supply them or exposed or possessed them for supply, he neither knew nor had reasonable grounds for believing that the goods failed to comply with the general safety requirement;

In 1991 it was known within the electrical industry that there were problems involving the ability of cooker hoods to withstand heat. The Technical Manager of New World Domestic Appliances, who was the Chairman of the British Standards Committee for Domestic Gas Cooking Appliances and a member of the European committee responsible for the Standards for gas cooking appliances, in his evidence said:

> The question of some cooker hoods not being able to withstand temperatures emitted by some gas cookers is a known problem. In 1990 [I] attended a meeting at BSI to look at the possibility of separate certification of cooker hoods for use with gas cookers.

From this it followed that Mr Mountford, Magnet's branch manager, should have appreciated that there was something unsafe about the hood. There was material information available in Whirlpool's industry that a potential problem existed with the combination of electrical hoods positioned over gas cookers.

It was contended that Mr Mountford was too junior a staff member to be aware of such knowledge. But counsel submitted that, as the manager of the branch, he was identified with the company because he was in charge. On this analysis the company were responsible because Mr Mountford was the company. Alternatively, it was argued, Magnet were still responsible because they had delegated all matters relating to safety to Mr Mountford; there was no requirement that he had to report anything relating to safety to the board. Furthermore, Magnet should have been aware of the problems with hoods used over gas cookers. The Court of Appeal took the view that the magistrates were fully entitled to find Magnet guilty of the offence laid against them under section 10, and their appeal failed.

Whirlpool were said to be only selling agents. They received orders from Magnet, which they passed on to the Dutch company which bought the goods from Italy. Whirlpool (UK) made only paper transactions and never actually handled the goods. The company relied on a due diligence defence which designers should fully appreciate. Section 39(1) of the Act reads:

> Subject to the following provisions of this section, in proceedings against any person for an offence to which this section applies it shall be a defence for that person to show that he took all reasonable steps and exercised all due diligence to avoid committing the offence.

The Technical Manager of Whirlpool (UK) said that they understood that CENELEC certificates were regarded as showing compliance with the EC safety standard. CENELEC is the European Committee for Electrotechnical Standardization and is based in Brussels. They also 'relied on an IMQ [the Istituto Italiano del Marchio di Qualita of Milan] certificate which assured the company that the product complies with safety standard'. Counsel for the prosecution submitted that, while this was indeed the case, Whirlpool (UK), being the importers, did not exercise all due diligence. They failed to appreciate that the existence of the certificates alone did not afford a defence to an offence under section 10. If they had made any enquiries at all they would have known that there was a potential problem and would have done something about it. In fact they simply relied upon the certificates and took no further steps to prevent the importation of goods that failed to comply with section 10. Their appeal was dismissed.

At the conclusion of the case a number of questions were posed. Again, one of them is of particular interest to designers. The High Court was asked 'Whether goods can probably be held to contravene the general safety requirement, imposed by section 10(1) of the Consumer Protection Act 1987, if they comply with the requirements of EC directives applicable to goods of that class and are certified as so complying, by an EC officially approved body'. It was submitted that it had been assumed 'in this and other industries' that the appropriate CENELEC or equivalent certificate was in effect a certificate of unity. As this was a criminal case the court was asked to certify that it was a question of public importance that should be determined by the House of Lords.

Their Lordships thought that the matter was clear 'beyond peradventure' and declined to certify.

Comment

A formal design review system would have ensured that safety information was a lead item in the programme. Hazard analysis and risk assessment would have identified the design risk of using the hood over a gas cooker. Simply providing the hood with adequate safety information would have made it safe. This case demonstrates very well the need for manufacturers and others to keep up-to-date in their field and that they are unwise to assume that third parties sought out such knowledge on their behalf.

Case History 2
Candy: The Fatal Washer/ Drier

In 1988 Mrs Eleanor Bellamy, a widow of 82, bought a Candy washer/drier, model 38WD, for her bungalow in Aston, near Sheffield. It gave 'first class' service until the evening of 17 February 1992 when it killed her. On that day her daughter, Mrs Marples, put some washing in the machine and then went out, leaving her mother to go to bed early at 17.30. When the daughter returned at 20.00 she found that there had been a fierce fire in the kitchen and that her mother was dead in bed, from the inhalation of smoke and carbon monoxide poisoning.

This domestic tragedy eventually involved the national press, the television news, a government minister and the Consumers' Association; it also produced some very serious criticisms about the design of the machine. Candy is a privately owned, Italian, white goods group founded by Peppino Fumagalli at the end of the Second World War in Monza; in 1980 it bought Kelvinator and in 1995 paid £106 million for Hoover.

At the beginning of 1991 Kelco, the British subsidiary of the Italian Candy, had placed advertisements in the national press headed 'Important Safety Announcement'. The first said:

> As part of our continuous Quality Control process it has come to our attention that if the washer/drier is used *not in accordance with the User Instruction Booklet* during the drying mode overheating could occur. In order to prevent this possibility we are offering to fit an additional component completely 'Free of charge'.

The announcement was placed in the *News of the World* and the *Sunday Express* on 17 March 1991 and in the *Daily Telegraph* on 22 March.

A second version, headed 'Important Safety Message' said:

Owners of Candy or Kelvinator washer/driers are urgently advised that under certain conditions it is possible for the machine to overheat during the drying cycle. In order to prevent this possibility we are offering to fit an additional component completely *free of charge.*

This advertisement was placed in the *Daily Mirror, Daily Express* and the *Sun* on 7 November 1991 and in the *Mail on Sunday, Sunday Mirror* and the *Sunday Post* on 10 November (see Figure C.2.1). Candy's Commercial Director said that the advertisements had been approved by the Department of Trade and Industry and the British Electrotechnical Approvals Board.

The Consumers' Association criticized the advertisements for the complicated instructions and for their failure to mention the ultimate risk of fire: 'The notice incorrectly stated that any case of overheating was due to owners not following the instructions correctly.' The retrofit was aimed at the 42 000 machines that had been sold but, by the time of the inquest on Mrs Bellamy, only 6700, or 16 per cent, had been modified. Hers was not one of them. According to the Consumers' Association they knew of 23 cases of the appliance overheating, with 12 of these being serious fires causing significant damage or injury.

The inquest on Mrs Bellamy was held in Rotherham on 5 August 1992. The Coroner heard from a number of expert witnesses, the first of which was Dr James Read, a Home Office forensic scientist, who described the situation in the bungalow in All Saints Way on the morning after the fire. He said that there had been 'a single seat of fire located in the top of the Candy washer/drier machine'. The extensive fire damage had destroyed all combustible material in that area of the kitchen so that no meaningful examination of individual components could be undertaken. There were no discernible remains of the machine's plastic laminate top and front fascia board. He was of the opinion that the fire was probably caused by the overheating of the electrical air heating unit of the clothes-drying facility. He did not think that overloading the machine would result in subsequently setting it on fire.

WARNING.
IMPORTANT SAFETY NOTICE

For owners of CANDY TC1000 AND TC1244 WASHER DRYERS.

Candy has decided to extend its recall campaign to encompass **all TC1000** and **all TC1244** washer dryers.

A fault can cause the programme timer to overheat and could cause a possible fire in the appliance. In order to prevent this, Candy will modify the appliance, free of charge.

PLEASE NOTE

This programme timer is only fitted to the **TC1000** and **TC1244**. No other models are involved.

To arrange a service engineer visit, owners of these models should contact Candy by dialling:

FREEPHONE 0800 373240

IF YOU THINK YOU HAVE ONE OF THESE MACHINES, PLEASE DO NOT USE THE APPLIANCE UNTIL YOU HAVE CONTACTED CANDY.

Alternatively, please complete the coupon below. You will then be contacted as soon as possible.

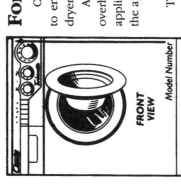

FRONT VIEW

Model Number

To: P.O. Box 88, Bromborough, Wirral, Merseyside L62 3QW.

Surname _____ Home Tel: _____ Daytime Tel: _____

Address. _____ Postcode _____

Brand _____ Model No. _____

Figure C.2.1 'Safety Notice' appearing in *The Times* on 7 December 1994.

The next witness, Michael Briskman, Technical Manager of the Consumers' Association, explained the drying components of the appliance. He said:

Basically, the machine dries by pushing hot air into the drum.

There is a fan which drives the hot air, it is driven into an aluminium chamber, which contains the heaters, and from the heaters the air is ducted into the drum. This is normally the principle used in hair driers, heaters, and the like. As a common arrangement in engineering, it is the thermostat which safeguards against overheating. Because, obviously should the fan fail or there be an obstruction in air flow, that would be sufficient to probably melt the casing and cause a hazard. The Candy machine has all these features; it has a thermostat.

Our contentions were, for [the heater element to melt] two things had to happen. First of all the air flow has to stop or be considerably reduced as a result of a fault, that is the breakdown of the fan or blockage. If that alone happened, the thermostat ought to prevent a catastrophe, but for that situation to happen to the thermostat also, for some reason or another, either would not work at all or be designed in such a way that they are not able to cope with it. Regarding Mrs Bellamy's machine, it was badly burned – the heater was quite clearly molten in the same way – suggesting again that there was combined failure of air flow and thermostat.

To confirm this argument tests were carried out in which the fan was disconnected, the ducting was blocked and the machine switched off halfway through a cycle. In each case the thermostat prevented a fire. Then the thermostat was shorted out, leaving the heater element constantly in circuit but unprotected. Smoke billowed from the machine in eight minutes, acid flames in ten, flames in 15 and a full-scale fire in 17 minutes. The witness said, 'We concluded that the fire we had seen previously, including Mrs Bellamy's fire, was the result of a combined failure of the thermostat and fan.'

The Coroner asked what would happen when the machine was switched off halfway through a cycle. The witness said:

The heater looks very similar to a grill element in an electric cooker, it is that kind of heater. It probably runs at 6 or 7 hundred degrees centigrade, and obviously when it is switched off, all the machine is now de-energised and that temperature is then dissipated in the surrounding area and therefore there is a temperature rise of the inner casing and it is likely that this may be the crux, that this is actually causing a gradual degeneration of the thermostat, for one of two reasons, either because the thermostat is made of plastic, deteriorating inside, or because the thermostat is designed to, say, operate at 100 degrees and is then pushed up to 200 degrees and the bimetallic strip is strained beyond its intended limit. But, at the same time, we were also able to obtain very high temperatures under conditions where the fan is disconnected, and the same would apply if somebody disconnected the supply valves to change a fuse or if there was a power failure and I would have thought that if that is a serious problem and is actually causing failures in that machine then there is a design issue here and you would expect the machine at some stage in its life to be switched off automatically [*sic*].

The witness said that the modification to the washer/drier by Candy was to fit a fuse link which would break down automatically on overheating. He did not see how that could safeguard against the problem of switching the machine off prematurely.

The Campaigns Executive of the Consumers' Association, Anthony Smith, told the court of his contact with Kelco and the letters the Association had received from users of the appliance. He said that the machine was designed to be run unattended, so that use could be made of the cheaper Economy 7 electricity available at night: 'People quite rightly set these machines, go to bed, and expect to wake up to find their washing dry.' He said that 'If something goes wrong with the dryer fan, by and large you know that something has gone wrong, because the machine ceases to work. It's much more difficult to see what is going wrong with the thermostat.' The letters received by the Association indicated quite clearly that there was a problem with the fans and thermostats. The first letter described an incident in September 1987 and the most recent fire was two weeks before the inquest. The emerging pattern was that of failing fans and failing thermostats. He believed that there were 25 000 to 30 000 machines still in use which were identical to that of Mrs Bellamy. He said that Mrs Bellamy's machine had been certified by an approvals body.

The National Service Manager of Kelco, Anthony Games, said that they became aware of fire incidents and the failure of two components at the same time: 'The thermostat was there to prevent any heat rise and should have done that and obviously it was not doing its job.' Analysis of the component showed that the failures were caused by it being subjected to temperatures above the specification. When a machine was stopped during the drying cycle the temperature would rise over 200 degrees, far above the design temperature of the thermostat. The company then initiated a recall and 15 000 letters were sent out.

The Coroner summarized the situation: 'What it really comes down to is that Candy, your company parent, has been buying fans which have shattered and thermostats which are not of sufficiently high quality, and putting them into Candy machines in Italy.' The witness accepted that was the case with the thermostats and that the fans were initially at fault. He said that the approvals body's certification was required for any appliance sold by the Electricity Boards.

The court was shown the section of the instruction booklet which said that the machine should be allowed to cool down if the cycle was interrupted prematurely. The witness agreed that there was no impression of danger and that more emphasis should have been added. Regarding the recall he said, 'The response has been far from what we could want. Of 42 000 machines at risk, we have modified 6 700 to date. We can only go to press again.'

The verdict was that Eleanor Bellamy died as a result of an accident.

The Consumer Affairs Minister, Baroness Denton of Wakefield, asked Kelco to consider issuing further warnings. A spokesman said, 'Meanwhile our advice is that anyone with a Candy washing machine should ring Freephone 0800 373 240 to get all the information to identify whether their machine is one affected.' A video of a Candy WD38 washer/drier in flames in a laboratory was given intensive media news coverage.

By 23 November Candy said that 30 231 machines, 72 per cent, had either been modified or booked to be retrofitted. The recall advertisements had been rerun four times and the company were working with the Association of Manufacturers of Domestic Appliances to develop a system whereby known purchasers of an appliance could be immediately located. By July 1993 79 per cent of purchasers had been traced.

Comment

Despite all the media coverage almost one-fifth of the purchasers had still to be found, pointing to the need to get it right first time. The design of domestic appliances which use energy should be such that they fail-to-safer. Hazard analysis and risk assessment methods such as Failure Mode Effects Analysis (FMEA) and Fault Tree Analysis (FTA) would have revealed the consequences of the failures in the Candy washer/drier (see Chapter 3).

During a design review of the washer/drier an FMEA would have looked at the effects of thermostat failure. The analysis would have warned that the possible outcome would be overheating and a fire. At the same time, a FTA could have started with overheating and a fire as the top event. By working back downwards from this situation, the combination of component failure which would cause the top event to occur would be discovered.

The case of the washer/drier illustrates that it is virtually impossible completely to recover a situation of this type. In the end some purchasers will remain at risk.

Sources

'Minister's plea after drier death', *The Times* 7 July 1992.
'The Killer Washer-Drier', *Which?*, London: Consumers' Association Ltd, September 1992.
'Candy scare shows recalls of faulty goods to be ineffective', *Fire Prevention*, Official Journal of the Fire Protection Association, London, October 1992.
'Improving recalls of unsafe goods', *Policy Report*, London: Consumers' Association Ltd, 1993.

Case History 3
The Deep-fat Frier with Design Problems

Even the most professional design review system is useless if it is ignored. The European multinational company, ITT Europe, was renowned for its rigorous approach to quality, with special emphasis on product safety. This case illustrates what happened when the system was bypassed, leading to the first product recall for a consumer appliance in Belgium.

A Belgian company Nova, part of ITT, manufactured a range of domestic appliances including a deep-fat frier called Fritex. The product consisted of an aluminium casting, electrically heated by a separately manufactured element fused into the base of the main body as part of the casting. The product worked well and caused no problems, but the manufacture of the casting, with the inclusion of the heating element, was difficult and costly. An independent consultant suggested that a channel should be cast into the base of the pan and the heating element clamped in as a separate operation. Production of this design started in August 1975, as Fritex 3. See Figure C.3.1.

On 6 January 1976 Nova after-sales received a defective Fritex from a customer. Investigation showed that the heating element had moved in its groove sufficiently to allow one of the ends to contact the aluminium casting. A test confirmed that this was a potentially repeatable failure. On 10 January a second customer complained that he had received electric shocks from his Fritex. Production was stopped and a recall was instituted.

An assessment of the Fritex 3 showed that it had two design defects. First, the thermal contact between the heating element and the aluminium casting was not as effective as in the previous design. This caused the heating element to reach a temperature

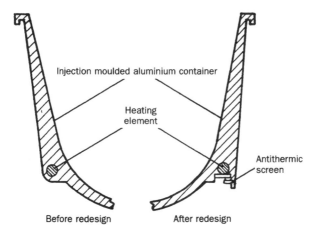

Figure C.3.1   The cost-reduction design defect of the Nova Fritex
© *Quality Assurance* June 1978.

about 180°C higher than previously. Second, the stresses caused by the excessive temperature and less firm clamping of the element allowed it to creep around the channel as it was switched on and off. But this did not necessarily make the Fritex dangerous. Clear instructions about the need for an earthed connection and the fitting of a three-lead flex should have protected the user from any short-circuit. Also the Fritex was sold with a standard European plug moulded on to the flex – the 'fail-safe' device. It was the Belgian kitchen that made the Fritex dangerous, as many do not have properly earthed outlets. The standard European three-pin plug could easily be forced into an unearthed two-pin outlet.

A risk analysis of Fritex 3 revealed that only 25 per cent of Belgian kitchens had an earth meeting legal standards, 25 per cent had a make-shift non-legal earth and 50 per cent had no earth at all. It was assumed that a short-circuited Fritex on a non-earthed outlet would give someone a shock sooner or later, and it was estimated that about 1 per cent of users receiving electric shocks would require medical treatment.

At this time ITT Europe had 190 000 employees in 12 different European countries. The Nova Fritex case was summed up by the senior managers responsible for the recall:[1]

Table C.3.1 Risk analysis of Nova Fritex 3

	Min %	Max %
Fritexes expected to short-circuit	25	50
Kitchens with no earth	50	75
Short-circuits giving electric shock	100	100
Shocked users needing medical attention	2	8
Overall product of proportions	0.25	3

The Fritex failure represented a serious breakdown of the ITT Product Qualification system. [The policy requires] each new product to be subjected to defined qualification tests to give assurance that it conforms to all of its specified requirements. Qualification testing is a formal quality assurance procedure additional to normal development testing. The important design change on the Fritex 3 was not subjected to this discipline and only a small amount of life testing was included in the development testing. Nova is a small company and at that time had staffing weaknesses in the Technical and Quality departments. The design change was proposed and tested by a consultant unfamiliar with the requirements for product qualification and this also contributed to the problem. The fact that the Fritex had been tested and approved by approval authorities in a number of countries only emphasises that there are no substitutes for rigorous internal qualification testing. The Fritex case led to a major re-emphasis on product qualification, particularly for consumer products.

There were only two accidents with the Fritex and probably neither was caused by a defective unit. In 1990 five Nova executives completed a management buy-out of the company, which became Nova Electro International NV, the third largest manufacturer of deep-fat friers in Europe (after Tefal and Moulinex), producing more than one million units per year.

Comment

Procedures are but so much paper unless they are enforced. Too often management are some distance from the action and assume that all is well, because of the procedures resting in the bulky files on their bookshelves. Not only should procedures be independently audited but also they must be tested, by introducing a notional rogue product and checking that it is appropriately detected.

Reference

1 Groocock, J. M., Clifton, P. and Mueller, A. K. (1978), 'The recall of the Nova Fritex', *Quality Assurance*, London: Institute of Quality Assurance.

Case History 4
The Power Tool with a Design Defect

Greenman v. Yuba Power Products Inc.
Supreme Court of California: 24 January 1963

In this case, the plaintiff, Mr Greenman, brought an action for damages against the retailer and the manufacturer of a Shopsmith, a combination power tool that could be used as a saw, drill and wood lathe. After seeing a Shopsmith demonstrated by the retailer and studying a brochure prepared by the manufacturer, he decided he wanted a Shopsmith for his home workshop, and his wife gave him one for Christmas in 1955. In 1957 he bought the necessary attachments to use the Shopsmith as a lathe for turning a large piece of wood he wished to make into a chalice. After he had worked on the piece of wood several times without difficulty, it suddenly flew out of the machine and struck him on the forehead, inflicting serious injuries. About ten and a half months later, he gave the retailer and the manufacturer written notice of claimed breaches of warranties and filed a complaint against them alleging such breaches and negligence.

The manufacturer's brochure included the following statements:

1 When Shopsmith is in horizontal position – Rugged construction of frame provides rigid support from end to end. Heavy centerless-ground steel tubing insures perfect alignment of components.
2 Shopsmith maintains its accuracy because every component has positive locks that hold adjustments through rough or precision work.

Our interest lies in the fact that the jury heard substantial evidence to show that the design was defective. Witnesses testified

195

that inadequate set screws were used to hold parts of the machine together, so that normal vibration caused the tailstock of the lathe to move away from the piece of wood being turned, permitting it to fly out of the lathe. They also testified that there were other more positive ways of fastening the parts of the machine together, the use of which would have prevented the accident.

In concluding his judgment Justice Traynor said:

> To establish the manufacturer's liability it was sufficient that plaintiff proved that he was injured while using the Shopsmith in a way it was intended to be used as a result of a defect in design and manufacture of which plaintiff was not aware that made the Shopsmith unsafe for its intended use.

The trial court had previously returned a verdict for the retailer against the plaintiff and for the plaintiff against the manufacturer in the amount of $65 000. The judgement was affirmed.

This US landmark case is frequently cited in connection with product liability matters. The court's decision was based on the concept of strict liability, and one result of the case was the inclusion of a new section in the American Law Institute's Restatement of the Law of Torts. This new section became the well known 402A of 1965, which was adopted by most US states in one form or another. The section said:

> Special Liability of Seller of Products for Physical Harm to User or Consumer
>> (1) One who sells any product in a defective condition unreasonably dangerous to the user or consumer or to his property is subject to liability for physical harm thereby caused to the ultimate user or consumer, or to his property, if
>>> (a) the seller is engaged in the business of selling such a product, and
>>> (b) it is expected to and does reach the user or consumer without substantial change in the condition in which it is sold.
>> (2) The rule stated in subsection (1) applies although
>>> (a) the seller has exercised all possible care in the preparation and sale of his product, and
>>> (b) the user and consumer has not bought the product from or entered into any contractual relation with the seller.

These words echo those of Justice Traynor in his judgment:

> A manufacturer is strictly liable in tort when the article he places on the market, knowing that it is to be used without inspection for defects, proves to have a defect that causes injury to human beings.

Comment

One of the factors in this case was that there was more than one way in which the tool could have been assembled. Indeed, the accident could have been prevented if one of them had been adopted by Mr Greenman. A similar defect was a contributory cause of the Brent Cross crane accident described in Case History 10. Another factor was that the product did not live up to the claims made for it. In a design review system product claims should feature in the programme from an early stage to ensure that they are fulfilled by the final design. Too often they are a marketing add-on at the end of the process by which time the designers may well have left the scene.

Source

Ashworth, J. S. (ed.) (1984), *Product Liability Casebook*, Colchester: Lloyd's of London Press Limited.

Case History 5

The £57 Million 'Mistake' in Persil Power

The European detergent market is worth £6 billion per year. There is a multiplicity of packs on the market, which cause 'more confusion in the soap aisle than in any other', according to the chief executive of a leading supermarket.

Soap powder wars have a high profile because of the attention devoted to them by the media. The chief protagonists, slugging it out in the high streets for market share, are the Anglo-Dutch Unilever and the US Procter & Gamble. Together they account for nearly 90 per cent of the £1 billion UK washing powder market. The occasionally ferocious claims and counter-claims provide the press with a rich supply of quotes and counter-quotes.

An indication of the problems that soap powder can cause was provided in September 1993 with Unilever's launch of New System Persil Automatic. The new product was enzyme-based – or biological – and aimed to take advantage of the low suds sector for the growing number of automatic washing machines, then found in half the homes in the country. The new powder's market share rose from 38 per cent to 50 per cent before its sales started to drop like a stone. The media ran stories of skin problems linked to the new product under headlines such as 'Washday alert on powder' and 'The big itch in your soap powder'. New System Persil Automatic had not used words like 'enzyme' or 'biological' but had relied on 'biocare', which is not to be found in technical dictionaries.

At the beginning of August 1994 Persil brought back the original Persil Automatic alongside the new version. The original was now 'Original Non Biological Persil Automatic' while the new product declared its biological provenance, to acknowledge the design difference between them.

While all this was going on, a far more serious design change was lurking to tarnish the Persil name, which goes back to the beginnings of the century. Persil Power was launched in the UK, and Omo Power on the Continent, in May 1994 to boost Persil's overall brand share which then stood at just over a quarter of the UK soap powder market. At first the new product overtook its arch rival, Procter & Gamble's Ariel, to become market leader of the sector. Then Procter & Gamble displayed photographs of clothes apparently ruined after being washed with the new Persil product. What followed became 'probably one of the biggest single consumer product controversies in history', according to Shandwick, the leading public relations agency which handled the Persil campaign.

Faithfully reported by the press, each company accused the other of foul play in a war of words. Both took out full-page advertisements knocking the other in newspapers and magazines. Writs for defamation were exchanged. The uproar was loud and extreme. Unilever changed the formulation of Persil Power by reducing the proportion of the ingredient that was responsible for the problem. The company stated that the 'defect only shows up under laboratory conditions and not under the two-year trial we conducted with 60,000 users. The new product meets all the industry standards.' It then delivered 11 million free packs of Persil Power to British housewives at a cost of £25 million. In response Procter & Gamble insisted:

> Persil should come clean to consumers on fabric damage. All our research and the findings of independent test institutions and consumer organisations in Europe show that reformulated Persil products continue to cause unacceptable levels of fabric damage.

Referring to the initial launch of Persil Power the co-chairman of Unilever said, 'We made a mistake. We launched a product which had a defect which we had not detected.' The Consumers' Association joined in with the statement: 'Any claim that the original Persil Power causes damage to clothes only under extreme conditions is nonsense.' The reports wiped 10 per cent off Unilever's share price.

The concept behind Persil Power was to use manganese compounds as catalysts at low temperatures, thereby improving the oxidation power by which clothes are bleached. Ordinary bleach, such as hydrogen peroxide, is most effective above 60°C but modern fabrics require lower temperatures than this. Unilever took out 35 patents to protect its new catalysts and invested £100 million in new plant, as well as spending £250 million on the Europe-wide launch of Persil Power. However, in practice, the manganese accelerator reacted with dark dyes in thin cotton fabrics causing weakening and colour fading.

When Unilever announced its year-end results in February 1995 the chairman conceded that Persil Power was 'the biggest marketing setback in the company's history'. It had cost £57 million in write-offs. A £42 million extraordinary charge to restructure the detergent business was needed, and Persil's market share had slipped from 29.2 per cent at the height of Persil Power's popularity in June 1994 to 20.2 per cent in April 1995.

In a masterly understatement Niall Fitzgerald, Unilever's head of detergents, said that the failure of the Persil Power products had proved to be a 'big disappointment'. He continued, 'All great businesses understand that enterprise involves risk, that occasionally there will be mistakes and that the true test of leadership is the ability to guide people through those moments of crisis.' He said that there had been no witch-hunt to allocate blame. Detergents accounted for only one-fifth of Unilever's worldwide activities, and the European concentrated powder comprised only 3 per cent of the world detergents market. In March 1996 Fitzgerald was named as the next chief executive of Unilever UK.

Customers were quickly offered New Generation Persil which did not contain the catalyst. In tests garments were washed 60 times compared to 15–25 times for earlier tests. The product was evaluated by six independent test institutes. The different varieties of Persil increased to eight with the launch of Persil Finesse, as brand segmentation was exploited to build market share.

In January 1995 Tesco became the first European supermarket to discontinue Persil Power and replace it with New Generation Persil, on which Unilever had spent most of the brand's £19 million promotion budget.

When Unilever's first quarter-year results were announced in May 1995 the chairman said that, with the failure of the Persil products, the performance of the European consumer business had been disappointing. Its impact was not disclosed separately.

Sensitivity about the failure was well demonstrated in an interview with Sir Michael Perry, the Chairman, reported in *Management Today*. Although the interviewer had been asked not to mention Persil Power, he asked him what had gone wrong to produce the £57 million write-off. Perry suddenly became 'rather quiet'. The report continued:

> Perry is unequivocal. 'I have nothing more to say than what we have already said umpteen times about Persil Power. It will be on the market as long as there is a consumer demand, it is an extremely effective product if used as recommended, and consumers all over Europe are doing just that.' Has there been a lot of internal soul-searching as to what went wrong? 'Yes.' Have people left the company because of what went wrong? 'No.' Is it something that has never happened before within Unilever? 'No.' Can you name me an equivalent problem? 'No. You know, you are only going to get monosyllables out of me on this subject.'
>
> Perry at this point looks firm but exasperated. A moment later he is trying to wrap the interview up with a brusque 'How long do we need now? Because we have really gone on for a long time . . .'. Eventually he regains his humour but it was an illuminating flashpoint. Others explain it thus: 'They've speeded up the pace of innovation and inevitably there are going to be accidents,' says one analyst. 'There is no business in the world that doesn't have accidents; the problem is they can ill-afford to have it in this area.'

The impact of the Persil Power launch was revealed when figures on Britain's top brands from *Checkout*/Neilsen were published. In the year to August 1995 sales in grocers of the Persil brand fell by 19.4 per cent, or £45 million, to £185.5 million. But the Ariel brand suffered too, because in the same period its sales fell by 7.4 per cent, or £17 million, to £216.7 million. What happened was that the consumers in their confusion turned to the own-labels such as Sainsbury's Novon and Safeway's Cyclon.

That figure of £57 million began to look like a serious underestimate of the loss. When Unilever's results were published in November 1995 *The Times* made the following comment:

> Unilever has been scrubbing hard to remove the stain on its reputation caused by last year's bungled Persil Power launch. The washing powder proved too powerful for its European customers to stomach and the City washed its hands of the company's shares. Estimates suggest that the debacle lost Unilever about £250 million and it lost its toe-hold in the £6 billion European washing powder market. Yesterday the company showed signs of modest recovery. Unilever indicated that Persil's market share was up by one third in the UK, although still below pre-Power days.

The *Financial Times* found that the key lessons to be learnt were:

1 Test products even more extensively to catch any flaws which could be used against it.
2 Do not neglect the brand while heavily promoting the product.
3 Cater to differences between national markets while drawing on any pan-European efficiencies in manufacturing and marketing.
4 Communicate more effectively about the company to the press, customers and bodies like consumers' associations rather than rely on product promotion.

In May 1996 it was reported that Unilever was to relaunch Persil in the UK with a £7 million budget.

Comment

The first lesson to be learnt from this example must be to make sure that design is managed effectively. If the design defect could be revealed in a washing machine no great scientific resources were necessary. It would seem that the problem was not so much one of soap powder technology but rather one of how that technology was organized. The £42 million cost of restructuring Unilever's detergent business is evidence of that.

Sources

The Times, 24 September 1994; 22, 25 February 1995; 10 May 1995; 11 November 1995; 13 December 1995; 22 March 1996; 29 April 1996.

Marketing, 26 July 1994; 29 September 1994; 23 February 1995; 25 May 1995.

Sunday Times, 23 April 1995; 19 May 1995; 25 September 1995.

Financial Times, 19 January 1995; 10 May 1995.

Management Today, May 1995; October 1995.

Daily Express, 24 September 1994.

Case History 6
Safe in Bed?

It is easy to imagine that one is safe in bed. But for many people in the United States that was an illusion. Tens of thousands of beds had a simple design defect which only became obvious when the mattress collapsed and deposited them on the floor. This case history illustrates the danger of overlooking the commonplace and obvious. If a product is literally part of the furniture we cease to take notice of it.

Towards the end of 1993 bunk beds, which had been imported into the United States from Malaysia, Taiwan and Mexico, were causing concern as they were a potential risk to those who slept in them. They were of tubular metal construction, usually painted in high gloss red, white, blue or black, sold for between $150 and $250 each and, importantly, frequently had no identifying marks of any description. By the summer of 1994 the Consumer Product Safety Commission (CPSC) had located at least nine companies which had imported a total of 300 000 beds.

The hazard was that the beds could unexpectedly collapse while in use, allowing the upper bunk to fall and cause injury, either to its occupant or the person below. The reason was a design defect in the mattress supports. One importer said that the upper bunk could fall suddenly, usually after squeaking or creaking which may not be recognized as warning sounds. The mattress frames were supported on metal tongues which were welded to the inside of the corner posts. A tab at the end of each side rail of a frame slid into its appropriate tongue. The design of the tongues was such that there could be an inadequate thickness of metal, or poor welding, which could lead to structural weakness (see Figure C.6.1).

The CPSC received 400 complaints about the bunk beds. Montgomery Ward had sold 13 000 at $199 each and had had 17

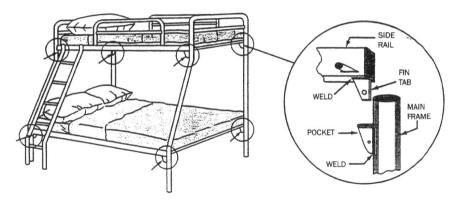

Figure C.6.1 Tubular bunk beds mattress supports

instances of the supports breaking, causing eight injuries. The Powell Company had imported 23 000 beds of which 36 were reported to have collapsed causing five injuries. Bernards had sold 11 000 and received 84 reports of supports breaking, with one injury. Gold Key had sold 50 000 at $160 to $300 and had received 100 reports of supports breaking, but no mention of injuries.

The CPSC advised people to examine the mattress support corners for cracks and to contact their retailer. If cracks were found the bed was not to be used: 'Do not wait for the bed to creak.' If cracks were present the bed would be replaced. If cracks were not present purchasers would receive a repair kit of reinforcement brackets.

In the summer of 1995 a different type of bunk bed was recalled by the CPSC. These were wooden bunk beds with openings on the top bunk which could present a potential entrapment hazard to young children. Twenty-four children died between 1990 and 1994 from being caught in such openings; 19 of these victims were aged two or under and four were three years of age. The spaces were large enough for a child's body to pass through but small enough to entrap a child's head.

The American Society for Testing and Materials's voluntary standard required that any space between the essential guard rails and the bed frame, and in the head and foot boards of the top bunk, had to be less than 3.5 inches. The recall programme involved 320 000 beds from 11 manufacturers.

Comment

If the incidents concerning the tabular steel bunk beds had taken place in Europe, the importer would be liable in the first instance for any compensation. Under the provisions of the EC Directive on Liability for Defective Products, the first importer into the EU takes over the responsibilities and liabilities of the producer as far as the purchaser is concerned, whatever recourse he may have against the actual manufacturer.

Second, inspection by a pragmatic engineer or a practical validation test before manufacture would have revealed the design weakness. As the corrective action could be carried out by the purchasers themselves the fault could have been easily discovered.

In the second instance, conformance to the voluntary standard would have prevented entrapment and the 24 deaths. This is an illustration of the need to make certain that designers always consult relevant standards.

Source

Safety News, a compilation of news releases and safety alerts by the US Consumer Product Safety Commission Washington September 1993, April, June, July, December 1994 and June 1995.

Case History 7
Safe on the Road?

We are familiar with car manufacturers' claims that their latest model has been exhaustively tested. Some will emphasize its safety as a particular attribute. It will have been driven millions of miles in snow and rain, subjected to the extremes of desert and tundra, while amazing wind tunnels and wonderful computer programs will have probed every eventuality. Grave engineers in white coats grasping clipboards appear in the advertisements, along with the pretty ladies. Yet despite all this up to 1 million cars are recalled in the UK each year for safety checks.

Virtually every car manufacturer has been involved in a recall. Between 1980 and 1995 some 36 manufacturers, including all the well known names, had to recall 11 352 908 vehicles for a retrofit in 1242 campaigns. The problems encountered in a six-month period, which are given below, are taken from the *Vehicle Recall Bulletin* of the Vehicle Inspectorate Executive Agency. The recall campaigns are launched and monitored as agreed in the voluntary Codes of Practice formulated from discussions between the Department of Transport and representative bodies of the motor industry. They provide an indication of their range and the action taken to overcome them. The recalls in other countries are taken from a survey undertaken by the Frankona insurance company and the US Department of Transportation publication *News*.

The *Vehicle Return Bulletin* reports the following:

- **Audi 80 and 100**. 624 cars. In some cases the alloy wheel retaining bolts may be of insufficient length and failed to achieve sufficient penetration into the threads of the hub. Suspect bolts were replaced with longer versions.
- **Citroen ZX and ZX Volcane**. 16 419 cars. It was possible for

the front brake pipe to be contacted by the anti-roll bar link rod and, in extreme conditions, this could have resulted in fluid leakage and partial loss of braking. After inspection the pipes were reset to give adequate clearance or replaced and correctly set.

- **Ford: some Escorts and Orions**. 17 608 cars. It was possible that the exhaust downpipe might separate from the upper flange and drop on to the starter motor terminal, damaging the wiring loom and causing the loss of various circuits. The exhaust downpipe was replaced with a new component.

- **Honda: some Civics**. 6680 cars. The transmission shaft cable lock pin might have become ineffective. In consequence the gear lever position might not have matched the actual gear position selected in the transmission. The lock pins were replaced with a modified type.

- **Mazda: some Xedos**. 1972 cars. The engine wiring harness might have chafed on the anti-lock braking control valve bracket, possibly causing the wiring to short, leading to failure of the ignition or fuel injection system and making the engine stop without warning. A plastic protector sleeve was installed on the wiring harness and any damaged harness repaired.

- **Porsche: some 911s and Carreras**. 248 cars. Under extreme circumstances wheel lock-up could occur during heavy braking because an incorrect brake modulator valve had been fitted. A modified valve was fitted.

- **Renault 19**. 29 658 cars. The bonnet catch securing bolts might have slackened in service allowing the lock mechanism to move and the bonnet to lift. The fixing bolts were replaced with screws and lock nuts.

- **Rover 800**. 32 361 cars. There was a possibility that the front seat belt long ends might not have been correctly secured to the anchorage on the seats. An inspection and correction was instituted.

- **Saab 9000**. 3461 cars. The fuel filler and ventilation rubber hoses might have cracked under the hose clamps and resulted in fuel leakage. The hoses were replaced by improved components and modified hose clips.

- **Seat Ibiza 021**. 35 325 cars. The handbrake cable might have chafed on the fuel filler pipe causing perforation and leakage of fuel. Perforated pipes were replaced and the cable repositioned and secured.

- **Vauxhall Cavalier Turbo Diesel**. 32 770 cars. Engine movement might have caused a wiring harness to chafe on a steel brake pipe adjacent to the brake master cylinder. This might have resulted in short-circuiting and possible loss of braking efficiency, should the brake fluid temperature rise as a result. A modified clip was fitted to the wiring harness, and it was sheathed for additional protection.
- **Vag: Golf and Passat VR6**. 306 cars. The hose clips securing the fuel supply pipe between the fuel rail and the injectors might have lost their tension and resulted in a fuel leakage. The fuel supply and return hoses were changed and secured with new spring clips.

Very briefly, car recalls in other countries, as reported by the German Frankona insurance company and US Department of Transport *News*, have included:

- **Austria. Volvo**. 1990, 30 000 cars. Reinforcing plates inserted in the front doors.
- **Denmark. Fiat Unos**. 1990, 10 000 cars. Check on the welding on the steering and suspension systems.
- **Germany. BMW 5 series**. 1990. Reduced power-assisted braking.
- **Japan. Toyota**. 1991. 32 956 trucks of five different models. Fault on front wheel brakes.
- **USA. Chrysler minivans**. 1995. 4 million vehicles. Faulty rear liftgate latches which are said to have caused 98 injuries and 37 deaths to occupants.
- **Worldwide. General Motors**. 1990. 616 000 cars. Faulty seat belts.

Comment

None of these data should cause surprise. Modern cars are complex products, driven in the UK by 30 million licence-holders. With such large-scale volume production, and the fierce competition in the marketplace, it is perhaps surprising that the problems are not even greater. Indeed, the fact that the defects are discovered and steps taken to rectify them should be a matter of reassurance. The lesson for other volume manufacturers is that they cannot afford to relax their attention to safety in design, even though they may have major resources and highly trained staff.

Sources

'*Vehicle Safety Recalls*', Bristol: Department of Transport, Vehicle Inspectorate Executive Agency, Vehicle Safety Branch, July 1994.
Product Recalls, Munich: Frankona Rückversicherungs-Aktien-Gesellschaft, 1993.
News, US Department of Transportation, October 1995.

Case History 8
Responsibility for Design of Bought-in Components

Richard Winward v. TVR Engineering Limited
Court of Appeal: 4 March 1986

The implications of this case concerning a bought-in component with an intrinsic design defect which caused damage to a producer's end-product are far-reaching for designers. The producer was found to be liable for the damage because he had not made efforts to discover any possible shortcomings in the component, preferring instead to rely on the supplier's reputation. The producer was a car manufacturer, TVR, and the component was an engine, made by Ford, with a Weber carburettor. It was the latter which had the inherent design defect concerning the push fit of a brass ferrule.

The case involved a car, manufactured by TVR Engineering in 1973 which caught fire in 1981 involving a certain Mrs Winward. The appeal was against the judgment of Her Honour Judge Mary Holt who had held the defendants liable in negligence and that the plaintiff could recover damages.

TVR's Managing Director, Mr Halstead, who had not held that office in 1973, explained the role of his company in purchasing components and incorporating them into their cars. He described the warranty that the firm used to get from Ford thus:

> We tend to ride on the back of Ford and go along with what they recommend . . . on matters of engineering we would be led by Ford Motor Company and use the parts which were recommended by them. We buy original equipment. Once led by people like Ford we cast an engineering eye over their equipment and if we are in agreement we use it.

TVR submitted that this was a reasonable standard of prudence and practice which discharged any legal obligation of reasonable care which lay upon them.

It was common ground that the fire which gave rise to the claim was ignited at, or directly proximate to, the carburettor which had partly melted.

The first explanation, proffered on behalf of the plaintiff, was accepted by the learned judge who had said:

> In my judgment one salient fact emerges namely that it was not good engineering practice, even though a commonly used commercial practice, to employ a push fit between metals having a different co-efficient of expansion. Mr Dias (an expert witness for the plaintiff) considered it a retrograde and risky practice and I accept his view of the matter. In the case of the ferrule in the Weber carburettor the push fit was used for a brass ferrule and a zinc alloy cased carburettor with a difference of 200° [sic] in rates of expansion. Moreover, I also accept Mr Dias' view that all push fits involve a manufacture to tolerance levels and that any movement of the ferrule will loosen the fit. Mr Makinson (an expert witness for the defendants) accepted that to be 100 per cent sure of avoiding risk a locking device was required.
>
> Given the fact that in service it could be expected that the fuel inlet pipes would be replaced and with a bevelled edge to the ferrule and the normal hardening of the pipes could be expected to be used to detach the pipes it appears to me to be clearly foreseeable that the ferrule would become loosened with the consequent risk of its becoming detached and a fire resulting.
>
> In my opinion [the defendants] manufactured a car in 1973 which was defective in design and which carried within its carburettor a push fit ferrule the retention force of which was likely to be diminished because of the differential expansion of the respective metals of the ferrule and casing of the carburettor and that it was a foreseeable risk that during servicing the ferrule might be loosened by twisting with the further risk of fire from detachment.
>
> In my judgment (the defendants) were negligent in failing to examine or make tests on the Weber carburettors which they used in their engines and in failing to modify the ferrule by inserting into it a locking or screwing device to prevent the risk of detachment and

in failing to warn owners of the relevant cars of the existence of the resultant danger.

In the Court of Appeal Sir Roualeyn Cumming-Bruce summed up this first explanation by saying it concerned:

> ... an inherent design fault in the fit of the brass ferrule which accounted for the eventual displacement of the ferrule after gradually [*sic*] over the years it had become loose in its seating so as to be subject to displacement upon the application, at the end of the day, of whatever fault it was which brought about the final unseating of the ferrule.

In a word, it was the unseating of the ferrule that caused the fire.

The second explanation, put forward by TVR, took the opposite view saying that the ferrule became unseated as a consequence of the fire, and was not a cause of it. The second explanation was summarized as

> ... being due to a defect in a pin within the chamber of a carburretor which in the ways described in the defendants' expert's report, produced ignition within the chamber of the carburettor such that the heat thereby produced caused the carburettor to melt and come apart.

The expert witness, Mr Makinson, had said that Ford and Reliant had used thousands of these carburettors.

> There was nothing in his experience to lead him to the inference that, in spite of the use of this carburettor with this kind of brass ferrule push fit for at least a dozen years in thousands of cars, there was any reason until this occasion, if at all, for suspecting the seating of the ferrule had ever caused any trouble at all, much less a fire, whereas there was some consensus of engineering opinion that other fires that had arisen when this carburettor was used could be traced to a quite different cause. Looking at all the possibilities, Makinson explained his reasons for thinking that the ferrule came out on this occasion as a consequence of the fire and not as a contributing cause.

Sir Roualeyn Cumming-Bruce agreed with the first explanation saying:

There was ample evidence on which the judge was entitled to conclude that, without postulating any esoteric engineering expertise, any manufacturer applying his mind to basic engineering principles should have appreciated that it was not good engineering practice to employ a push fit instead of a screw fit between two metals having a different co-efficient of expansion. The judge was entitled to accept Mr Dias' opinion that such a practice was a retrograde and risky one, and accept it the learned judge did.

A quite separate proposition, on which TVR relied, was that there was no reasonably foreseeable risk which imposed upon them any obligation either to minimize the risk, by taking such action as introducing a pin, or to warn the users of manufactured vehicles. Sir Roualeyn Cumming-Bruce explained:

These manufacturers were not insurers. Their duty of care was limited to take reasonable care for the safety of the consumer who drove the car. The duty of care, of course, varies with the particular facts and Lord Justice Asquith (as he then was) neatly expressed the equation when he contrasted the magnitude of the risk with the gravity of the consequences if risk supervened. The appellant's case here is that, on the history disclosed before the judge, the defendants, when purchasing and incorporating in their motorcar a Ford engine with a Weber carburettor, were entitled to take the view which they did that there was absolutely nothing in the history of this carburettor to put the defendants on enquiry before incorporating a carburettor and a Ford engine in a motorcar which they had designed and proceeded to assemble . . .

The learned judge had disagreed because she accepted that it was simply not good engineering practice to rely on the push fit. Mr Makinson, giving evidence on behalf of the defendant, agreed that, if the ferrule came out, it would be a catastrophe, but he described the relevant practical equation as being a smallish risk. He said it was a commercial risk.

The submission on behalf of the plaintiff maintained that it was not necessary to embark on heavy expenditure, or any particular refinement of engineering knowledge, in order to minimize the risk. There were many simple alternative ways in which the ferrule could be locked, so that the risk of displacement could be removed altogether. In the familiar cases over the past 30 or 40 years, in which the duty of care has been examined in different contexts, it had rightly been held that it is a material consideration to consider how much trouble and how much expense a manufacturer or an employer should have to undertake in order to minimize, or altogether remove, quite a small risk in terms of the incidence of a risk carrying with it the gravity of a major catastrophe in the event of the risk supervening.

Sir Roualeyn Cumming-Bruce said in his judgment:

> In my view, on the evidence before the judge, she was right to hold that the defendant as a manufacturer was under an obligation to address his mind to the safety of the components that he was proposing to purchase and incorporate and was not entitled blindly to purchase and incorporate such materials and gadgets as Ford or other manufacturers such as Weber were putting on the market. It was his duty to apply such engineering skill and knowledge as is appropriate to the manufacturer and marketer of a motor car and, on the evidence of the plaintiff's experts which the learned judge accepted, a manufacturer, with a reasonably appropriate degree of knowledge and expertise, should address his mind to the suitability of this particular push fit, relying on different metal components to operate in circumstances of high temperature, and should have considered that there was a problem resulting from a potential gradual developing instability which might, in an appropriate combination of circumstance and forces, ultimately give rise to a displacement in a ferrule during the operation of the engine with an obvious serious risk of fire. There is no evidence that the defendants ever addressed their minds to the risk at all and, on the evidence of Mr Halstead himself, who presented the evidence of the policy of the company, it was open to the judge to hold, as she did, that, when the defendants cast what Mr Halstead described as an engineering eye over the equipment, they were under a duty to observe what Dias described as a clearly retrograde practice. If they had addressed their minds, then, even though the risk was, on the history, obviously a risk of low incidence, they were under a duty to minimize it by some simple device by reason of the gravity of the circumstances that might or would supervene in the event of a ferrule becoming displaced.

The appeal was dismissed.

Comment

It is the responsibility of the designer of the final product to ensure that the components which he specifies are acceptable. If a component turns out to be faulty its manufacturer may be exposed to liability, along with the producer of the final product. In such a case the producer of the final product could not escape liability by seeking to shift responsibility on to the component manufacturer. The message is clear. The designer who specifies certain components, which are to be comprised into his final product, is responsible for the contribution they make to overall safety. Therefore he must assess them for safety and not rely on their provenance as evidence of it.

Case History 9
The Austin Allegro and the Rear Hub Bearing

Victor and Margaret Walton v. British Leyland (UK) Limited, Dutton Forshaw (North East) Limited and Blue House Lane Garage Limited
High Court, Queens Bench Division: 12 July 1978

The first Austin Allegros were sold in May 1973. This case about them is important because of the evidence of the deputy chairman, the chief engineer and the withering comments of the judge in his summing up. The message is very clear: if there is a design defect don't treat the symptoms; cure the disease.

A significant alteration in the design of the Allegro, compared with the Maxi and the 1300 range, was the use of tapered roller bearings in the rear hub assembly. These had to be adjusted in a different way from earlier models which had been fitted with roller bearings. The tapered roller bearings, designed by Timken, were fitted not only to the Allegro and Marina but also to many cars worldwide. Their proper adjustment involved 'end float', which allowed a certain amount of play in the wheel. This was apparent on rotating and rocking the wheel after it had been properly adjusted.

On 17 October 1973, five months after the Allegro first went on the market, a British Leyland (BL) Product Bulletin was sent to accredited dealers. It drew attention to the method of adjusting the new rear hub bearings and emphasized the risk of them seizing up if insufficient end float was provided. The document was marked 'Confidential'.

On 12 December 1973 BL authorized a 'major' modification to the Allegro – the fitting of a special washer 'to provide an additional bearing retention safety feature'. A Bulletin of 9 August 1974 contained a diagrammatic illustration of the import- ance of the difference between torque tightening for ball bearings and end float for roller bearings. Another Bulletin of 25 September 1974 concerned all cars produced since 16 September 1974. They now incorporated a larger retaining washer in the rear hub assembly 'to improve bearing security'. It also urged the importance of fitting the washers 'when servicing the rear brake hub bearings or brakes of earlier vehicles'. This document was to figure significantly in the subsequent trial.

By now BL had realized that they had a very serious problem on their hands with the Allegro. In fact, the only company witness at the trial said that he could recall nothing similar in scope and seriousness in his entire experience with BL, which went back to 1940. The development of the defects was revealed in BL's Product Problem Progress Card which tracked the 'Rear bearing failure – wheel adrift' events. In the trial the judge selected some of the entries for illustration:

- In the month to 22 August 1974 not less than 10 cases of bearing failure, some with wheel adrift, were reported from the Continent.
- By 5 September 1974 a total of 50 cases had been reported.
- By 26 October 1974 'no less than 100 cases of wheel adrift to date' were recorded.
- In January 1975 three further failures 'thought to be due to corrosion' were reported.

Within BL the experts put the blame on mechanics who were careless and unfamiliar with end float adjustment, which caused overtightening. This would lead to overheating, bearing collapse and, in the worst cases, the wheel coming off. The design was satisfactory, there was little evidence of corrosion and greasing the bearings was accepted as having been carried out properly at the factory. The conclusion was that the fault lay with the mechanics at garages, particularly during the 12 000 mile service. The judge found that this did not explain why similar problems did not appear to be affecting the Marinas, which had been launched before the Allegro and had similar bearings.

A test of 2 October 1974 concluded that 'The [larger] washer is effective in preventing the wheel coming adrift when bearing failure occurs'. The washer was incorporated in all Allegros made after 16 September 1974. But the larger washer was a 'palliative' and could not prevent a bearing failure. A limited education programme was initiated for distributors' mechanics.

On 10 September 1974 the deputy chairman wrote to senior BL engineers after a serious accident involving an Allegro in Italy. He said:

> I am still not satisfied with the solution to the loss of rear wheels on the Allegro. The larger washer will certainly stop the wheels coming off in some cases but there has been at least one example of the hub itself fracturing and the larger washer obviously cannot help when that happens. To my untutored eye it looks as if the bearing is not up to the job. Will you please have this investigated.

A week later the chief engineer's response was:

> *Rear Hubs and Bearings.* The design was introduced to satisfy perform- ance demands at lower costs, and it is true to state that provided design requirements are adhered to no problem would be experi- enced. Unfortunately the design is not idiot proof and therefore will continuously involve risk. The risk becomes greater as vehicles become older and evermore carelessly maintained. Had we incorpor- ated the large washer from the commencement the risk would have been tolerable. . . . Engineering have considered the possibility of recall action but do not favour it owing to the fact that it would damage the product, and historically the response is too low to guarantee fixing the problem and thereby removing our liability.

The judge commented that 'damaging the product' was a euphemism for 'be bad for sales'.

A month later a television programme referred to a single case of a wheel 'becoming detached'. On 15 October 1974 a BL press release stated:

> We have had a small number of rear wheel bearing failures reported and the evidence shows that failure can be brought about by cor- rosion arising from water ingress and/or maladjustment during vehicle servicing. Action has already been taken to correct any

irregularities in new vehicle production and any cases in service are being dealt with as necessary.

The judge called this 'commercial camouflage' of the true state of affairs. At this time BL's Engineering and Service were recommending that a recall campaign at a cost of £300 000 was not justified. An intensive education campaign for 'franchise outlets' was recommended with authority to fit the larger washer when rear hub or rear brake servicing was being carried out: 'This should protect the customer against subsequent malpractice.'

Albert Walton bought an Allegro in November 1974. It had been manufactured in February that year and so did not have the larger washers fitted. Throughout 1975 the car was in and out of Dutton Forshaw, BL's distributor from whom the car had been purchased, for a number of warranty claims including four clutch replacements. Then, in January 1975, Mr Walton noticed a noise from the rear offside wheel. He took it back again to Duttons, who fitted the larger washer when they replaced the bearing. The car had a 6000-mile service in June 1975 and a 12 000-mile service, by Blue House Garage, in March the following year, when the bearings were adjusted on each side.

During the evening of 22 April 1976 Albert Walton was driving north along the M1 motorway near Newport Pagnell at 50 to 60 mph. In the car were Victor and Margaret Walton, his brother and sister-in-law, who were on holiday from Australia. The rear nearside wheel came off and the car hit the central crash barrier. Victor Walton was thrown clear and escaped with minor injuries but his wife was very seriously hurt and was left as a quadraplegic. A police vehicle examiner found that the outer bearing had collapsed and the inner cone had been welded by excessive heat on to the stub axle.

After the accident the car was repaired by a BL dealer on a special Allegro jig. Mr Walton had only driven it for 200 miles when he heard a grinding noise from the rear offside wheel. Taking no chances he got a low loader to take the vehicle to Blue House. They found that, although the outer bearing had collapsed, the washer had prevented the wheel from coming off.

Victor and Margaret Walton brought an action against BL,

Dutton Forshaw and Blue House. It was heard at the Teeside Crown Court before Mr Justice Willis on 12 July 1978. The case against Duttons was that they should have fitted the larger washer to both hubs in January 1975, and not just to the rear offside hub. At that time Duttons had the Product Bulletin of 25 September 1974 and the letter of 24 October 1974, mentioned above. The judge found that these documents did not suggest any real gravity in the problem and that the letter was at best ambiguous and at worst misleading. The sole BL witness was unable to criticize Duttons and the judge found them blameless.

Blue House had serviced Albert Walton's cars for 30 years but, as they were not an authorized dealer they had not received the Product Bulletins. They had no knowledge of the larger washer modification nor the importance of end float, apart from the Handbook and Workshop Manual. The garage's mechanic, Mr Ransome, had been with them for 14 years and was completely familiar with the difference between torque and end float. The judge rejected the contention that the defect had been caused by overtightening at Blue House during the service.

The judge held that BL's responsibility was total. He said:

It is not being wise after the event to state that had the larger washer been fitted to Mr Walton's car the accident would, in all probability, not have happened. Over a period of about a year, until October 1974, Leylands were faced with mounting and horrifying evidence of Allegro wheels coming adrift. Any of the cases reported to them could have had fatal results for the occupants of the cars concerned and other road users. They assumed, rightly or wrongly, that apart from isolated cases of corrosion, human error on the part of mechanics was the cause of the bearing failures. The Deputy Chairman was gravely disturbed; the view of the Chief Engineer of 16 September, 1974 was that the design, not being 'idiot proof', would continuously involve risk, a risk which he thought would have been tolerable had the larger washer been fitted from the start.

From that date, therefore, if not before, the Engineering Section considered the risk, to those who were driving Allegros which had not been fitted with larger washers on both rear hub assemblies, of their wheels coming adrift to be 'intolerable'. What, in such circumstances, is the standard of care towards users of their products to be expected of a manufacturer in the position of Leylands? They were entirely satisfied that the larger washer provided a safety factor which could confidently be expected, following stringent tests, to prevent a wheel coming adrift if a bearing failed. All cars manufactured after 16 September 1974 were fitted with the approved safety device. Some steps, in my view totally inadequate, were taken to give instructions on the lines of what Dutton Forshaw were recommended to do but only to dealers. Outside this limited safety net were left, in ignorance of the risk to which Leylands knew they were subject, a very large number of Allegro owners, including Mr Walton and his passengers. In my view, the duty of care owed by Leylands to the public was to make a clean breast of the problem and recall all cars which they could in order that the safety washers could be fitted.

I accept, of course, that manufacturers have to steer a course between alarming the public unnecessarily and so damaging the reputation of their products, and observing their duty of care toward those whom they are in a position to protect from dangers of which they alone are aware. The duty seems to me to be higher when they can palliate the worst effects of a failure which, if Leyland's view is right, they could never decisively guard against.

They knew the full facts; they saw to it that no one else did. They seriously considered recall and made an estimate of the cost at a figure which seems to me to have been in no way out of proportion to the risks involved. It was decided not to follow this course for commercial reasons. I think this involved a failure to observe their duty of care for the safety of the many who were bound to remain at risk, irrespective of the recommendations made to Leyland's dealers and to them alone.

If I am wrong in equating the duty to take reasonable care in the circumstances of this case with the obligation to recall the cars for fitting of safety washers, and so have put it too high, it was in my view at least their duty to ensure that all cars still in stock were fitted with this safey feature before sale. It is sufficient for Mr Walton's purposes that the duty is put no higher than that. This would have saved Mr Walton and his passengers and, in my judgment, Leyland were negligent in having failed to do so.

Judgment was given for Mr Walton against BL.

Comment

An important part of this case was the internal BL documents. These had to be available because each party must disclose to the other their relevant papers, unless they can claim privilege for them. A party must disclose not only documents which assist his case but also documents which damage his case. Designers should be fully aware of the consequences of discovery and realize that their documentation could one day appear as evidence in the High Court. Marginal comments scribbled in haste are as much part of a document as the text itself.

Source

Ashworth, J. S. (ed.) (1984), *Product Liability Casebook*, Colchester: Lloyd's of London Press Limited.

Case History 10
The Brent Cross Crane Failure

This case history concerns a mixture of design, information and manufacturing failures, with a number of contributing factors. These failures resulted in death and injury to many people who had no connection with the equipment which caused the accident.

The works outing to Southend for Rutherford Geake, joinery manufacturers of Feltham, ended in tragedy on Saturday 20 June 1964. The coach, in which the 40 employees were travelling, was slowing down as the traffic lights changed at the junction of Hendon Way and the North Circular Road just north of London, when the accident happened. The 40-foot-high Brent Cross flyover, intended to carry Hendon Way over the North Circular, was under construction, and a mobile crane was being used to erect a large Scotch Derrick crane for the main works contractors, the Cleveland Bridge and Engineering Company.

The base of the tripod of the derrick was 20 foot high, and the mobile crane was being used to place the king post on top of the tripod Because of the length of the king post and the height to which it had to be lifted the mobile crane had been fitted with an extension jib. It had lifted the king post 2–3 inches from the ground when it slewed about two feet to one side and collapsed on the passing coach.

Afterwards Mr H. Jones, the crane driver with 25 years' experience, said, 'I noticed the jib of my crane beginning to bend. I lent out of my cab and shouted and waved the traffic to keep away.' The 7.75 ton, 50-foot king post crushed the rear half of the vehicle. Seven people were killed and the 32 injured were taken to hospital in eight ambulances. On the Tuesday after the accident the Parliamentary Secretary from the Ministry of Transport, made a statement in the House of Commons. The public inquiry, ordered by the Ministry of Labour, was held at Holborn Town Hall under Edgar Fry QC.

The 15-ton Coles, lorry-mounted, diesel electric, mobile crane could be fitted with an 80-foot jib. The basic jib was constructed from two sections, each 15 feet long, called the head and heel or top and bottom sections. In between these two sections it was possible to fit two extra sections – one of 20 feet and one of 30 feet. Varying the sections could give jib lengths of 50, 60 and 80 feet.

The 1962 Road Traffic Act imposed severe restrictions on vehicles having a forward projection of more than 6 foot. To meet this requirement a hinge section could be arranged in the top and bottom jib sections, if it was ordered by the customer. This allowed a jib to be hinged back about its mid-point, so halving its effective length and enabling transit by road.

The hinged section was a discontinuity in the structure and thus a potential source of weakness. For this reason it had to be placed at the point of lowest stress, next to the top section. But there was a failure to tell crane owners where the hinged section had to be fitted. In practice it was always fitted to the bottom section, as that was more convenient. In this position it had to carry greater loads than those for which it was designed. Nevertheless the first crane with this configuration operated without mishap. See Figure C.10.1.

To provide the Court of Inquiry with information many tests were carried out by the British Crane and Engineering Corporation, which had manufactured the crane, and the Building Research Station. The Brent Cross crane was the second one ordered with a hinged section, but it was not manufactured as designed. The central lug of the hinge was designed with a rectangular shape, so that compressive forces were transmitted straight through metal-to-metal contact. The second crane ordered had central lugs which were triangular in shape, which transmitted compressive forces through the hinge pin well out of the centre line. This induced serious local bending stresses

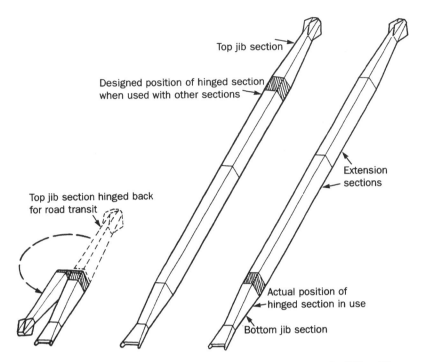

Top jib section

Designed position of hinged section when used with other sections

Extension sections

Top jib section hinged back for road transit

Actual position of hinged section in use

Bottom jib section

Figure C.10.1   Basic jib with hinged section, and extended jib with hinge in design and actual position

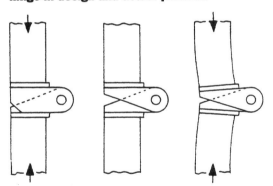

Figure C.10.2   Mobile crane: hinge detail
Left, the hinge as designed with thrust transmitted straight through. Centre, as manufactured. Right, bending stresses occurring as a result of thrust being taken through offset pin.

Source: Booker, P. J. (1965), 'Brent Cross crane failure', *The Engineering Designer,* November 1965.

which were transmitted to the adjacent members of the jib, where the failure occurred. See Figure C.10.2.

A Ministry of Labour investigation concluded that the accident was primarily due to the design of a hinged section of the jib. At the Court of Inquiry the Cleveland Bridge and Engineering Company admitted responsibility for the fact that a safe load indicator was not working and there was some overloading of the mobile crane. However, the Court found that a principal cause of the accident was the insertion of the hinged section in a position for which it was not designed. Immediately below the top section the bending force on it would have been less than a quarter of that obtaining at the lower position. The hinged section had not been manufactured as designed and there were a number of other minor contributing causes.

Commenting on the report of the Court one expert wrote 'Between the lines this report gives a dismal story of bad organisation and bad lines of communication. It is interesting ... to speculate as to how much blame for this accident lays [*sic*] with the designers and how much with management.'

Since 1964 there have been two important developments:

■ The Health & Safety at Work etc Act 1974 demands that employers have safe systems of work, as far as is reasonably practicable.

■ The publication in 1989 of the British Standard Code of Practice for the Safe Use of Cranes, BS 7121 Part 1. This gives advice to organisations, wishing lifting operations to be carried out, on ways of meeting their legal responsibilities. It details who is responsible and what their duties are.

Nevertheless, in 1994 it was reported that in a recent 12-month period incidents involving the use of cranes, investigated by the Factories, Agriculture & Quarries Inspectorate, had resulted in 17 fatalities.

The latest edition of the *Mobile Crane Operators' Safety Guide* recommends that every crane operator should have a personal copy of the 52-page booklet. It refers to BS 7121 Code of Practice for the Safe Use of Cranes and includes a 35-point safety checklist.

Comment

It would have been advisable if the crane used at Brent Cross had been designed in such a manner that there was only one – safe – way in which the jib could be assembled. The fact that the hinged section could be fitted incorrectly was foreseeable misuse. This is something for which designers have to provide. People do not always use products in the way in which the designer intended, but the designer must take this into account and be aware of the possibilities.

Case History 11
Raychem: Reducing the Fire Risk in Electric Cabling

Although this book is concerned with management programmes to reduce design risks, the Raychem case history is included to illustrate the technical aspects of such a programme, the aim of which was to reduce the risk of fire in sensitive situations. The means by which the hazard could arise were defined and then a programme established to reduce its risks. The authorities consulted are mentioned in the text by their more familiar acronyms; the full versions can be found in the List of Abbreviations on page xiii.

The US Raychem Corporation has 11 000 employees in more than 40 countries with headquarters in California. It is a materials science company manufacturing products based on the physical properties of polymers. chemicals and ceramics. These products include pipeline coatings, leak detectors for liquids and overcurrent sensors. The safety products include wire and cable insulation and heat-shrinkable tubing.

The European Corporate Technology Centre and European Electronics Division are based at Swindon, UK. They produce high-performance wire and cable and heat-shrinkable tubing, markers and moulded parts. Their particular interest is in the use of cables for military purposes and the development of low fire hazard materials for the jacketing of complex cables for application in the Royal Navy and offshore installations.

The rapid spread of electronic devices in domestic and industrial areas makes the use of fire-resistant cables of wider importance. Most modern cables are insulated with jackets based on natural polymers (for example, rubber) or synthetic polymers (for example, polyethylene (PE) or polyvinyl chloride (PVC)). Being organic polymers these insulation materials can burn and thus contribute very significantly to the overall fireload in any given environment.

When a polymer on a cable core is exposed to a fire a complicated chain of chemical events is initiated. If the polymer has a relatively low melting point it could begin to melt and drip when first exposed to the heat of the fire. As the temperature rises the ignition temperature of the polymer will eventually be reached and burning will commence. Drips of burning polymer could fall from the cable and, if they do not self-extinguish immediately, could fall on to other ignitable material and start another fire. If there is insufficient oxygen available, or it is not hot enough to cause complete combustion of the organic polymer, the off gases will be heavily contaminated with unburned carbon particles thus forming a dense smoke. The flames of the burning polymer could propagate rapidly along the cable length, due to the potential flammability of the polymer and the conduction of heat along the copper core of the cable. The off gases from the burning of certain polymers can contain significant quantities of gases that could cause corrosion damage to other equipment or structures, or be hazardous to human beings by causing irritation, inflammation or malfunction of soft tissues in the eyes, nose and lungs.

To lower the overall fire hazard each of these interrelated events had to be studied separately and action taken to reduce the risk it presented. At the same time critical mechanical and electrical properties had to be retained for the material to function as a high-quality cable jacket. To test a specially developed new material five parameters need to be considered:

1. **Ease of ignition**. A sample of the material is exposed to an incident heat flux and the time taken for ignition is measured. Ignition time can be measured as a function of the incident flux and the maximum heat flux which will not cause ignition within, for example, 10 minutes can be found. The higher the

value of this heat flux, the more resistant the material is to ignition. Tests such as the ISO 5657 Ignitability Apparatus, or the Cone Calorimeter (ISO 5660, ASTM E1354) can be used to obtain this information.

2. **Flame propagation**. There are a number of flame propagation tests for wire and cable products ranging from small-scale tests on single specimens – for example, IEC 332–1 and UL 1581 VW-1 – to large-scale tests such as IEC 332–3 in which 3.5 m lengths of cable are tested in a vertical tray.

   Heat release rate measurements on relatively small samples using the Cone Calorimeter have been shown to correlate with large-scale flame propagation tests. Indeed, it is now generally accepted that the single most important fire property is the rate of heat release.

3. **Smoke generation**. Smoke consists of a suspension of fine particles which obscures vision. The hazard associated with dense smoke is that it makes it extremely difficult for victims trapped in a fire to find their way to an exit, and equally it makes it difficult for members of the rescue services to locate victims in a fire-enveloped area. Most tests for comparison of smoke generated from burning polymers rely on some optical method for measuring the degree of obscuration of a light path caused by the smoke. The traditional NBS smoke chamber is the basis of several standard tests such as NES 711, and ASTM E662. In these tests smoke accumulates in a chamber from a sample exposed to a heat flux of 25 kWm^{-2}. ISO 5659 is a recent improvement to the NBS chamber which tests horizontal samples under a cone heater with heat fluxes between 10 kWm^{-2} and 50 kWm^{-2}. A larger-scale test is the '3 metre cube' which was originally designed by London Underground (IEC 1034). In this test a horizontal cable sample is burned over a tray of burning alcohol and the optical density of the accumulating smoke is measured.

   Smoke generation can also be measured in dynamic tests which measure the rate of smoke production. This can be done using the cone calorimeter (ASTM E1354) as well as in larger-scale tests.

4. **Corrosivity of fire gases**. A major part of the corrosion caused

by fire gases from burning polymers is due to the formation of acidic gases. There are relatively simple tests which assess the amount of acid gas by absorption into a solution of alkali or by measurement of the pH and conductivity of a solution of the acid gases (IEC 754). Polymers containing chlorine or bromine generate hydrogen chloride and hydrogen bromide, respectively. These acids can arise from the polymer (for example, PVC), or from some of the conventional additives used to treat polymers to make them less flammable. New low fire hazard materials specifically avoid additives or polymers that can generate these acids.

More recent tests are being developed which measure directly the effects of corrosive fire gases on an exposed copper circuit board. One such test is the Cone Corrosimeter proposed by ASTM D09.21.04.

5. **Toxic hazard**. For general testing purposes it is neither practicable nor desirable to undertake animal testing. The approach used is to carry out a straightforward chemical analysis for the gases generally considered to be hazardous (for example, acid gases, hydrogen cyanide, carbon monoxide and so on) and then use some agreed formula to compute a hazard rating from the measured concentrations. However, it should be noted that small-scale toxic potency tests as we know them today are inappropriate for regulatory purposes. Toxic hazard analysis is a complex problem and much work is currently underway in standards committees to develop improved test methods. IEC 695–7–1 is a useful guidance document on the subject.

Using tests of the type described above, new materials have been and are being developed which are superior to rubber, polyethylene or polyvinyl chloride in that they have a good balance of mechanical and electrical properties and present a low fire hazard.

Comment

This is a practical example of how hazards are identified and measured so that their risks can be tackled by the designer. It is an illustration of the type of information required in a design review system to ensure that a safer product will be developed.

Case History 12
The Foreseeability of Risk and the Duty of Care

Crow v. Barford (Agricultural) Limited and H. B. Holttum & Company Limited
Court of Appeal: 8 April 1963

It is the responsibility of the designer to take into account foreseeable risks. The classic snail in the ginger beer bottle case (*Donaghue* v. *Stevenson*) was based on the principle that a defect had to be both hidden and unknown in order for the duty of care to apply. This case history turns on whether or not the risk of injury from the blades of a rotary grass cutter was foreseeable by the plaintiff, or whether the risk was so concealed that the designer should have done something about protecting users.

In December 1958 Mr Crow, a farmer, bought a rotary grass cutter, called a Barford 18-inch Rotomo, from light tractor specialists, H. B. Holttum & Co. The machine had revolving blades, covered by a guard, and was driven by a Villiers 2-stroke motor. The guard had an opening, on the right-hand side of the machine, through which the cut grass was expelled. The engine was mounted on top of the mower with a recoil starter, also on the right-hand side. To start the engine the user had to hold the handle of the mower with his or her left hand while using the right hand to pull the starter, the right foot being on the guard to the side and rear of the opening.

When Mr Holttum demonstrated the machine to Mr Crow it would have been obvious that the blades were revolving within about one eighth of an inch of the opening. To put a hand or foot into the aperture would have been dangerous.

On Easter Saturday, 28 March 1959, Mr Crow found that he

could not start the machine. He cured an air lock in the petrol feed and tried again, following Mr Holttum's instructions with his right foot adjacent to the opening. When the engine started his foot slipped into the opening and the blades severed two of his toes.

As a result, he brought an action against the manufacturer, Barford, for negligence and breach of duty in failing to give warning of the true nature of the machine – in other words, that the machine was intrinsically dangerous or, alternatively, that there had been a failure to take reasonable care in design and manufacture to prevent the blades causing injury. He also sued the retailer, Holttum, for breach of merchantable quality (today amended to satisfactory quality) under the Sale of Goods Act 1893.

Counsel had argued in the original hearing that the physical design of the machine was not the defect. The defect was the danger that a foot might slip when starting the machine, in the usual way. But this meant that the risk had to be reasonably foreseeable to Barford but not so to Mr Crow. Thus the risk was either reasonably foreseeable or it was not. The trial judge, who had seen the machine demonstrated and heard the witnesses, said that he did not think that Barford could reasonably have foreseen the accident to Mr Crow, or that there was any foresee-able risk of danger. If, then, it was not a foreseeable risk there was no lack of care on the part of Barford. Alternatively, if it was a risk sufficiently likely to be foreseeable it could not be a hidden defect.

In his judgment Lord Justice Diplock said that the physical design of the machine was in no sense hidden.

> It was perfectly obvious on looking at the machine that there was an aperture as large as life, there were the knives, and there was the starting handle. It was quite obvious that if you were going to use the machine and start the blades revolving, it would be very dangerous indeed to allow your foot or any part of your body to get in the aperture.

The rule in *Donaghue* v. *Stevenson* did not apply.

The appeal against both defendants failed.

Comment

The effect of the case on designer liability for negligence can be summarized as follows:

- If the risk of injury is not reasonably foreseeable the designer cannot be liable and
- if the risk of injury is reasonably foreseeable and obvious the designer will not be liable.

Source

Ashworth J. S. (ed.) (1984), *Product Liability Casebook*, Colchester: Lloyd's of London Press Limited.

Case History 13
The Pentium Design Flaw

The first commercial microprocessor was invented in 1971 by Intel, which became the largest manufacturer of semiconductors in the world. Intel architecture is at the core of over 80 per cent of personal computers. Its Pentium chip, launched in March 1993, enabled a computer to run 400 times faster than the original IBM PC of 12 years previously. The target was to sell 7 million units per year to manufacturers such as IBM, Dell and Campaq; in Europe £30 million was spent on advertising.

To produce the Pentium a simultaneous engineering concept was chosen in which design and development operated in parallel, using a design team which included customers. The Pentium's predecessor, the 486, had a number of design defects, 60 per cent of which were discovered by users. The general manager in charge of developing the Pentium, Vin Dham, said, 'This time I had the goal of finding all the errata on my processor in-house.' They turned out to be unfortunate words. He wanted 'no more talking in corridors to decide things. I wanted standardised procedures, formal design reviews, and documentation every step of the way.' A better way of testing design, called programmable logic gates, was introduced.

The launch literature, *Inside Intel*, said:

> We put each Intel processor through literally millions of tests before it's shipped. That's our assurance you're getting the highest quality engine to drive your PC. We also test each new chip on hundreds of today's most popular software applications, so you know your favourite software will run smoothly.

Professor Thomas Nicely, a mathematician at Lynchburg College in Virginia, found that the Pentium's special mathematics could make mistakes. When dividing by certain long numbers, particularly those above 824 billion and those with nine or more digits after the decimal point, it would get the first eight or so digits of the answer right but then add the rest more or less at random. For instance, to divide 4 195 835 by 3 145 727, and then multiply by the second number again, would produce an answer 256 too high – an error of 0.006 per cent.

The Pentium element responsible for the calculation is called the double precision floating point processor; it is important to statisticians, mathematicians and economists. It works out part of the answer itself and then completes it from a 'look-up table', which stores common calculations. The table should have been the same as that in the previous chip, the 486, but some numbers were wrongly copied over and the highly praised testing methods did not find the error.

It took Dr Nicely four months to confirm that he had found a mistake. He then put his conclusions on the Internet computer network. The media headlines tell what happened next: 'Chips fault raises worldwide fears of computer errors'; 'Calculators that can't do their sums properly'; 'Intel to replace millions of faulty chips'; 'Intel fights to recover from Pentium fiasco'; 'Chips are down at Intel as IBM pulls plug on flawed Pentiums'; 'How not to manage a crisis'; 'Fuzzy Logic'; and 'Intel foots £310m Pentium bill'.

Intel claimed that it had detected the defect four months previously and had corrected it in subsequent production. It had not told the purchasers of the 4 million chips already sold since, according to their estimates, a spreadsheet user doing random calculations would only find an error once every 27 000 years. This claim was disputed by IBM when it announced that it was stopping production of products containing the Pentium. It said that the average spreadsheet user was likely to find an error once every 24 days. Dr Nicely countered that this claim was 'almost ludicrous'. A British computer magazine, *PC Week*, said the defect could produce wrong answers once every two months to once every ten years.

In response, an Intel spokesman stated:

We have not encountered a single case of this problem occurring in real life. We have shipped thousands of corrected chips to people who have asked for them, but this is a minor technical flaw. We have had more significant flaws in previous generations of chips.

Purchasers could have an installation kit and a replacement chip to fit to their own computers or have the work done by a dealer. In its year-end figures Intel set aside $474 million for the worldwide replacement of Pentium, in what one expert termed the largest recall in computer history.

Andrew Grove, Intel's President and Chief Executive Officer, admitted that the company's attitude had seemed 'arrogant and uncaring'. He apologized for 'what we view as an extremely minor technical problem [that] has taken on a life of its own'. These words were echoed in full-page advertisements:

> We at Intel wish sincerely to apologise for our handling of the recently publicised Pentium processor flaw. What Intel continues to believe in is that an extremely minor flaw has taken on a life of its own.

Steve Poole, European Vice-President of Intel, said:

> With hindsight I agree with the criticisms. We are an engineering company and we are not used to dealing with this kind of issue. We have learned that we must be very careful when we think one thing and the public disagrees.

Grove's remarks go straight to the root of this design defect: had it been managed professionally it could have passed by virtually unnoticed. Intel's attitude gave its competitors an opportunity to exploit: NexGen with its Nx586, AMD with its K5, Cyrix with its M1 and IBM with PowerPC were all on the track of Pentium. Harold Thimbleby, Professor of Computing Science at Middlesex University, said that the only novel thing about the incident was that the company had come clean. Steve Poole said that they would be reviewing how they handled public relations.

In 1995 Intel launched the P6 chip which contains 5.5 million transistors in a technique that made it twice as fast as the Pentium.

In May 1995 it was reported that Intel had made an out-of-court settlement in 13 product liability cases. The company refused to comment but rumours suggested the figures ran into tens of millions of dollars. Another report said that the company was offering to settle 11 lawsuits to include lawyers' fees and maintaining a lifetime warranty.

Comment

One of the great truths is that business success comes from doing the little things right, every day. Simultaneous engineering, programmable logic gates, formal design reviews and all the documentation associated with them should have picked up the copying error. The mistake was compounded by a lack of awareness that it could become a monster – so much so that, instead of Intel managing the incident, the incident ended up managing Intel. Realistic simulation exercises are valuable in training senior executives in the consequences of overlooking one of the little things.

Sources

The Times, 10 October 1994; 25, 28 November 1994; 19, 21 December 1994.
Sunday Times, 18 December 1994; 23, 30 January 1995; 12 February 1995; 2 April 1995.
Management Today, May 1994; March 1995.
Economist, 3 December 1994.
Lloyd's List, 3 May 1995.
International Risk Management, April 1995.
Intel literature.

Case History 14
Exploding Office Chairs

In the early 1970s swivel office chairs with height adjustment for the seat were introduced. The seat was mounted on a central column with a gas-operated, stepless system, to provide up and down movement, controlled by a lever (see Figure C.14.1). There were two designs, side-entry levers and top-entry levers for the cylinders, which allowed the vertical movement at a touch. The gas cylinder had an internal pressure of 40 bar.

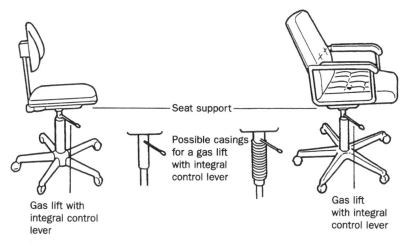

Seat support

Possible casings for a gas lift with integral control lever

Gas lift with integral control lever

Gas lift with integral control lever

Figure C.14.1 Exploding office chairs

The side-entry cylinder had an actuating lever which passed through the side of the cylinder to operate the central valve. The top-entry cylinder was actuated by a lever and linkage mechanism which was part of the chair base, rather than part of the gas cylinder itself.

The weakness in the side-entry design was the point at which the integrated adjustment lever was inserted into the cylinder.

Accidents occurred when the central column broke and the contents of the cylinder were fired out explosively, as the pressure was suddenly released. The chair seat and back assembly could suddenly detach from the pedestal, leaving the cylinder as a compressed gas weapon capable of firing a large projectile a considerable distance. The danger of serious injury could be greatly increased if the expulsion of the inner parts of the mechanism was delayed, by burrs on the inner face of the cylinder, allowing time for curious bystanders to crowd round. Numerous incidents were reported, some of which were very serious, as in Belgium where a death resulted from the failure of a gas-lift chair.

In Germany there were three designs of gas cylinder: the Type 1, Type 2 and Type 3. The manufacturers were two companies in Germany, which sold the cylinders to chair manufacturers, with 30 per cent being exported. In Germany, before 1978, the Type 1 and Type 2 had caused some accidents, although without any personal injury. They were replaced in 1980 by the Type 3, which was considered safe. One of the cylinder manufacturers, which had 170 000 chairs with Type 1 and Type 2 cylinders, replaced 50 000 of them with the Type 3, at a cost of DM3 million.

More than 3.1 million of the apparently safe Type 3 had been sold to 44 chair manufacturers in Germany. A German test centre had authenticated its safety with the Geprüfte Sicherheit-Zeichen mark, upon which UK chair manufacturers initially would rely. But there was very little objective experience on which to base the test procedure. An estimate had to be made of the protocol to be followed to replicate users standing up and sitting down in a chair. The test was based on a total of 200 000 load instances, at 80 a day for 250 days per year, giving a life expectancy of ten years. This proved to be a serious underestimate, and the figure was later changed to a total of two million load instances.

In 1982 at a Bonn police station five of eight gas-lift office chairs were 'destroyed' by the explosion of the cylinders in a short period of time. The chairs were in use 24 hours a day by eight policemen whose task was to monitor video screens. The chairs were all less than one year old and were fitted with Type 3 cylinders. An examination of the damaged chairs concluded that it was not possible to determine whether the failures were due to incorrect installation or a design defect.

In 1983 an employee at a Hanover bank found that his chair had become unsteady. As he was examining it to discover the cause, the gas cylinder exploded and drove a steel bolt into his head, penetrating his eye and brain. The accident resulted in much media interest and public concern. A tabloid newspaper claimed that swivel office chairs were a time bomb which could explode at any time.

Three different German test institutes investigated what was now recognized as a design defect and subsequently recommended the fitting of a safety clamp. This was given great publicity in the general and trade press, and 435 000 leaflets explaining the situation were distributed. In 1984 a large advertisement appeared in the national daily press. One also appeared in the Dutch papers explaining how to check office chairs and gave details for retrofitting 'dangerous' chairs. It was estimated that there were 140 000 chairs with gas-lifts in the Netherlands where ten accidents had been reported without any injuries.

In Germany 1000 dealers were told of the problem and how to correct it by fitting a safety clamp. The cost, at DM35 per chair, had to be borne by the individual chair owners due to a loophole in the law. By July 1984 the safety clamp had been fitted to 400 000 chairs in Germany. By 1986 60 per cent of the total number had been retrofitted, but there had been 20 accidents with serious head and hand injuries.

Eventually, damage or injury was said to occur at between 0.1 and 0.3 per 1000 chairs and, it was claimed that 80 per cent of potential accidents had been eliminated by the safety clamp. Up to 1990 there had been 1000 accidents in Germany. It was not possible to take action against the manufacturer of the gas cylinders as they were not classified as a work tool ready for use under the Equipment Safety Act.

New gas cylinders with top-entry levers were developed to meet the stricter requirements of the 1984 standard, DIN45450/51. In 1988 these became mandatory.

In the UK the first indication that there was a safety problem with gas-lift office chairs had come through an informal warning from the Swedish Mobelsinstitute in 1982. The German Type 3 cylinder, imported for Germany, was used by the UK chair manufacturers. Two million side-entry cylinder chairs, relying on the German safety mark, had been made before their production was stopped. Between 1983 and 1988 a total of 23 accidents occurred in the UK, of which nine caused serious personal injury.

The UK Furniture Industry Research Association (FIRA) and the Health and Safety Executive investigated the problem. In a major project, FIRA looked at the work that had been carried out in Germany by the test institutes and the manufacturers. It concluded that one design of side-entry cylinder was 'considerably more dangerous than other recent types because it is significantly weaker and tends to fail more suddenly and violently. . . .' It also said:

> The problem of gas cylinder fatigue in pedestal chairs was enounterd in Germany and might not have become a problem elsewhere if the German research and testing had been satisfactory in the first place.
>
> The British standards of that time would not, however, detect the fault and change of standards' philosophy for furniture for the work place was well overdue.
>
> The service failures are the direct result of overstressing the critical parts of the gas springs. Expulsive disassembly follows as a matter of course if the fracture is in the full diameter part of the cylinder. This could be prevented by simple design changes. . . .

FIRA and the Health and Safety Executive launched a leaflet campaign which recommended that office chairs should be examined by an expert and either replaced or fitted with a safety clamp at a cost of £5. There was an urgent recommendation that people weighing over 100 kg (16 st) should not use gas-lift chairs. Government departments changed their specification to top-entry cylinder chairs. In 1987 only two accidents were reported following the introduction of these measures.

Comment

This case history gives a clear message to designers that even safety Standards can be seriously wrong. There is perhaps also a greater reliance in Germany on technical safety standards to guarantee safety. Today many Standards concerning safety are being produced to support the 'essential requirements' of the New Approach directives. Further, some Standards are mandatory and thus have legal authority. There has to be a possibility that some may be inadequate in one way or another.

This warns the designer to be cautious about accepting conformance to a Standard as a cast-iron defence against a defective design.

If the injuries caused by the exploding office chairs had taken place ten years later the law would have been different. The concept of strict liability in the EC Directive for Liability for Defective Products was adopted by the UK in 1987, by Germany in 1989 and by the Netherlands in 1990. This would have meant that those injured in the explosions could have sued the relevant manufacturer under the strict liability provisions, if necessary. It would not have been essential to prove negligence to recover compensation; they would only have had to prove the causal link between the defective product and the injury.

Sources

Micklitz H-W. *et al.* (1994), *Federalism and Responsibility*, London: Graham & Trotman.

Gulliver, W. C. (1990), *Integrity of Gas Cylinder Pedestal Office Chairs*, Stevenage: Furniture Industry Research Association, April.

Case History 15
The Flixborough Chemical Plant Disaster

Just before five o'clock in the afternoon of the first Saturday in June 1974 an explosion at the Nypro plant at Flixborough, Humberside, killed 28 people and injured about 40. The flames rose 200 feet into the air as the control building was reduced to rubble, killing the 18 men inside. Some 2000 houses were damaged as were 167 shops and factories.

The plant, jointly owned by Dutch State Mines and the National Coal Board, produced over 50 000 tonnes a year of caprolactam for use in the manufacture of nylon. The £18 million, 20-acre site was totally destroyed with the pall of smoke still visible 20 miles away the following day. Forty-five fire engines tackled the blaze as 3000 people were evacuated from the neighbouring villages. In the City £20 million was wiped off the value of Courtaulds, the fibres and textiles group, which was one of Nypro's biggest customers; shares also fell in British Enkalon and in the carpet makers Allied Textiles and Youghal.

In the plant, cyclohexane was heated under pressure in six reactors, each of which was about 10m high and 3m in diameter. The reactors were usually connected in series but, at the time of the explosion, number five was out of commission; on 30 March it had been lifted off its platform by a crane and placed nearby. To keep the plant in operation reactor number four had been connected to reactor number six by a specially made bypass pipe (see Figures C.15.1 and C.15.2).

The gap between reactor four and reactor six was about 6m and the outlet from reactor four was 0.35m higher than the inlet to reactor six. To accommodate these differences a dog-leg shaped pipe was made in the Nypro workshop. The bypass had

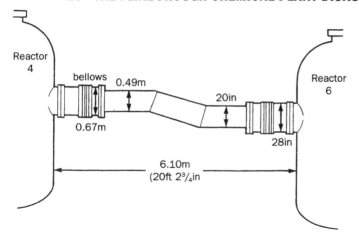

Figure C.15.1   The bypass pipe in the Nypro plant, Flixborough

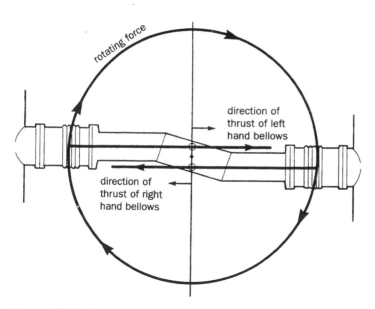

Figure C.15.2   The couple on the bypass pipe in the Nypro plant, Flixborough

bellows at each end to take up the expansion and contraction of the system. The six reactors together were 60m long and the difference in length between 0°C and the operating temperature of 150°C was 135mm. The bypass was fitted and tested – though not adequately – on 1 April.

After the explosion the bypass was found bent double on the

concrete plinth below the reactors. The bellows at each end had torn apart, leaving 0.67m openings in each of the reactors through which the gas had escaped.

The subsequent Court of Inquiry found that in designing the bypass, no one had appreciated that the pressurized assembly would be subjected to a turning moment, imposing forces on the two bellows connections for which bellows are not designed. Neither had it been appreciated that the hydraulic thrust of the bellows would tend to make the dog-leg buckle at the mitre joints. No calculations were made to determine whether the bellows or pipe would withstand these forces. The relevant British Standard (BS 3351 1971) was not consulted, nor was the designer's guide issued by the bellows' manufacturer; the complete bypass was not pressure-tested before use to the safety valve pressure. BS 3351 requires the test pressure to be 1.3 times the design pressure.

In operation the forces on either end of the bypass were not opposite each other, because of the dog-leg shape necessitated by the difference in height of reactor four and reactor six. Each bellows exerted a force of 20 kilonewtons on its end of the bypass but they exerted a couple, which is a system of two equal but directly opposite parallel forces. This would have caused the bellows to 'squirm' (which happens when an accordion is played) and then to burst; parts of the bellows were found afterwards which had completely lost their corrugation. The combination of the forces exerted by the bursting bellows caused the pipe to jack-knife. This failure left the reactors open to the atmosphere and 40 tonnes of vapour were released to the atmosphere in 45 seconds.

Comment

The series of failures was so elementary that some basic design management would have prevented the disaster. Perhaps the simplest precaution would have been to test the bypass before use but this was not done. This case history illustrates that, in even major operations, the obvious can be overlooked and thus provides a warning always to question underlying principles.

Sources

Marshall, V. C. (1979), *Disaster at Flixborough* Exeter: A Wheaton & Son.
The Flixborough Disaster: Report of the Court of Inquiry London: HMSO, May 1975.
The Times 3, 4 and 6 June 1974.

Case History 16
The Tay Bridge Disaster

The cause of this disaster was the failure of the bridge's design to take into account the environment of use. There were a number of contributory factors, but the fundamental error lay in ignoring the wind pressure on an exposed bridge two miles long. One lesson from that December night in 1879 was that big engineering projects had become too complex to be the responsibility of one man. What had started with men like Joseph Paxton, Isambard Brunel and Robert Stephenson ended with Sir Thomas Bouch. Much has been written about the circumstances – including William McGonagal's awful poem – but here we focus on the design aspects.

In 1870 the North British Railway Company obtained the assent of Parliament to the construction of a bridge two miles long over the estuary of the River Tay. It took six years to build and was the longest bridge in the world when the government inspector from the Board of Trade declared the bridge to be safe and fit for use in 1878.

On Sunday 29 December 1879 the 5.27pm train from Burntisland to Dundee was crossing the 1060 yards of the Firth when 13 spans, and the 12 towers that supported them, were carried away. The locomotive, five carriages and a brake van together with 75 men, women and children plunged to their deaths. The storm that night had a ferocity that few had experienced before.

The Board of Trade inquiry examined 120 witnesses and asked 20 000 questions. There was a speed limit of 25 mph on the bridge and the five engine-drivers who gave evidence all denied they had ever exceeded it, or had raced the ferryboats across the water below. The thirteen high central-spans were supported on towers of six cast iron columns. Each column was built of seven pipes bolted together through their flanges.

The inquiry heard from the workmen at the Wormit Foundry, which had cast the columns, that there was a great lack of what we would now call quality control. Blow holes and faults in the castings were filled with Beaumont Egg – a mixture of beeswax, fiddler's resin, iron borings and lamp black. Before leaving Wormit's the columns were painted or covered with white lead and grease which disguised the defects.

The bridge had been designed by Sir Thomas Bouch who had asked the advice of the Astronomer Royal on wind pressure, when he was making preliminary plans for a bridge across the Forth. The Astronomer Royal had written in a letter, 'I think we may say the greatest wind pressure to which a plane surface like that of the bridge will be subjected on its whole extent is 10 lb per square foot.'

During the inquiry the Wreck Commissioner asked the designer the following questions:

'Sir Thomas, did you in designing this bridge make any allowance at all for wind pressure?'

'Not specially.'

'Was there not a particular pressure had in view by you at the time you make the design?'

'I had the report of the Forth Bridge.'

Preparations for starting the contract to build the Tay Bridge were well advanced in 1870. The letter from the Astronomer Royal was written in 1873.

The Secretary of the Meteorological Council told the inquiry that the wind pressure down the Tay, along a front of 250 feet, could be more than 50 lb per square foot and the velocity more than 90 mph. After the disaster the Astronomer Royal published a paper on winds and bridges in which he wrote, 'all calculations for the strength of the proposed structure should be based on the assumption of a pressure of 120 lb to the square foot'. He called this 'establishing a modulus of safety'.

The government inspector from the Board of Trade did not test the bridge for the effects of wind pressure.

The report of the inquiry blamed Sir Thomas Bouch for the design defects and for failing to supervise the construction of the bridge. Some of the girders from Bouch's bridge were used in the second Tay bridge which was opened in 1887. Today the stumps of old piers can still be seen acting as cutwaters for the new piers.

The locomotive, a 4–4–0 No 224, which pulled the ill-fated train was recovered from the Tay and afterwards worked for 39 years. A relief fund was set up to help the families of those who died, and the last application for assistance was received in the late 1930s. It was from the sister of one of the two guards who had travelled on that 5.27pm train from Burntisland to Dundee.

In December 1985 Professor Iain MacLeod of Strathclyde University said that new research showed that the disaster was the result of poor design, which could not have been avoided by higher standards of construction. Modern analysis techniques revealed that the bolts used in the bridge were not strong enough to hold it in a Force 10 wind.

Comment

Behind this tragedy is the message that designers must be particularly careful of safety considerations when designing to a tight budget. Bouch had a reputation for building cut-price railways: cheap, lightly constructed but reliable lines. To get agreement to bridge the Tay he claimed that he could do it for £200 000; although the final figure was £300 000. When he died a broken man, less than a year after the disaster, the Institution of Civil Enginers said, 'In his death the profession has to lament one who though carrying his works nearer to the margin of safety than many other would have done . . .'. Bouch's work on the Forth Bridge design was abandoned and renewed after new designers had prepared a fresh scheme. The massive structure we can see today is in great contrast to the spidery lattice and slender piers of the original Tay Bridge.

Sources

Thomas, J. (1972), *The Tay Bridge Disaster*, Newton Abbot: David & Charles.

Perkins, J. (1975), *The Tay Bridge Disaster*, The City of Dundee District Council.

Prebble, J. (1980), *The High Girders*, London: Secker & Warburg.

The Times 29 December 1879; 11 December 1985.

Case History 17
Product Safety in the Space Programme

The events of the year 1967 may now be difficult to remember with accuracy. The names in the news included Martin Luther King who led protest marches in New York, Dr Christian Barnard who performed the first heart transplant in Cape Town and the Shah of Iran who was crowned in Tehran. Harold Wilson was Prime Minister, the Six-Day War was fought between Israel and the Arab nations and President de Gaulle made his 'free Quebec' speech in Canada. But something happened in Florida at the end of January which many *will* remember with horror. It was 'a disaster waiting to happen'.

To overtake the Soviet Union's successes in space, between 1957 and 1961, President Kennedy, in May 1961, pledged Congress that America would, by the end of the decade, land a man on the moon and bring him safely back to earth. Considerable study was required to determine which of the possible techniques would give the best chance of success. The method eventually employed was that of a lunar-orbit rendezvous, by which a launch vehicle, Saturn V, placed a 50-ton spacecraft in a lunar trajectory. The Apollo spacecraft released the lunar module which landed on the moon. Kennedy's promise was achieved by Apollo 11 in 1969. In total there were 400 000 people involved in Project Apollo.

Back on 27 January 1967, on Complex 34 at the Kennedy Space Centre in Florida, three men were sealed in the Apollo 1 command module on the top of a Saturn rocket. They were taking part in a simulated countdown for the first manned Apollo flight, set to orbit the earth for the following month.

Simulated countdowns were a regular feature of the training

of astronauts and were not considered dangerous. There was no fuel in the Saturn rocket. The command module had many faults when it left the factory and the simulator itself was a constant source of problems. On that Friday at the end of January there had been a series of problems ever since the astronauts had entered the module at 1 pm. It was pressurized with pure oxygen and was sealed by a two-piece hatch. Difficulties with communications with the ground continued until 6.31pm, when the controllers heard one brief word from the module: 'Fire'.

The closed-circuit television monitor at Cape Kennedy had a picture of the command module's hatch window filled with flame. The next message was 'We've got a fire in the cockpit'. The monitor showed one of the astronauts trying to undo the bolts on the hatch. Then 'We've got a bad fire . . . We're burning up'. The last sound was a cry of pain. The technicians outside the module could not open the hatch because it was too hot.

The temperature had rapidly reached 1000°F and 14.7 seconds after that first word astronauts Grissom, White and Chaffee died of asphyxiation. The fire lasted for 25.5 seconds before consuming all the oxygen. In the 'white room' surrounding the command module there was no proper emergency equipment nor a rescue team available. The first firemen arrived 8 minutes 55 seconds after the fire call and the first medical doctors after 11 minutes 55 seconds.

The fire was designated the Apollo 204 Accident and NASA immediately established the Apollo 204 Review Board. Its seven members were heavily weighted with NASA personnel because of the complex nature of the Apollo project. It formed 21 working panels to review the many spacecraft subsystems, components and materials, and conducted numerous tests and studies. In addition, the US Senate Committee on Aeronautical and Space Sciences carried out a full analysis of the Apollo 204 Accident and examined the procedures and findings of the Review Board.

The front page of *The Times* on 28 January led with 'Three Spacemen Die in U.S. Fire During Tests for Apollo flight'. It was seen as a severe setback to the moon landing programme. All the Soviet newspapers carried reports and pictures of the disaster, and Moscow said that the spacemen's courage had won the hearts of the Soviet people. Two days later Sir Bernard Lovell, Director of the Jodrell Bank Experimental Radio Astronomy Station, wrote on the risks of space exploration. Grissom and Chaffee were buried on 31 January in Arlington National Cemetery and White at West Point military academy. At the end of February the interim report of the Review Board stimulated the headline 'Apollo Fire Blamed on Complacency. Fire Hazards Underestimated'. The third leader in *The Times* concluded that 'safety should be allowed much more weight'.

In April the Review Board's report 'revealed many deficiencies in design and engineering, manufacturing and quality control'. The Board said that the precise failure would probably never be positively identified, but the central conclusion was that 'the Apollo team . . . in its devotion to the many difficult problems of space travel . . . failed to give adequate attention to certain mundane but equally vital questions of crew safety'.

The Senate report criticized NASA for overconfidence and complacency and its failure to recognize the hazards of the test in an all-oxygen atmosphere. Some members of the committee were disturbed by the possibility that shortcomings in design, production and quality control would not have come to light if there had been no disaster. The Space Agency was also criticized for failing to advise Congress of the shortcomings of (what became) North American-Rockwell Corp, the prime contractor, which had been the subject of a secret report in 1965.

The conditions which led to the disaster were:

1 **Failure to identify the test as hazardous**. The cabin atmosphere, of 100 per cent pure oxygen at 16.7 psi, was not determined to be hazardous but the Review Board's view was that 'the test conditions were extremely hazardous'. The previous successful Mercury and Gemini programmes had used pure oxygen over hundreds of hours of testing and this had led to a false sense of confidence and complacency.

It appears that everyone associated with the design and test of the spacecraft simply failed to understand fully the dangers and the co-operative effect of an ignition source, the combustible materials and the pure oxygen atmosphere in a sealed spacecraft cabin.

2 **The spacecraft hatch**.

'Apollo spacecraft 012 had an inward opening hatch which required at least 90 seconds for either internal or external removal and crew egress.'

The 16.7 psi test atmosphere, and the increase in pressure created by the fire, did not allow the hatch to be opened without cabin depressurization and there was no means of doing so quickly. NASA had considered a quick-opening hatch, as had been used in Mercury and Gemini spacecraft, but the risk of it possibly accidentally releasing in space was regarded as to be in excess of the benefit to be gained from installing it.

3 **Ground safety procedures**. The training of personnel in safety procedures and the availability of emergency equipment were completely inadequate.

4 **Operational test procedures**. These were subject to last-minute changes which were only agreed verbally and not put in writing. However, they did not contribute to the fire.

5 **Communications**. There were problems with the voice link between the command module and the Manned Spaceflight Operations Building over five miles away. Despite attempts to solve the problem, communications remained unsatisfactory. However, the communications difficulties did not contribute to the fire.

6 **Control of combustible material**. Combustible materials were present inside the spacecraft. They included nylon netting installed underneath the couches to catch dropped equipment, foam pads to protect the interior during the test, and Velcro fasteners – some of which were normally considered flame-resistant but nevertheless burned in the fire. At the time of the test there were non-flight materials in the cabin.

7 **Engineering, workmanship and quality control deficiencies**. An unnecessarily hazardous condition was created by deficiencies in design, workmanship and quality control, including

■ problems in the design and installation of electric wiring

- chronic failure of components of the environmental control system
- failure to conduct vibration tests of a complete flight-configured spacecraft
- improper design protection of electric cabling
- deficiencies in the management of engineering, such as change orders, configuration control and the general status of hardware
- lack of an adequate level of workmanship in manufacturing, installation and rework appropriate to the technical sophistication of the Apollo spacecraft – for example, a wrench socket was found in the command module during the disassembly process.

A detailed design review of the entire spacecraft communications system was proposed; combustible material in the capsule had to be severely restricted and controlled; full-scale mock-up fire tests were recommended and the time required for the crew to get out reduced and the procedures simplified. The Board found that 113 significant engineering orders had not been carried out when the capsule was delivered to NASA.

There is another memory of the space story that will be recalled with horror. It concerned an 'accident rooted in history'. In 1986 television showed the almost standard picture of the latest space shuttle blasting off from the Kennedy Space Centre. Then, the vehicle exploded in an appalling white cloud which sent out pretty streamers in a dreadful firework display. The seven crew were killed, including Christa McAuliffe the teacher whose schoolchildren were watching the launch that freezing Tuesday morning in January.

The investigations that followed identified the O-rings as the immediate cause of the disaster. They were used in the joints between the 11 segments of the solid booster rockets, which provided the additional thrust needed to escape the pull of the earth. A design defect in the clevis joints allowed a blow-by of hot gases which turned *Challenger* into a giant blowtorch.

The investigations revealed that the O-rings were but the symptom of a very serious management disease – one that was chillingly similar to that found in the Apollo tragedy 19 years previously. The House of Representatives Committee on Science and Technology found that the fundamental problem was poor technical decision-making over a period of several years by top NASA and contractor personnel: 'Existing contract incentives used by NASA do not adequately address or promote safety and quality concerns.' The Committee found that safety, reliability and quality assurance programmes within NASA were grossly inadequate. They recommended that NASA should review its risk management activities to define a complete risk management programme.

The Committee concluded, 'What we . . . must realize is that the lessons learned by the *Challenger* accident are universally applicable, not just for NASA but for governments and society.'

The dreadful parallel is that the tragedy of 1986 was due to the same basic mistakes as the tragedy of 1967. Despite all the experts and resources the obvious was overlooked because of a failure in management. The technology to have prevented the accidents was available. What was missing was the will to apply it. Some of the mistakes that were made seem to have been devastatingly simple, perhaps because the wood was concealing the trees.

Comment

The message for designers is never to take anything for granted. Rigorously enforce design reviews, preferably by a panel which includes personnel not engaged in the project they are assessing. Independent product safety audits, concerned not with quality but on safety and its management, are valuable in checking the effectiveness of the management of product safety.

Perhaps the most significant conclusion, from the investigation into the *Challenger* disaster, was that the fundamental problem started at the top level of management. For industry this means that a board of directors cannot dodge responsibility for managing design safety. It is a decision area that should not be delegated. Senior executives have to make a direct, active contribution to ensuring that their products are as safe as possible.

Sources

Report of the Apollo 204 Review Board to the Administrator, National Aeronautics and Space Administration, Washington DC, 4 April 1967.

Report of the Committee on Aeronautical and Space Sciences, Apollo 204 Accident, Washington DC: US Senate 30 January 1968.

Chaikin, A (1994), *A Man on the Moon*, London: Michael Joseph.

Case History 18
The DC-10 Cargo Door

Turkish Airlines flight 981 from Ankara took off from Paris at 12.30 pm on 3 March 1974 and headed for London. Five minutes later it crashed in the Forest of Ermenonville, 30 miles north-east of Paris, killing everyone on board. It was the world's worst civil air disaster up to that time with 345 dead, including 11 crew and 200 British passengers. They had been transferred to the flight in Paris by British Airways because a strike by 400 ground engineers at Heathrow had caused the cancellation of some of their flights. Bodies from the aircraft were found six and nine miles away from the site of the crash. The cargo door was found seven miles away.

The airline had bought three DC-10s for £25 million in 1973, and the one that crashed was the first to be delivered. More than 100 of the type were in service. In June 1972 a DC-10 had been badly damaged by cargo door failure while flying over Windsor, Ontario. Modifications, recommended by McDonnell-Douglas the manufacturers, were designed to make sure that the cargo door was always closed properly; if it was not, the aircraft interior could not be pressurized. But one of the key modifications had not been made to the aircraft that crashed near Paris, despite certificates confirming that they had been carried out. New door mechanisms were being installed in DC-10s as a matter of urgency.

The mechanism which operated the cargo door is shown in Figure C.18.1. A torque tube revolves to drive a latch hook over its spool, while the top of the latch swings through an arc of about 90° until it comes to rest against the metal stop. Provided that the top part of the latch passes beyond the centre point of its arc, the force created by pressurization (within the aircraft) will be transmitted to the door structure. A locking-pin system

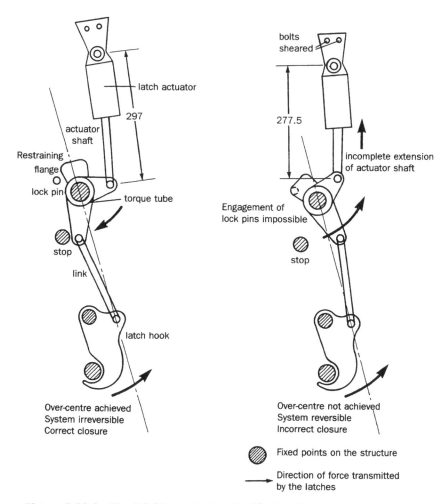

latch actuator

297

actuator shaft

Restraining flange

lock pin

torque tube

stop

link

latch hook

Over-centre achieved
System irreversible
Correct closure

bolts sheared

277.5

incomplete extension of actuator shaft

Engagement of lock pins impossible

stop

Over-centre not achieved
System reversible
Incorrect closure

Fixed points on the structure

Direction of force transmitted by the latches

Figure C.18.1   The DC-10 cargo door locking system

was incorporated to ensure that the top part of the latch actually did go over-centre.

In theory, if the latches were not fully home the locking-pins would jam and the resistance would be transmitted back to the handle on the outside of the door. In addition, the vent-door (which allowed access to the locking handle) would not close. McDonnell-Douglas designed a support plate to prevent the torque tube distorting. This could occur if the handle on the outside of the cargo door was forced down. Furthermore, the linkages in the system were re-rigged so that the locking-pins would be driven further over the top of the latches. But the support plate which should have been fitted was missing, although there was something far more seriously wrong with the cargo door than this. Someone had misrigged the locking-pins so that even in the fully closed position they barely covered the lugs at all.

What in fact happened was that the travel of the pins was reduced, so that a child could have beaten the safety system. Even with the latches only partly closed, and with the locking-pins jammed up against them, it would only have needed a force of 13 lbs to operate the locking handle successfully, and close the vent door.

At Paris Orly Airport, Turkish Airlines used a private concern to provide it with ground service. A 39-year-old Algerian expatriate had been instructed how to close and lock the DC-10 cargo door. First, he had to activate the electrical power circuits and press a button which would bring the door down on its rubber seal. He held the button for a further ten seconds to give time for the actuators to move the latches over the spools on the door sill. He verified this by closing down the locking handle alongside the small vent door. If the latches were home the locking handle would move and the vent door would simul-taneously close.

If the latches had not gone home the locking handle would encounter resistance and the vent door would not close. He did not understand the mechanics and neither could he read the instructions on the door, which warned him against using force on the locking handle, because they were printed in English. He thought he had to get the locking handle down and the vent door closed which meant it was safe. But, because of the misrigging of the locking-pins, the actuators had not driven the latches over the spool and, although the handle was down, the door was not safe.

At 11 500 feet, the pressure differential inside the DC-10 would have been 4.5 psi. There would have been almost five tons of air pressing against the inside of the door, competing directly against the ability of the partially closed latches to hold it shut.

Because the latches were not over-centre all of that force was transmitted to two bolts, a quarter of an inch in diameter, which held the latch actuator to the inside of the door. The bolts gave way, the latch talons were pulled from the spools and the door blew open, to be ripped from its hinges by the slipstream.

Comment

The surprising thing about this disaster is that such a high-tech product could be destroyed by a simple mechanical linkage. The complexity of an aircraft is an amalgam of many different specialities, all of which had been operating successfully in the DC-10. Yet it was defeated by a low-tech failure. Its source ultimately lay in the original design, compounded by failures in carrying out the modification and in maintenance. This case history is another illustration of the fact that the biggest disaster can have a seemingly trivial cause and the need always to pay attention to the detail, however mundane it may be.

Sources

Eddy, P. Potter, E. and Page, B. (1976), *Destination Disaster*, London: Hart-Davis. *The Times*, 4, 9 and 16 March 1974.

Case History 19
The Supertanker's Design Weakness

This case history, concerning the supertanker *Amoco Cadiz*, demonstrates the practical application of the hazard analysis and risk assessment technique, Fault Tree Analysis, which is described in Chapter 3. The engineering detail may be unfamiliar to many designers but the principles of FTA are illustrated very clearly. The following quote from the reference paper is apposite for many design situations:

> It is not unusual for the steering system of a ship to consist of many elements produced by different manufacturers. There may be minimal exchange of information between them, except through the shipyard ordering the equipment.
>
> It is therefore difficult to see how a failure mode analysis can be made for a steering system as a whole except by the shipyard engineers or the owners. If a steering system is to give good reliable service over a number of years it is reasonable to expect that some form of failure analysis is undertaken before the equipment is installed.

The court judgment included some interesting comments on the division of responsibility between the shipbuilder and the operator, which also have wider implications. The grounding of the 109 700-tonne supertanker *Amoco Cadiz* contaminated 20 miles of the French coast and led to newspaper headlines such as 'Black tide fouls beach in Brittany'. The ship was registered in Monrovia and had been built in Cadiz in 1973; she was the flagship of the Amoco Transport company, the carrier for Amoco Phillips Petroleum.

At 9.45 am on 16 March 1978 the steering-gear of the *Amoco Cadiz* broke down in rough seas, about ten miles from the Isle of Ushant, off Brest. The cause was the failure of a pipe flange on the main steering-gear hydraulic circuit which allowed the oil in the system to be discharged into the steering-gear compartment. The crew were unable to recharge the system and regain control of the steerage before the ship grounded at 21.04. Over the next few days the entire cargo of 226 000 tonnes of crude oil polluted hundreds of miles of the French coastline.

The steering-gear and related equipment of the *Amoco Cadiz* complied with all existing international regulations; this raised doubts about their adequacy. The disaster highlighted both the basic weakness of the single hydraulic circuit, almost universally employed in the ram and rotary vane types of steering-gear, and the drastic potential consequences of the failure of the steering-gear of a large tanker.

Following the *Amoco Cadiz* casualty new international regulations were developed as a matter of urgency for the steering-gears of all ships, but with particular emphasis on large tankers. The new regulations concentrated on the importance of maintaining the integrity of at least part of the hydraulic circuit after a single failure of pressure parts, so that steering capability could be maintained or be rapidly recovered after a fault. The regulations envisaged automatic changeover of separate identical systems or means to separate automatically a single hydraulic circuit in order to isolate fault in pressure parts.

The simple Fault Tree Analysis, in Figure C.19.1, of the type of steering-gear used in the *Amoco Cadiz* shows the route to failure in a qualitative manner direct through the OR gates. Figure C.19.2 shows a Fault Tree Analysis of a conventional four-ram steering-gear with six failure modes leading through the OR gates. Figure C.19.3 shows a Fault Tree Analysis of the same type of steering-gear designed in accordance with the new regulations, and fitted with separate and independent power actuating systems, and shows the failure modes through the OR gates reduced to two.

The result of the grounding of the *Amoco Cadiz* was a series of complex international lawsuits which were consolidated into a single court action. A 111-page opinion was issued by Judge Frank McGarr of the Eastern Division of the Northern Circuit, Court

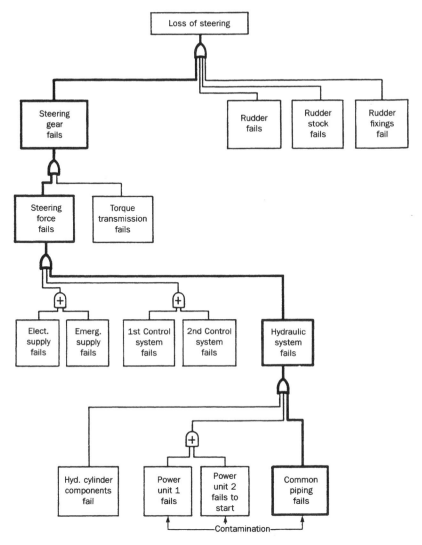

Figure C.19.1 Simple Fault Tree Analysis showing the route to failure of an *Amoco Cadiz*-type steering-gear. The heavy black line shows that a failure in the common piping must result in a loss of steering. There is no back-up mechanism.
Source: Cowley (1982).

of Illinois. He said that Amoco was entitled to damages against Astilleros, the Spanish shipyard which built the *Amoco Cadiz,* 'to the extent that its own liability was contributed to by the negligence and fault of the shipbuilder'.

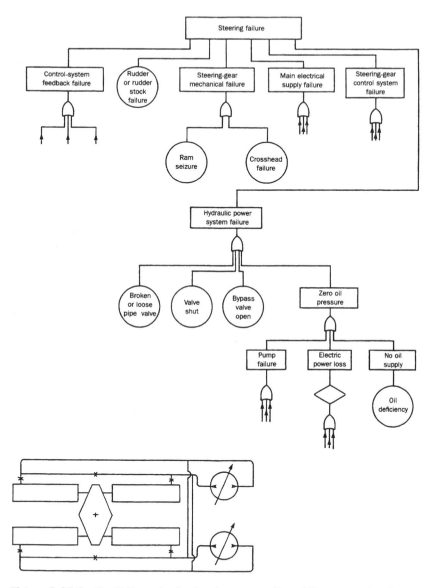

Figure C.19.2   Fault Tree Analysis of a conventional four-ram steering-gear showing the six failure modes through the OR gates leading to loss of steering. Compare this with Figure C.19.3 which has the failure modes reduced to two.
Source: Cowley (1982).

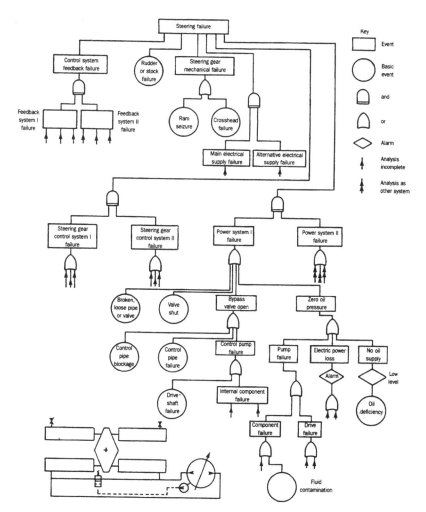

Figure C.19.3 Fault Tree Analysis of a four-ram steering-gear, with separate and independent power actuating systems, showing only two failure modes through the OR gates leading to loss of steering. Compare this with Figure C.19.2 which has six failure modes leading to loss of steering.
Source: Cowley (1982).

The judge concluded that Amoco International Oil Company (AIOC), the operator, 'negligently performed its duty to ensure that the *Amoco Cadiz* in general and its steering-gear in particular were seaworthy, adequately maintained and in proper repair'.

He noted that AIOC 'negligently performed its duty to ensure that the crew of the *Amoco Cadiz* was properly trained', and failed in its duty to ensure that the design and construction of the *Amoco Cadiz* was 'properly carried out so as to result in a seaworthy vessel'. He said AIOC was negligent in operating the *Amoco Cadiz* without a redundant steering system, or any other means of controlling the rudder, in the event of the complete failure of the hydraulic steering system.

In arriving at his decision Judge McGarr outlined the history and operation of the *Amoco Cadiz*. These indicated that, from the outset, there were problems with its steering-gear which were not adequately comprehended or repaired. In addition, the oil company failed to follow the maintenance instructions for the steering-gear, which ultimately caused the disaster.

Judge McGarr listed several areas where AIOC failed to maintain the steering-gear of the *Amoco Cadiz* properly. The company did not act to ensure that the filters on the steering-gear were cleaned according to the instruction manual; it did not act to ensure that the oil in the steering-gear was changed; it did not arrange to have samples of the hydraulic fluid analysed; it did not require the ship's steering-gear system to be purged to remove air.

In addition he faulted the company for accepting the ship from the Spanish shipyard with acknowledged defects in its steering-gear. In particular the ship was delivered with cast-iron steering-gear ram bushings. It arranged to have bronze bushings installed on its own vessels and placed additional bushings on board the *Amoco Cadiz*. These were not installed.

The judge noted that *Amoco Cadiz*'s steering-gear in the last four months of its life was losing 7 to 12 litres of hydraulic fluid per day. This was 'greatly in excess of what would occur with a properly maintained system'. The report said:

This excessive consumption was known to AIOC which in the exercise of ordinary skill and prudence, should have recognised it as symptomatic of a progressive degradation of the system's reliability.

With both steering-gear pumps secured, the *Amoco Cadiz* and her sister-ships experienced as much as 15 degrees of rudder movement while in port: 'This fact was well known among AIOC engineers and should have signalled a serious malfunction of the two-sided restrain system of the *Amoco Cadiz* steering mechanism.' The unexplained rudder movement of the tanker was neither properly investigated nor corrected. AIOC also failed to instruct the *Amoco Cadiz* crew in emergency steering-gear drills and procedures to be followed in the event of a steering-gear breakdown.

Comment

There were so many failures that led to this accident that one significant fact can easily be overlooked. The ship's vital rudder mechanism had the elementary weakness of no redundancy – a back-up system to take over if there was a failure of the primary system. Yet it still conformed to the international regulations then in force. This is another example of the warning that designers should not rely entirely on conformance with standards and regulations as the sole evidence of safety.

Sources

Cowley, J. (1982), 'Steering gear: new concepts and requirements', *Transactions of the Institute of Marine Engineers*, Vol. 94, Paper 23.
Financial Times, 21 April 1984.

Case History 20
The Ro-ro Ferries and Design

Specifying a safer design will not necessarily bring about a safer product. This is true even when a recognized, international organization representing 137 countries is involved. A panel of experts in the UN's International Maritime Organization (IMO), the specialized agency which deals with maritime matters, reporting on ro-ro safety in 1995,[1] said: 'Establishing a safety centred culture cannot . . . be established by regulations.'

The *Herald of Free Enterprise* disaster will be remembered by the pictures in the media of the ro-ro ferry lying on its side at Zeebrugge. It rolled over on 6 March 1987 because of a failure to close the bow doors, which allowed the sea to enter the car deck at a rate of 20 tonnes per minute. The public inquiry into the deaths of over 190 people who perished said 'From top to bottom the body corporate was infected with the disease of sloppiness'.

A book[2] on the *Herald of Free Enterprise* says:

> The basic premise behind ro-ros is a commercial one. A ro-ro ferry is essentially a raft over which superstructures are built. The economics of their design require that cargo decks are large and there are no bulkheads to divide the space. The fewer divides there are, the easier it is to load and unload vehicles: also more can be carried. As ferries have increased in size this basic commercial structure has remained. No one seems to have questioned the safety implications.

In 1988 the relevant regulations of the International Convention for the Safety of Life at Sea (SOLAS) were amended, by the IMO, in the light of the Zeebrugge disaster. A new(!) regulation required that 'cargo loading doors shall be locked before the ship proceeds on any voyage and remain closed until the ship is at its next berth'. The implementation of the new SOLAS 90 Standard to existing ships would result in a large part of the world's ro-ro fleet being modified: 'In some cases the changes could be extensive and the high cost involved could lead to some of them being scrapped and replaced by new tonnage.'[3]

By 1989 all ferries using British waters had installed the additional devices but much of the rest of the world did not follow suit. The Department of Transport commented, 'The agreement derives from work undertaken in the International Maritime Organization's Maritime Safety Committee but which failed to secure support for its world-wide application.'[4]

One vessel not covered by the new regulations was the *Estonia*, because it operated in part of the Baltic not included in the agreement. The 15 500 tonne ro-ro ship was sailing from Tallinn to Stockholm at the end of September 1994. It sank within 45 minutes of the bow visor being ripped off by the 10 metre-high waves, as she forced her way at 15 knots against a fierce westerly gale. The visor formed the flared prow of the ship and, in harbour, lifted up to allow vehicles access to the car deck. It consisted of 56 tonnes of stainless steel depending on two hinges at the bottom and two latches at the top held in place by 300 mm pins. The visor, and the bow ramp behind it which formed an inner door, had a common hydraulic locking system with no redundancy – that is, no secondary back-up system to take over if the primary system failed. The death toll was 910 passengers and crew. The shipowner's liability for the deaths was estimated at $75 million, with 5000 registered claimants from 16 countries.

An underwater robot camera revealed that the missing visor lay some distance from the ship itself in 230 feet of water, but the inner door behind it was still in position. There was a 3 foot gap along its top edge which had allowed the sea to enter the car deck and capsize the vessel. Although it was decided not to raise the *Estonia*, the visor was recovered.

The tragedy reopened the discussion about the introduction of bulkheads in open deck ferries to restrict the effect of water entering and upsetting the stability of the vessel. In 1995 a report[1] to the IMO proposed major changes to ro-ro ferries. Draft regulations made provision for the use of longitudinal and transverse bulkheads to divide the open decks into watertight compartments. The Panel of Experts said that it was aware 'that some of its proposals will have severe implications to existing ro-ro passenger ships and may even lead to some ships being forced out of service'. It was of the firm opinion that a 'major improvement in the safety of passenger ships will be accomplished if all its proposals are adopted and brought into force'. It stressed that the full value of the proposals will not be felt unless 'a change in the basic philosophy is brought about among those engaged in the operation of such ships, both aboard and ashore'.

The Panel also said:

> Technical requirements alone, both constructional and operational, will not establish a safe environment in the areas of passenger ships. It is, therefore, necessary that every person with a professional interest in passenger ships feels reponsible for their safety.

The Transport Select Committee of the House of Commons, set up after the *Estonia* disaster, reported in July 1995. It called for an urgent overhaul of the 'inadequate' safety standards for ro-ro ferries, because their design made them vulnerable to sinking if water flooded the car decks. Expert witnesses had stated that just one foot of water on the car deck could could lead to the capsize of a large ferry. One member of the Committee said, 'The ferry industry needs to be reminded that they have been looking after their profits rather than their passengers.' Three MPs who had served on the Committee vowed never to travel on a ro-ro ferry again. The report's proposals were considered by the IMO at a meeting in November 1995. It failed to agree to set a global standard on water on the car deck.

In 1996 an agreement between 14 European maritime nations agreed a new standard on ferry safety. By 2002 all ships operating in northwest Europe must be capable of staying afloat to allow orderly evacuation, even after being holed below the waterline and having up to 20 ins of water on the car deck. About 100 ro-ros using British ports will be affected.

Comment

Even the widespread use and apparent acceptance of a product does not make its design safe. Designers should always question the commonplace.

References

1 'Ro-ro ferry safety: Panel of Experts report to IMO' *International Maritime Organisation Briefing*, 11 April 1995.
2 Crainer S. (1993), *Zeebrugge: Learning from Disaster*, London: Herald Charitable Trust.
3 'SOLAS: the International Convention for the Safety of Life at Sea, 1974', *Focus on IMO*, London, August 1994.
4 *The Times*, 28 July 1995; 29 September 1994; 30 November 1995; 29 February 1996; 28 June 1996.

Case History 21
Miss Jay Jay: accident or design?

J. J. Lloyd Instruments Ltd v. Northern Star Insurance Co Ltd
Court of Appeal: October 15 1986

As we saw in Chapter 6, insurance can be a complicated business. When it is compounded with design defects and a marine policy, the resolution of a claim can demand expert legal argument. In this case, although it was accepted that there were design defects in the product, these were not the only cause of the loss. It was the way in which the policy was worded which determined the result of the case.

The motor cruiser *Miss Jay Jay* left Deauville about lunchtime on 15 July 1980 to cross the English Channel to Hamble. There was a heavy wind and a choppy, confused sea with waves three metres high. The voyage was made at 15 knots so that the vessel would plane from wave to wave as far as possible. This produced a slamming effect on the hull as the waves were not evenly spaced. At Hamble it was found that £30 000 worth of damage had been caused.

The cruiser was owned by J. J. Lloyd Instruments who had insured her with Northern Star Insurers. The policy provided indemnification 'against all loss or damage to the insured craft . . . which is directly caused by external accidental means'. Subsequently those last three words became very important. Under this standard form of policy for pleasure craft it was impractical for Northern Star to survey such craft. Lloyd Instruments successfully sued the insurers in 1985, whereupon the insurers went to appeal.

Northern Star claimed that there had been nothing accidental about the loss. It was due to the admitted faulty design of the cruiser which was not suitable for the sea conditions of 15 July 1980. The loss could have been recovered under a product liability policy not under a marine policy.

On appeal, the insurer claimed that the loss was not caused by 'accidental external means'; that the cruiser was unseaworthy due to its design defects; and that it was the design defects, and not the adverse sea, that were the prime cause of the loss.

Lord Justice Lawton, in his judgment, said that a properly designed and built cruiser should not have been damaged by the conditions which the *Miss Jay Jay* encountered. This was enough to make what happened 'accidental'. The cause was the frequent and violent impacts of a badly designed hull upon an adverse sea but the design defects were not the sole cause of the loss. It was settled law that if there were two concurrent and effective causes of a marine loss, and only one came within the terms of a policy but the other did not, the insurer was liable.

Northern Star were not aware of the design defects nor that the cruiser was unseaworthy on 15 July 1980. As these were not excluded in the policy as contributing to a loss, without being the sole loss, the claim fell within the policy – provided the sea conditions were a proximate cause of the loss.

As the cause of the damage came within the terms of Lloyd Instruments' insurance policy they were entitled to the compensation available under it. It was established that the combination of unseaworthiness due to the design defects and an adverse sea was responsible for the damage to the cruiser. One without the other would not have caused the loss.

The appeal was dismissed.

Comment

Insurance can be a complex business for a designer when considering what is covered and what is not. This case illustrates just how complicated it can be. Professional advice is always advisable.

Case History 22
Almost Safer by Design

In Greek mythology Daedalus built a retreat for King Minos at Knossus in Crete; it was called the Labyrinth and seemed to have neither beginning nor end, like the river Meander which returns on itself. Daedalus fell out of favour with the king who locked him up in a tower, together with his son Icarus. Minos kept all his own ships under military guard so that escape by sea was impossible; but the king could not control the air.

Daedalus was a very skilled craftsman and set to work to make wings for himself and Icarus. He used quill feathers threaded together, with the smaller ones held in place by wax.

When all was ready for the flight the father said, 'My son, be warned! Neither soar too high, lest the sun melt the wax; nor sweep too low, lest the feathers be wetted by the sea.' They flew away from the island; the fishermen, shepherds and ploughmen looking upwards mistook them for gods. They passed Samos and Delos on the left and Lebynthos on the right.

Then Icarus disobeyed his father's warning and began to soar towards the sun. The heat softened the wax, which allowed the feathers it held to come free, and he plunged into the sea and was drowned. Daedalus carried the body to a nearby island which is now called Icaria, and which gave its name to the surrounding sea.

Comment

Later, Daedulus was able to settle his account with Minos. This he did by fixing a pipe in the roof of a bathroom used by the king. While Minos luxuriated in a warm bath Daedalus poured boiling water upon him down this pipe.

A cursory examination of this case could ascribe Icarus's death to a design defect. But in fact it was caused by his contributory negligence in ignoring a specific product warning. A cost-benefit analysis would show that the benefit of escaping from the clutches of Minos outweighed the risks associated with the only mode that could be used. Daedalus applied the best state of the art available and his design must be judged by the knowledge in Crete at that time. The circumstances of his position were such that the product could not be assessed for development risks, as only one attempt was possible.

APPENDICES

Appendix I
Council Decision Concerning Modules for Conformity Assessment for CE Marking

COUNCIL DECISION
of 22 July 1993
concerning the modules for the various phases of the conformity assessment procedures and the rules for the affixing and use of the CE conformity marking, which are intended to be used in the technical harmonization directives
(93/465/EEC)

THE COUNCIL OF THE EUROPEAN COMMUNITIES,
Having regard to the Treaty establishing the European Economic Community, and in particular Article 100a thereof,

Having regard to the proposal from the Commission[1],

In cooperation with the European Parliament[2],

Having regard to the opinion of the Economic and Social Committee[3],

Whereas Council Decision 90/683/EEC of 13 December 1990 concerning the modules for the various phases of the conformity assessment procedures which are intended to be used in the technical harmonization directives[4] needs to be substantially amended in various places; whereas, it is necessary, in a spirit of clarity and rationality, to consolidate its provisions by means of this Decision;

Whereas the Council adopted a Resolution on 21 December 1989 concerning a global approach to conformity assessments[5];

Whereas the introduction of harmonized methods for the assessment of

---

(1) OJ No C 160, 20. 6. 1991, p. 14; and OJ No C 28, 2. 2. 1993, p. 16.
(2) OJ No C 125, 18. 5. 1992, p. 178; OJ No C 115, 26. 4. 1993, p. 117; and Decision of
     14 July 1993 (not yet published in the Official Journal).
(3) OJ No C 14, 20. 1. 1992, p. 15; and OJ No C 129, 10. 5. 1993, p. 3.
(4) OJ No L 380, 31. 12. 1990, p. 13.
(5) OJ NO C 10, 16. 1. 1990, p. 1.

conformity and the adoption of a common doctrine for their implementation are likely to facilitate the adoption of future technical harmonization directives concerning the placing on the market of industrial products and thus be conducive to the implementation of the internal market;

Whereas such methods should ensure that products are in full conformity with the essential requirements laid down in the technical harmonization directives, in order to provide, in particular, for the health and safety of users and consumers;

Whereas such conformity should be assured without imposing unnecessarily onerous conditions on manufacturers, and by means of clear and comprehensible procedures;

Whereas limited flexibility should be introduced as regards use of additional modules, or variations in the modules, when the specific circumstances of a particular sector or directive so warrant, but not to such a degree as to undercut the purpose of the current Decision and only when explicitly justified;

Whereas in the abovementioned Resolution of 21 December 1989 the Council approved as a guiding principle the adoption of common rules on the use of the CE marking;

Whereas in its Decision 90/683/EEC the Council laid down that the industrial products covered by the technical harmonization directives can be placed on the market only after the manufacturer has affixed the CE marking to them;

Whereas a single CE marking should be used in order to facilitate controls on the Community market by inspectors and to clarify the obligations of economic operators in respect of marking under the various Community regulations;

Whereas the aim of the CE marking is to symbolize the conformity of a product with the levels of protection of collective interests imposed by the total harmonization directives and to indicate that the economic operator has undergone all the evaluation procedures laid down by Community law in respect of his product.

HAS DECIDED AS FOLLOWS:

Article 1

1. The procedures for conformity assessment which are to be used in the technical harmonization directives relating to the marketing of industrial products will be chosen from among the modules listed in the Annex and in accordance with the criteria set out in this Decision and in the general guidelines in the Annex.

These procedures may only depart from the modules when the specific circumstances of a particular sector or directive so warrant. Such departures from the modules must be limited in extent and must be explicitly justified in the relevant directive.

2. This Decision lays down rules for affixing the CE conformity marking

provided for in Community legislation concerning the design, manufacture, placing on the market, entry into service or use of industrial products.

3. The Commission shall report periodically on the functioning of this Decision, and on whether conformity assessment and CE marking procedures are working satisfactorily or need to be modified.

No later than the end of the transitional period in 1997, or earlier if the matter is found to be urgent, the Commission shall also report back on any special problems raised by the incorporation of Council Directive 73/23/EEC of 19 February 1973 relating to electrical equipment designed for use within certain voltage limits within the scope of CE marking procedures, and, in particular, whether safety is being compromised. It shall also review any problems raised by the issue of overlapping Council directives, and whether any further Community measures are required.

Article 2

1. Decision 90/683/EEC is hereby repealed.

2. References to the Decision repealed shall be construed as references to this Decision.

Done at Brussels, 22 July 1993.

For the Council
The President
M. OFFECIERS-VAN DE WIELE

ANNEX

CONFORMITY ASSESSMENT PROCEDURES AND CE MARKING IN THE TECHNICAL HARMONIZATION DIRECTIVES

I. GENERAL GUIDELINES

A. The principal guidelines for the use of conformity assessment procedures in technical harmonization directives are the following:

(a) the essential objective of a conformity assessment procedure is to enable the public authorities to ensure that products placed on the market conform to the requirements as expressed in the provisions of the directives, in particular with regard to the health and safety of users and consumers;

(b) conformity assessment can be subdivided into modules which relate to the design phase of products and to their production phase;

(c) as a general rule a product should be subject to both phases before being able to be placed on the market if the results are positive (*);

(d) there are a variety of modules which cover the two phases in a variety of ways. The directives must set the range of possible choices which can be considered by the Council to give the public authorities the high level of safety they seek, for a given product or product sector;

(e) in setting the range of possible choices open to the manufacturer, the directives, will take into consideration, in particular, such issues as the appropriateness of the modules to the type of products, the nature of the risks involved, the economic infrastructures of the given sector (e.g. existence or non-existence of third parties), the types and importance of production, etc. The factors that have been taken into account must be explicitly spelled out by the Commission in these directives;

(f) the directives will, in setting the range of possible modules for a given product or product sector, attempt to leave as wide a choice to the manufacturer as is consistent with ensuring compliance with the requirements.

The directives will set out the criteria governing the conditions in which the manufacturer chooses the most appropriate modules for his production from the modules laid down by the directives;

(g) the directives should avoid imposing unnecessarily modules which would be too onerous relative to the objectives of the directive concerned;

(h) notified bodies should be encouraged to apply the modules without unnecessary burden for the economic operators. The Commission,

(*) The specific directives may provide for different arrangements.

in cooperation with the Member States, must ensure that close cooperation is organized between the notified bodies in order to ensure consistent technical application of the modules;

(i) in order to protect the manufacturers, the technical documentation provided to notified bodies has to be limited to that which is required solely for the purpose of assessment of conformity. Legal protection of confidential information is required;

(j) whenever directives provide the manufacturer with the possibility of using modules based on quality assurance techniques, the manufacturer must also be able to have recourse to a combination of modules not using quality assurance, and *vice versa*, except where compliance with the requirements laid down by the directives requires the exclusive application of a certain procedure;

(k) for the purposes of operating the modules, Member States must notify on their own responsibility bodies under their jurisdiction which they have chosen from the technically competent bodies complying with the requirements of the directives. This responsibility involves the obligation for the Member States to ensure that the notified bodies permanently have the technical qualifications required by the directives and that the latter keep their competent national authorities informed of the performance of their tasks. Where a Member State withdraws its notification of a body, it must take appropriate steps to ensure that the dossiers are processed by another notified body to ensure continuity;

(l) in addition, with regard to conformity assessment, the sub-contracting of work shall be subject to certain conditions guaranteeing:
   – the competence of the establishment operating as sub-contractor, on the basis of conformity with series EN 45 000 standards, and the capability of the Member State that has notified the sub-contracting body to ensure effective monitoring of such compliance,
   – the ability of the body notified to exercise effective responsibility for the work carried out under sub-contract;

(m) notified bodies which can prove their conformity with harmonized standards (EN 45 000 series), by submitting an accreditation certificate or other documentary evidence, are presumed to conform to the requirements of the directives. Member States having notified bodies unable to prove their conformity with the harmonized standards (EN 45 000 series) may be requested to provide the Commission with the appropriate supporting documents on the basis of which notification was carried out;

(n) a list of notified bodies must be published by the Commission in the *Official Journal of the European Communities* and constantly updated.

B. The principal guidelines for the affixing and use of the CE marking are the following:

(a) The CE marking symbolizes conformity to all the obligations incumbent on manufacturers for the product by virtue of the Community directives providing for its affixing.

Thus, such conformity is not limited to the essential requirements relating to safety, public health, consumer protection, etc., as certain directives may impose specific obligations not necessarily forming part of the essential requirements.

(b) The CE marking affixed to industrial products symbolizes the fact that the natural or legal person having affixed or been responsible for the affixing of the said marking has verified that the product conforms to all the Community total harmonization provisions which apply to it and has been the subject of the appropriate conformity evaluation procedures.

(c) Where the industrial products are subject to other directives concerning other aspects and which also provide for the affixing of the CE marking, the latter must indicate that the products are also presumed to conform to the provisions of those other directives.

However, where one or more of these directives allow the manufacturer, during a transitional period, to choose which arrangements to apply, the CE marking indicates conformity to the provisions only of those directives applied by the manufacturer. In this case, particulars of the directives applied, as published in the *Official Journal of the European Communities*, must be given in the documents, notices or instructions accompanying the products or, where appropriate, on the data plate.

(d) 1. The CE conformity marking must consist of the initials 'CE' taking the following form:

If the CE marking is reduced or enlarged the proportions given in the above graduated drawing must be respected:

2. Where the directive concerned does not impose specific dimensions, the CE marking must have a height of at least 5 mm.

3. The CE marking must be affixed to the product or to its data plate. However, where this is not possible or not warranted on

account of the nature of the product, it must be affixed to the packaging, if any, and to the accompanying documents, where the directive concerned provides for such documents.

4. The CE marking must be affixed visibly, legibly and indelibly.

(e) Any industrial product covered by the technical harmonization directives based on the principles of the global approach must bear the CE marking, save where the specific directives provide otherwise; such exceptions constitute derogations not from the marking requirement but from the administrative procedures for conformity evaluation, which may in certain cases be considered too cumbersome. Appropriate grounds must accordingly be given for any exception to or derogation from the marking requirement.

The CE marking is the only marking which certifies that the industrial products conform to the directives based on the principles of the global approach.

Member States must refrain from introducing into their national regulations any reference to a conformity marking other than the CE marking in connection with conformity to all the provisions contained in the directives on CE marking.

(f) The CE marking must be affixed at the end of the production control phase.

(g) The CE conformity marking must be followed by the identification number of the notified body within the meaning of paragraph I.A where the said body is involved in the production control phase within the meaning of this Decision.

Such identification numbers must be assigned by the Commission as part of the body notification procedure. The Commission must publish lists of the notified bodies in the *Official Journal of the European Communities*; such lists must be updated regularly.

A notified body must be assigned the same number when it is notified under several directives. The Commission must ensure that each notified body receives a single identification number, however many directives it is notified under.

(h) It is necessary to lay down provisions concerning the use of certain products. In this case, the CE marking and the identification number of the notified body may be followed by a pictogram or any other mark indicating, for example, the category of use.

(i) The affixing for any other marking liable to deceive third parties as to the meaning and form of the CE marking must be prohibited.

(j) A product may bear different marks, for example marks indicating conformity to national or European standards or with traditional optional directives provided such marks are not liable to cause confusion with the CE marking.

Such marks may therefore only be affixed to the product, its packaging or the documentation accompanying the product on condition that the legibility and visibility of the CE marking are not thereby reduced.

(k) The CE marking must be affixed by the manufacturer or his agent established within the Community. In exceptional, duly warranted cases, the specific directives may provide that the CE marking can be affixed by the person responsible for placing the product on the Community market.

  The identification number of the notified body must be affixed under its responsibility either by the body itself or by the manufacturer or his agent established within the Community.

(l) Member States must take all provisions of national law necessary to exclude any possibility of confusion and to prevent abuse of the CE marking.

  Without prejudice to the provisions in the directive concerned relating to the application of the safeguard clause, where a Member State establishes that the CE marking has been affixed unduly, the manufacturer, his agent or, exceptionally, where the specific directives so provide, the person responsible for placing the product in question on the Community market is obliged to make the product comply and to end the infringement under conditions imposed by the Member State. Where non-compliance continues, the Member State must take all appropriate measures to restrict or prohibit the placing on the market of the product in question or to ensure that it is withdrawn from the market in accordance with the procedures laid down in the safeguard clauses.

II. MODULES FOR CONFORMITY ASSESSMENT

Explanatory notes

Specific directives may allow the CE marking to be affixed to the packaging or the accompanying documentation, instead of to the product itself.

The declaration of conformity or the certificate of conformity (whichever of the two applies in the directive concerned) must cover either individual or several products and shall either accompany the product(s) covered or be kept by the manufacturer. The appropriate solution for the directive concerned will be specified.

References to Articles refer to the standard paragraphs of Annex II.B to the Council resolution of 7 May 1985 (OJ No C 136, 4. 6. 1985, p. 1), which have become standard Articles in the 'new approach' directives.

The development of computerized communication of certificates and other documents issued by notified bodies is envisaged within INSIS.

Specific directives may use modules A, C and H with additional provisions containing supplementary requirements which figure in the boxes in the modules.

Module C is designed to be used in combination with module B (EC type-examination). Modules D, E and F will also normally be used in combination with module B; however, in special cases (for example, when dealing with certain products of very simple design and construction) they may be used on their own.

Module A (internal production control)

1. This module describes the procedure whereby the manufacturer or his authorized representative established within the Community, who carries out the obligations laid down in point 2, ensures and declares that the products concerned satisfy the requirements of the directive that apply to them. The manufacturer or his authorized manufacturer established within the Community must affix the CE marking to each product and draw up a written declaration of conformity.

2. The manufacturer must establish the technical documentation described in paragraph 3 and he or his authorized representative established with the Community must keep it for a period ending at least 10 years(*) after the last product has been manufactured at the disposal of the relevant national authorities for inspection purposes.

    Where neither the manufacturer nor his authorized representative is established within the Community, the obligation to keep the technical documentation available is the responsibility of the person who places the product on the Community market.

3. Technical documentation must enable the conformity of the product with the requirements of the directive to be assessed. It must, as far as relevant for such assessment, cover the design, manufacture and operation of the product(**).

(*) The specific directives may alter this period.
(**) The content of the technical documentation shall be laid down directive by directive in accordance with the products concerned.

   For example, the documentation must contain so far as relevant for assessment:
   – a general description of the product,
   – conceptual design and manufacturing drawings and schemes of components, sub-assemblies, circuits, etc.,
   – descriptions and explanations necessary for the understanding of said drawings and schemes and the operation of the product,
   – a list of the standards referred to in Article 5, applied in full or in part, and descriptions of the solutions adopted to meet the essential requirements of the directive where the standards referred to in Article 5 have not been applied,
   – results of design calculations made, examinations carried out, etc.,
   – test reports.

4. The manufacturer or his authorized representative must keep a copy of the declaration of conformity with the technical documentation.

5. The manufacturer must take all measures necessary in order that the manufacturing process ensures compliance of the manufactured products with the technical documentation referred to in point 2 and with the requirements of the directive that apply to them.

Module Aa

This module consists of module A plus the following supplementary requirements:

For each product manufactured one or more tests on one or more specific aspects of the product must be carried out by the manufacturer or on his behalf (*). The tests are carried out on the responsibility of a notified body chosen by the manufacturer.

On the responsibility of the notified body, the manufacturer must affix the former's identification number during the manufacturing process.

(*) If this option is adopted in a specific directive, the products concerned and the tests to be carried out must be specified.

---

or:

A notified body chosen by the manufacturer must carry out or have carried out product checks at random intervals. An adequate sample of the final products, taken on site by the notified body, must be examined and appropriate tests as set out in the relevant standard(s) referred to in Article 5, or equivalent tests, must be carried out to check the conformity of the product with the relevant requirements of the directive.

In those cases where one or more of the products checked do not conform the notified body must take appropriate measures.

The product checking must include the following aspects:

(Relevant aspects must be specified here such as for example the statistical method to be applied, the sampling plan with its operational characteristics, etc.)

On the responsibility of the notified body, the manufacturer must affix the former's identification number during the manufacturing process.

Module B (EC type-examination)

1. This module describes that part of the procedure by which a notified body ascertains and attests that a specimen, representative of the production envisaged, meets the provisions of the directive that apply to it.

2. The application for the EC type-examination must be lodged by the manufacturer or his authorized representative established within the Community with a notified body of his choice.

    The application must include:

    – the name and address of the manufacturer and, if the application is lodged by the authorized representative, his name and address in addition,

    – a written declaration that the same application has not been lodged with any other notified body,

    – the technical documentation, as described in point 3.

    The applicant must place at the disposal of the notified body a specimen, representative of the production envisaged and hereinafter called 'type'(*). The notified body may request further specimens if needed for carrying out the test programme.

3. The technical documentation must enable the conformity of the product with the requirements of the directive to be assessed. It must, as far as relevant for such assessment, cover the design, manufacture and operation of the product(**).

4. The notified body must:

    4.1. examine the technical documentation, verify that the type has been manufactured in conformity with the technical documentation and identify the elements which have been designed in accordance with the relevant provisions of the standards referred to in Article 5, as well as the components which have been designed without applying the relevant provisions of those standards;

(*) A type may cover several versions of the product provided that the differences between the versions do not affect the level of safety and the other requirements concerning the performance of the product.

(**) The content of the technical documentation must be laid down by directive in accordance with the products concerned.

For example the documentation must contain as far as is relevant for assessment:

– a general type-description

– conceptual design and manufacturing drawings and schemes of components, sub-assemblies, circuits etc.

– descriptions and explanations necessary for understanding of said drawings and schemes and the operation of the product.

– a list of the standards referred to in Article 5, applied in full or in part, and descriptions of the solutions adopted to meet the essential requirements of the directive where the standards referred to in Article 5 have not been applied,

– results of design calculations made, examinations carried out, etc.,

– test reports.

4.2. perform or have performed the appropriate examinations and necessary tests to check whether where the standards referred to in Article 5 have not been applied, the solutions adopted by the manufacturer meet the essential requirements of the directive;

4.3. perform or have performed the appropriate examinations and necessary tests to check whether where the manufacturer has chosen to apply the relevant standards, these have actually been applied;

4.4. agree with the applicant the location where the examinations and necessary tests will be carried out.

5. Where the type meets the provisions of the directive, the notified body must issue an EC type-examination certificate to the applicant. The certificate must contain the name and address of the manufacturer, conclusions of the examination, conditions for its validity and the necessary data for identification of the approved type(*).

A list of the relevant of the technical documentation must be annexed to the certificate and a copy kept by the notified body.

If the manufacturer is denied a type certification, the notified body must provide detailed reasons for such denial.

Provision must be made for an appeals procedure.

6. The applicant must inform the notified body that holds the technical documentation concerning the EC type-examination certificate of all modifications to the approved product which must receive additional approval where such changes may affect the conformity which the essential requirements or the prescribed conditions for use of the product. This additional approval is given in the form of an addition to the original EC type-examination certificate.

7. Each notified body must communicate to the other notified bodies the relevant information concerning the EC type-examination certificates and additions issued and withdrawn(**).

8. The other notified bodies may receive copies of the EC type-examination certificates and/or their additions. The Annexes to the certificates must be kept at the disposal of the other notified bodies.

9. The manufacturer or his authorized representative must keep with the technical documentation copies of EC type-examination certificates and their additions for a period ending at least 10 years(***) after the last product has been manufactured.

Where neither the manufacturer nor his authorized representative is established within the Community, the obligation to keep the technical documentation available is the responsibility of the person who places the product on the Community market.

(*) The specific directives may provide for the certificate to have a period of validity.
(**) The specific directives may provide for different arrangements.
(***) The specific directives may alter this period.

Module C (conformity to type)

1. This module describes that part of the procedure whereby the manufacturer or his authorized representative established within the Community ensures and declares that the products concerned are in conformity with the type as described in the EC type-examination certificate and satisfy the requirements of the directive that applies to them. The manufacturer or his authorized representative established within the Community must affix the CE marking to each product and draw up a written declaration of conformity.

2. The manufacturer must take all measures necessary to ensure that the manufacturing process assures compliance of the manufactured products with the type as described in the EC type-examination certificate and with the requirements of the directive that apply to them.

3. The manufacturer or his authorized representative must keep a copy of the declaration of conformity for a period ending at least 10 years(*) after the last product has been manufactured.

   Where neither the manufacturer nor his authorized representative is established within the Community the obligation to keep the technical documentation available is the responsibility of the person who places the product on the Community market.

Possible supplementary requirements:

For each product manufactured one or more tests on one or more specific aspects of the product must be carried out by the manufacturer or on his behalf (*). The tests must be carried out on the responsibility of a notified body, chosen by the manufacturer.

   On the responsibility of the notified body, the manufacturer must affix the former's identification number during the manufacturing process.

(*) If this option is adopted in a specific directive, the products concerned and the tests to be carried out must be specified.

---

or:

A notified body chosen by the manufacturer must carry out or have carried out product checks at random intervals. An adequate sample of the final products, taken on site by the notified body, must be examined and appropriate tests as set out in the relevant standard(s) referred to in Article 5, or equivalent tests, must be carried out to check the conformity of production with the relevant requirements of the directive.

(*) The specific directives may alter this period.

In those cases where one or more of the products checked do not conform the notified body must take appropriate measures.

The product checking must include the following aspects:

(Relevant aspects must be specified here such as for example the statistical method to be applied, the sampling plan with its operational characteristics, etc.)

On the responsibility of the notified body, the manufacturer must affix the former's identification number during the manufacturing process.

Module D(*), (production quality assurance)

1. This module describes the procedure whereby the manufacturer who satisfies the obligations of point 2 ensures and declares that the products concerned [are in conformity with the type as described in the EC type-examination certificate and] satisfy the requirements of the directive that apply to them. The manufacturer or his authorized representative established within the Community must affix the CE marking to each product and draw up a written declaration of conformity. The CE marking must be accompanied by the identification symbol of the notified body responsible for EC monitoring as specified in point 4.

2. The manufacturer must operate an approved quality system for production, final product inspection and testing as specified in paragraph 3 and is subject to monitoring as specified in point 4.

3. *Quality system*

   3.1. The manufacturer must lodge an application for assessment of his quality system with a notified body of his choice, for the products concerned.

      The application must include:

      – all relevant information for the product category envisaged,

      – the documentation concerning the quality system,

      – if applicable, the technical documentation of the approved type and a copy of the EC type-examination certificate.

   3.2. The quality system must ensure compliance of the products [with the type as described in the EC type-examination certificate and] with the requirements of the directive that apply to them.

      All the elements, requirements and provisions adopted by the manufacturer shall be documented in a systematic and orderly manner in the form of written policies, procedures and instructions.

(*) Where this module is used without module B:

   – points 2 and 3 of module A must be added between points 1 and 2 in order to incorporate the need for technical documentation,

   – the words in square brackets must be deleted.

The quality system documentation must permit a consistent interpretation of the quality programmes, plan, manuals and records.

It must contain in particular an adequate description of:

- the quality objectives and the organizational structure, responsibilities and powers of the management with regard to product quality,
- the manufacturing, quality control and quality assurance techniques, processes and systematic actions that will be used,
- the examinations and tests that will be carried out before, during and after manufacture, and the frequency with which they will be carried out,
- the quality records, such as inspection reports and test data, calibration data, qualification reports of the personnel concerned, etc.,
- the means to monitor the achievement of the required product quality and the effective operation of the quality system.

3.3. The notified body must assess the quality system to determine whether it satisfies the requirements referred to in point 3.2. It presumes conformity with these requirements in respect of quality systems that implement the relevant harmonized standard(*).

The auditing team must have at least one member with experience of evaluation in the product technology concerned. The evaluation procedure must include an inspection visit to the manufacturer's premises.

The decision must be notified to the manufacturer. The notification must contain the conclusions of the examination and the reasoned assessment decision.

3.4. The manufacturer must undertake to fulfil the obligations arising out of the quality system as approved and to uphold it so that it remains adequate and efficient.

The manufacturer or his authorized representative shall keep the notified body that has approved the quality system informed of any intended updating of the quality system.

The notified body must evaluate the modifications proposed and decide whether the amended quality system will still satisfy the requirements referred to in paragraph 3.2 or whether a re-assessment is required.

It must notify its decision to the manufacturer. The notification must contain the conclusions of the examination and the reasoned assessment decision.

4. *Surveillance under the responsibility of the notified body*

4.1. The purpose of surveillance is to make sure that the manufacturer duly fulfils the obligations arising out of the approved quality system.

(*) This harmonized standard will be EN 29 002, supplemented, if necessary, to take into account the specific nature of the products for which it is implemented.

4.2. The manufacturer must allow the notified body entrance for inspection purposes to the locations of manufacture, inspection and testing, and storage and must provide it with all necessary information, in particular:
 - the quality system documentation,
 - the quality records, such as inspection reports and test data, calibration data, qualification reports of the personnel concerned, etc.

4.3. The notified body must periodically(*) carry out audits to make sure that the manufacturer maintains and applies the quality system and must provide an audit report to the manufacturer.

4.4. Additionally the notified body may pay unexpected visits to the manufacturer. During such visits the notified body may carry out, or cause to be carried out, tests to verify that the quality system is functioning correctly, if necessary. The notified body must provide the manufacturer with a visit report and, if a test has taken place, with a test report.

5. The manufacturer must, for a period ending at least 10 years(**) after the last product has been manufactured, keep at the disposal of the national authorities:
 - the documentation referred to in the second indent of point 3.1,
 - the updating referred to in the second paragraph of point 3.4,
 - the decisions and reports from the notified body which are referred to in the final paragraph of point 3.4, points 4.3 and 4.4.

6. Each notified body must give the other notified bodies the relevant information concerning the quality system approvals issued and withdrawn(***).

Module E(****) (product quality assurance)

1. This module describes the procedure whereby the manufacturer who satisfies the obligations of point 2 ensures and declares that the products concerned [are in conformity with the type as described in the EC type-examination certificate and] satisfy the requirements of the directive that apply to them. The manufacturer or his authorized representative established within the Community must affix the CE mark to each product and draw up a written declaration of conformity. The CE mark must be accompanied by the identification symbol of the notified body responsible for surveillance as specified in point 4.

(*) In the specific directives, the frequency may be specified.
(**) The specific directives may alter this period.
(***) The specific directives may provide for different arrangements.
(****) When this module is used without module B:
 - points 2 and 3 of module A must be added between points 1 and 2 in order to incorporate the need for technical documentation,
 - the words in square brackets must be deleted.

2. The manufacturer must operate an approved quality system for final product inspection and testing as specified in paragraph 3 and must be subject to surveillance as specified in point 4.

3. *Quality system*

   3.1. The manufacturer must lodge an application for assessment of his quality system for the products concerned, with a notified body of his choice.

   The application must include:
   - all relevant information for the product category envisaged,
   - the quality system's documentation,
   - if applicable, the technical documentation of the approved type and a copy of the EC type-examination certificate.

   3.2. Under the quality system, each product must be examined and appropriate tests as set out in the relevant standard(s) referred to in Article 5 or equivalent tests shall be carried out in order to ensure its conformity with the relevant requirements of the directive. All the elements, requirements and provisions adopted by the manufacturer must be documented in a systematic and orderly manner in the form of written policies, procedures and instructions. This quality system documentation must ensure a common understanding of the quality programmes, plans, manuals and records.

   It must contain in particular an adequate description of:
   - the quality objectives and the organizational structure, responsibilities and powers of the management with regard to product quality,
   - the examinations and tests that will be carried out after manufacture,
   - the means to monitor the effective operation of the quality system,
   - quality records, such as inspection reports and test data, calibration data, qualification reports of the personnel concerned, etc.

   3.3. The notified body must assess the quality system to determine whether it satisfies the requirements referred to in point 3.2. It presumes conformity with these requirements in respect of quality systems that implement the relevant harmonized standard(*).

   The auditing team must have at least one member experienced as an assessor in the product technology concerned. The assessment procedure must include an assessment visit to the manufacturer's premises.

   The decision must be notified to the manufacturer. The notification must contain the conclusions of the examination and the reasoned assessment decision.

   3.4. The manufacturer must undertake to discharge the obligations arising

(*) This harmonized standard will be EN 29 003, supplemented if necessary to allow for the specific features of the products for which it is implemented.

from the quality system as approved and to maintain it in an appropriate and efficient manner.

The manufacturer or his authorized representative must keep the notified body which has approved the quality system informed of any intended updating of the quality system.

The notified body must evaluate the modifications proposed and decide whether the modified quality system will still satisfy the requirements referred to in paragraph 3.2 or whether a re-assessment is required.

It must notify its decision to the manufacturer. The notification must contain the conclusions of the examination and the reasoned assessment decision.

4. *Surveillance under the responsibility of the notified body*

   4.1. The purpose of surveillance is to make sure that the manufacturer duly fulfils the obligations arising out of the approved quality system.

   4.2. The manufacturer must allow the notified body entrance for inspection purposes to the locations of inspection, testing and storage and shall provide it with all necessary information, in particular:
   – the quality system documentation,
   – the technical documentation,
   – the quality records, such as inspection reports and test data, calibration data, qualification reports of the personnel concerned, etc.

   4.3. the notified body must periodically(*) carry out audits to ensure that the manufacturer maintains and applies the quality system and must provide an audit report to the manufacturer.

   4.4. Additionally, the notified body may pay unexpected visits to the manufacturer. At the time of such visits, the notified body may carry out tests or have them carried out in order to check the proper functioning of the quality system where necessary; it must provide the manufacturer with a visit report and, if a test has been carried out, with a test report.

5. The manufacturer must, for a period ending at least 10 years(**) after the last product has been manufactured, keep at the disposal of the national authorities:
   – the documentation referred to in the third indent of point 3.1,
   – the updating referred to in the second paragraph of point 3.4,
   – the decisions and reports from the notified body which are referred to in the final paragraph of point 3.4, points 4.3 and 4.4.

6. Each notified body must forward to the other notified bodies the relevant information concerning the quality system approvals issued and withdrawn(***).

(*) The intervals between audits may be specified in the specific directives.
(**) The specific directives may alter this period.
(***) The specific directives may provide for different arrangements.

Module F(*) (product verification)

1. This module describes the procedure whereby a manufacturer or his authorized representative established within the Community checks and attests that the products subject to the provisions of point 3 [are in conformity with the type as described in the EC-type examination certificate and] satisfy the requirements of the directive that apply to them.

2. The manufacturer must take all measures necessary in order that the manufacturing process ensures conformity of the products [with the type as described in the EC type-examination certificate and] with the requirements of the directive that apply to them. He shall affix the CE marking to each product and shall draw up a declaration of conformity.

3. The notified body must carry out the appropriate examinations and tests in order to check the conformity of the product with the requirements of the directive either by examination and testing of every product as specified in point 4 or by examination and testing of products on a statistical basis, as specified in point 5, at the choice of the manufacturer(**).

3a. The manufacturer or his authorized representative must keep a copy of the declaration of conformity for a period ending at least 10 years(***) after the last product has been manufactured.

4. *Verification by examination and testing of every product*

   4.1. All products must be individually examined and appropriate tests as set out in the relevant standard(s) referred to in Article 5 or equivalent tests shall be carried out in order to verify their conformity with [the type as described in the EC-type examination certificate and] the requirements of the directive that apply to them.

   4.2. The notified body must affix or cause to be affixed, its identification symbol to each approved product and draw up a written certificate of conformity relating to the tests carried out.

   4.3. The manufacturer or his authorized representative must ensure that he is able to supply the notified body's certificates of conformity on request.

5. *Statistical verification*

   5.1 The manufacturer must present his products in the form of homogeneous lots and shall take all measures necessary in order that the manufacturing process ensures the homogeneity of each lot produced.

   5.2. All products must be available for verification in the form of homo-

---

(*) Where this module is used without module B:
  – it must be supplemented by points 2 and 3 of module A (between points 1 and 2), so as to introduce the need for technical documentation,
  – the text in square brackets must be deleted.
(**) The manufacturer's discretion may be limited in the specific directives.
(***) The specific directives may alter this period.

geneous lots. A random sample shall be drawn from each lot. Products in a sample shall be individually examined and appropriate tests as set out in the relevant standard(s) referred to in Article 5, or equivalent tests, shall be carried out to ensure their conformity with the requirements of the directive which apply to them and to determine whether the lot is accepted or rejected.

5.3. The statistical procedure must use the following elements:
(Relevant elements must be specified here such as, for example, the statistical method to be applied, the sampling plan with its operational characteristics, etc.)

5.4. In the case of accepted lots, the notified body must affix, or cause to be affixed, its identification symbol to each product and shall draw up a written certificate of conformity relating to the tests carried out. All products in the lot may be put on the market except those products from the sample which were found not to be in conformity.

If a lot is rejected, the notified body or the competent authority must take appropriate measures to prevent the putting on the market of that lot. In the event of frequent rejection of lots the notified body may suspend the statistical verification.

The manufacturer may, under the responsibility of the notified body, affix the latter's identification symbol during the manufacturing process.

5.5. The manufacturer or his authorized representative must ensure that he is able to supply the notified body's certificates of conformity on request.

Module G (unit verification)

1. This module describes the procedure whereby the manufacturer ensures and declares that the product concerned, which has been issued with the certificate referred to in point 2, conforms to the requirements of the directive that apply to it. The manufacturer or his authorized representative established within the Community must affix the CE marking to the product and draw up a declaration of conformity.

2. The notified body must examine the individual product and carry out the appropriate tests as set out in the relevant standard(s) referred to in Article 5, or equivalent tests, to ensure its conformity with the relevant requirements of the directive.

The notified body must affix, or cause to be affixed, its identification number on the approved product and shall draw up a certificate of conformity concerning the tests carried out.

3. The aim of the technical documentation is to enable conformity with the

requirements of the directive to be assessed and the design, manufacture and operation of the product to be understood(*).

Module H (full quality assurance)

1. This module describes the procedure whereby the manufacturer who satisfies the obligations of paragraph 2 ensures and declares that the products concerned satisfy the requirements of the directive that apply to them. The manufacturer or his authorized representative established within the Community must affix the CE marking to each product and draw up a written declaration of conformity. The CE marking must be accompanied by the identification symbol of the notified body responsible for the surveillance as specified in point 4.

2. The manufacturer must operate an approved quality system for design, manufacture and final product inspection and testing as specified in point 3 and shall be subject to surveillance as specified in point 4.

3. *Quality system*

   3.1. The manufacturer must lodge an application for assessment of his quality system with a notified body.

      The application must include:

      – all relevant information for the product category envisaged,

      – the quality system's documentation.

   3.2. The quality system must ensure compliance of the products with the requirements of the directive that apply to them.

      All the elements, requirements and provisions adopted by the manufacturer must be documented in a systematic and orderly manner in the form of written policies, procedures and instructions. This quality system documentation shall ensure a common understanding of the quality policies and procedures such as quality programmes, plans, manuals and records.

      It must contain in particular an adequate description of:

      – the quality objectives and the organizational structure, responsi-

---

(*) The content of the technical documentation shall be laid down directive by directive in accordance with the products concerned. As an example, the documentation shall contain so far as relevant for assessment:
- a general description of the product,
- conceptual design and manufacturing drawings and schemes of components, sub-assemblies, circuits, etc.,
- descriptions and explanations necessary for the understanding of said drawings and schemes and the operation of the product,
- a list of the standards referred to in Article 5, applied in full or in part, and descriptions of the solutions adopted to meet the essential requirements of the directive where the standards referred to in Article 5 have not been applied,
- results of design calculations made, examinations carried out, etc.,
- test reports.

bilities and powers of the management with regard to design and product quality,

– the technical design specifications, including standards, that will be applied and, where the standards referred to in Article 5 will not be applied in full, the means that will be used to ensure that the essential requirements of the directive that apply to the products will be met,

– the design control and design verification techniques, processes and systematic actions that will be used when designing the products pertaining to the product category covered,

– the corresponding manufacturing, quality control and quality assurance techniques, processes and systematic actions that will be used,

– the examinations and tests that will be carried out before, during and after manufacture, and the frequency with which they will be carried out,

– the quality records, such as inspection reports and test data, calibration data, qualification reports of the personnel concerned, etc.,

– the means to monitor the achievement of the required design and product quality and the effective operation of the quality system.

3.3. The notified body must assess the quality system to determine whether it satisfies the requirements referred to in point 3.2. It shall presume compliance with these requirements in respect of quality systems that implement the relevant harmonized standard(*).

The auditing team must have at least one member experienced as an assessor in the product technology concerned. The evaluation procedure shall include an assessment visit to the manufacturer's premises.

The decision must be notified to the manufacturer. The notification must contain the conclusions of the examination and the reasoned assessment decision.

3.4. The manufacturer must undertake to fulfil the obligations arising out of the quality system as approved and to uphold it so that it remains adequate and efficient.

The manufacturer or his authorized representative must keep the notified body that has approved the quality system informed of any intended updating of the quality system.

The notified body must evaluate the modifications proposed and decide whether the amended quality system will still satisfy the requirements referred to in paragraph 3.2 or whether a re-assessment is required.

It must notify its decision to the manufacturer. The notification

(*) This harmonized standard shall be EN 29 001, completed if necessary to take into consideration the specificity of the products for which it is implemented.

shall contain the conclusions of the examination and the reasoned assessment decision.

4. *EC surveillance under the responsibility of the notified body*

4.1. The purpose of surveillance is to make sure that the manufacturer duly fulfils the obligations arising out of the approved quality system.

4.2. The manufacturer must allow the notified body entrance for inspection purposes to the locations of design, manufacture, inspection and testing, and storage, and shall provide it with all necessary information, in particular:
   - the quality system documentation,
   - the quality records as foreseen by the design part of the quality system, such as results of analyses, calculations, tests, etc.,
   - the quality records as foreseen by the manufacturing part of the quality system, such as inspection reports and test data, calibration data, qualification reports of the personnel concerned, etc.

4.3. The notified body must periodically(*) carry out audits to make sure that the manufacturer maintains and applies the quality system and shall provide an audit report to the manufacturer.

4.4. Additionally the notified body may pay unexpected visits to the manufacturer. At the time of such visits the notified body may carry out tests or have them carried out in order to check the proper functioning of the quality system where necessary; it must provide the manufacturer with a visit report and, if a test has been carried out, with a test report.

5. The manufacturer must, for a period ending at least 10 years(**) after the last product has been manufactured, keep at the disposal of the national authorities:
   - the documentation referred to in the second indent of the second subparagraph of point 3.1,
   - the updating referred to in the second subparagraph of point 3.4,
   - the decisions and reports from the notified body which are referred to in the final subparagraph of point 3.4, points 4.3 and 4.4.

6. Each notified body must forward to the other notified bodies the relevant information concerning the quality system approvals issued and withdrawn(***).

   Possible supplementary requirements:

(*)In the specific directives, the frequency may be specified.

(**) The specific directives may alter this period.

(***) The specific directives may provide for different arrangements.

Design examination

1. The manufacturer must lodge an application for examination of the design with a single notified body.

2. The application must enable the design, manufacture and operation of the product to be understood, and shall enable conformity with the requirements of the directive to be assessed.

    It must include:

    – the technical design specifications, including standards, that have been applied,

    – the necessary supporting evidence for their adequacy, in particular where the standards referred to in Article 5 have not been applied in full. This supporting evidence must include the results of tests carried out by the appropriate laboratory of the manufacturer or on his behalf.

3. The notified body must examine the application and where the design meets the provisions of the directive that apply to it must issue an EC design examination certificate to the applicant. The certificate shall contain the conclusions of the examination, conditions for its validity, the necessary data for identification of the approved design and, if relevant, a description of the product's functioning.

4. The applicant must keep the notified body that has issued the EC design examination certificate informed of any modification to the approved design. Modifications to the approved design must receive additional approval from the notified body that issued the EC design examination certificate where such changes may affect the conformity with the essential requirements of the directive or the prescribed conditions for use of the product. This additional approval is given in the form of an addition to the original EC design examination certificate.

5. The notified bodies must forward to the other notified bodies the relevant information concerning:

    – the EC design examination certificates and additions issued,

    – the EC design approvals and additional approvals withdrawn (*).

(*) The specific directives may provide for different arrangements.

CONFORMITY ASSESSMENT PROCEDURES IN COMMUNITY LEGISLATION

	A. (internal control of production)	B. (type examination)	C. (conformity to type)	D. (production quality assurance) EN 29002	E. (product quality assurance) EN 29003	F. (product verification)	G. (unit verification)	H. (full quality assurance) EN 29001
DESIGN	Manufacturer Keeps technical documentation at the disposal of national authorities Aa Intervention of notified body	Manufacturer submits to notified body — Technical documentation — Type Notified body — Ascertains conformity with essential requirements — Carries out tests, if necessary — Issues EC type-examination certificate					Manufacturer — Submits technical documentation	Manufacturer — Operates an approved quality system (QS) for design. Notified body — Carries out surveillance of the QS — Verifies conformity of the design (¹) — Issues EC design examination certificate (¹)
PRODUCTION	A. Manufacturer — Declares conformity with essential requirements — Affixes the CE marking Aa Notified body — Tests on specific aspects of the product(¹) — Product checks at random intervals (¹)		Manufacturer — Declares conformity with approved type — Affixes the CE marking Notified body — Tests on specific aspects of the product (¹) — Product checks at random intervals (¹)	Manufacturer — Operates an approved quality system (QS) for production and testing — Declares conformity with approved type — Affixes the CE marking Notified body — Approves the QS — Carries out surveillance of the QS	Manufacturer — Operates an approved quality system (QS) for inspection and testing — Declares conformity with approved type, or to essential requirements — Affixes the CE marking Notified body — Approves the QS — Carries out surveillance of the QS	Manufacturer — Declares conformity with approved type, or with essential requirements — Affixes the CE marking Notified body — Verifies conformity — Issues certificate at conformity	Manufacturer — Submits product — Declares conformity — Affixes the CE marking Notified body — Verifies conformity with essential requirements — Issues certificate of conformity	Manufacturer — Operates an approved QS for production and testing — Declares conformity — Affixes the CE marking Notified body — Carries out surveillance of the QS

(¹) Supplementary requirements which may be used in specific Directives.

Appendix II
Consumer Protection Act 1987: Part I

1987 CHAPTER 43

An Act to make provision with respect to the liability of persons for damage caused by defective products; to consolidate with amendments the Consumer Safety Act 1978 and the Consumer Safety (Amendment) Act 1986; to make provision with respect to the giving of price indications; to amend Part I of the Health and Safety at Work etc. Act 1974 and sections 31 and 80 of the Explosives Act 1875; to repeal the Trade Descriptions Act 1972 and the Fabrics (Misdescription) Act 1913; and for connected purposes.

[15th May 1987]

Be it enacted by the Queen's most Excellent Majesty, by and with the advice and consent of the Lords Spiritual and Temporal, and Commons, in this present Parliament assembled, and by the authority of the same, as follows:–

PART I
PRODUCT LIABILITY

Purpose and construction of Part I.

1. – (1) This Part shall have effect for the purpose of making such provision as is necessary in order to comply with the product liability Directive and shall be construed accordingly.

(2) In this Part, except in so far as the context otherwise requires –

'agricultural produce' means any produce of the soil, of stockfarming or of fisheries;

1976 c. 30.
1976 c. 13.

'dependant' and 'relative' have the same meaning as they have in, respectively, the Fatal Accidents Act 1976 and the Damages (Scotland) Act 1976;

'producer', in relation to a product, means –

(a) the person who manufactured it;

(b) in the case of a substance which has not been manufactured but has been won or abstracted, the person who won or abstracted it;

308

(c) in the case of a product which has not been manufactured, won or abstracted but essential characteristics of which are attributable to an industrial or other process having been carried out (for example, in relation to agricultural produce), the person who carried out that process;

'product' means any goods or electricity and (subject to subsection (3) below) includes a product which is comprised in another product, whether by virtue of being a component part or raw material or otherwise; and

'the product liability Directive' means the Directive of the Council of the European Communities, dated 25th July 1985, (No. 85/374/EEC) on the approximation of the laws, regulations and administrative provisions of the member States concerning liability for defective products.

(3) For the purposes of this Part a person who supplies any product in which products are comprised, whether by virtue of being component parts or raw materials or otherwise, shall not be treated by reason only of his supply of that product as supplying any of the products so comprised.

2. – (1) Subject to the following provisions of this Part, where any damage is caused wholly or partly by a defect in a product, every person to whom subsection (2) below applies shall be liable for the damage.

Liability for defective products.

(2) This subsection applies to –

(a) the producer of the product;

(b) any person who, by putting his name on the product or using a trade mark or other distinguishing mark in relation to the product, has held himself out to be the producer of the product;

(c) any person who has imported the product into a member State from a place outside the member States in order, in the course of any business of his, to supply it to another.

(3) Subject as aforesaid, where any damage is caused wholly or partly by a defect in a product, any person who supplied the product (whether to the person who suffered the damage, to the producer of any product in which the product in question is comprised or to any other person) shall be liable for the damage if –

(a) the person who suffered the damage requests the supplier to identify one or more of the persons (whether still in existence or not) to whom subsection (2) above applies in relation to the product;

(b) that request is made within a reasonable period after the damage occurs and at a time when it is not reasonably practicable for the person making the request to identify all those persons; and

(c) the supplier fails, within a reasonable period after receiving the request, either to comply with the request or to identify the person who supplied the product to him.

(4) Neither subsection (2) nor subsection (3) above shall apply to a person in respect of any defect in any game or agricultural produce if the only supply of the game or produce by that person to another was at a time when it had not undergone an industrial process.

(5) Where two or more persons are liable by virtue of this Part for the same damage, their liability shall be joint and several.

(6) This section shall be without prejudice to any liability arising otherwise than by virtue of this Part.

Meaning of 'defect'.

3. – (1) Subject to the following provisions of this section, there is a defect in a product for the purposes of this Part if the safety of the product is not such as persons generally are entitled to expect; and for those purposes 'safety', in relation to a product, shall include safety with respect to products comprised in that product and safety in the context of risks of damage to property, as well as in the context of risks of death or personal injury.

(2) In determining for the purposes of subsection (1) above what persons generally are entitled to expect in relation to a product all the circumstances shall be taken into account, including –

(a) the manner in which, and purposes for which, the product has been marketed, its get-up, the use of any mark in relation to the product and any instructions for, or warnings with respect to, doing or refraining from doing anything with or in relation to the product;

(b) what might reasonably be expected to be done with or in relation to the product; and

(c) the time when the product was supplied by its producer to another;

and nothing in this section shall require a defect to be inferred from the fact alone that the safety of a product which is supplied after that time is greater than the safety of the product in question.

Defences.

4. – (1) In any civil proceedings by virtue of this Part against any person ('the person proceeded against') in respect of a defect in a product it shall be a defence for him to show –

(a) that the defect is attributable to compliance with any requirement imposed by or under any enactment or with any Community obligation; or

(b) that the person proceeded against did not at any time supply the product to another; or

(c) that the following conditions are satisfied, that is to say –

(i) that the only supply of the product to another by the person proceeded against was otherwise than in the course of a business of that person's; and

(ii) that section 2(2) above does not apply to that person or applies to him by virtue only of things done otherwise than with a view to profit; or

(d) that the defect did not exist in the product at the relevant time; or

(e) that the state of scientific and technical knowledge at the relevant time was not such that a producer of products of the same description as the product in question might be expected to have discovered the defect if it had existed in his products while they were under his control; or

(f) that the defect –

(i) constituted a defect in a product ('the subsequent product') in which the product in question had been comprised; and

(ii) was wholly attributable to the design of the subsequent product or to compliance by the producer of the product in question with instructions given by the producer of the subsequent product.

(2) In this section 'the relevant time', in relation to electricity, means the time at which it was generated, being a time before it was transmitted or distributed, and in relation to any other product, means –

(a) if the person proceeded against is a person to whom subsection (2) of section 2 above applies in relation to the product, the time when he supplied the product to another;

(b) if that subsection does not apply to that person in relation to the product, the time when the product was last supplied by a person to whom that subsection does apply in relation to the product.

5. – (1) Subject to the following provisions of this section, in this Part 'damage' means death or personal injury or any loss of or damage to any property (including land).

Damage giving rise to liability.

(2) A person shall not be liable under section 2 above in respect of any defect in a product for the loss of or any damage to the product itself or for the loss of or any damage to the whole or any part of any product which has been supplied with the product in question comprised in it.

(3) A person shall not be liable under section 2 above for any loss of or damage to any property which, at the time it is lost or damaged, is not –

(a) of a description of property ordinarily intended for private use, occupation or consumption; and

(b) intended by the person suffering the loss or damage mainly for his own private use, occupation or consumption.

(4) No damages shall be awarded to any person by virtue of this Part in respect of any loss of or damage to any property if the amount which would fall to be so awarded to that person, apart from this subsection and any liability for interest, does not exceed £275.

(5) In determining for the purposes of this Part who has suffered any loss of or damage to property and when any such loss or damage occurred, the loss or damage shall be regarded as having occurred at the earliest time at which a person with an interest in the property had knowledge of the material facts about the loss or damage.

(6) For the purposes of subsection (5) above the material facts about any loss of or damage to any property are such facts about the loss or damage as would lead a reasonable person with an interest in the property to consider the loss or damage sufficiently serious to justify his instituting proceedings for damages against a defendant who did not dispute liability and was able to satisfy a judgment.

(7) For the purposes of subsection (5) above a person's knowledge includes knowledge which he might reasonably have been expected to acquire –

    (a) from facts observable or ascertainable by him; or

    (b) from facts ascertainable by him with the help of appropriate expert advice which it is reasonable for him to seek;

but a person shall not be taken by virtue of this subsection to have knowledge of a fact ascertainable by him only with the help of expert advice unless he has failed to take all reasonable steps to obtain (and, where appropriate, to act on) that advice.

(8) Subsections (5) to (7) above shall not extend to Scotland.

Application of certain enactments etc.
1976 c. 30.

6. – (1) Any damage for which a person is liable under section 2 above shall be deemed to have been caused –

    (a) for the purposes of the Fatal Accidents Act 1976, by that person's wrongful act, neglect or default;

1940 c. 42.

    (b) for the purposes of section 3 of the Law Reform (Miscellaneous Provisions) (Scotland) Act 1940 (contribution among joint wrong-doers), by that person's wrongful act or negligent act or omission;

1976 c. 13.

    (c) for the purposes of section 1 of the Damages (Scotland) Act 1976 (rights of relatives of a deceased), by that person's act or omission; and

1982 c. 53.

    (d) for the purposes of Part II of the Administration of Justice Act 1982 (damages for personal injuries, etc. – Scotland), by an act or omission giving rise to liability in that person to pay damages.

    (2) Where –

    (a) a person's death is caused wholly or partly by a defect in a product, or a person dies after suffering damage which has been so caused;

    (b) a request such as mentioned in paragraph (a) of subsection (3) of section 2 above is made to a supplier of the product by that person's personal representatives or, in the case of a person whose death is caused wholly or partly by the defect, by any dependant or relative of that person; and

(c) the conditions specified in paragraphs (b) and (c) of that subsection are satisfied in relation to that request,

this Part shall have effect for the purposes of the Law Reform (Miscellaneous Provisions) Act 1934, the Fatal Accidents Act 1976 and the Damages (Scotland) Act 1976 as if liability of the supplier to that person under that subsection did not depend on that person having requested the supplier to identify certain persons or on the said conditions having been satisfied in relation to a request made by that person.

1934 c. 41.

(3) Section 1 of the Congenital Disabilities (Civil Liability) Act 1976 shall have effect for the purposes of this Part as if –

1976 c. 28.

(a) a person were answerable to a child in respect of an occurrence caused wholly or partly by a defect in a product if he is or has been liable under section 2 above in respect of any effect of the occurrence on a parent of the child, or would be so liable if the occurrence caused a parent of the child to suffer damage;

(b) the provisions of this Part relating to liability under section 2 above applied in relation to liability by virtue of paragraph (a) above under the said section 1; and

(c) subsection (6) of the said section 1 (exclusion of liability) were omitted.

(4) Where any damage is caused partly by a defect in a product and partly by the fault of the person suffering the damage, the Law Reform (Contributory Negligence) Act 1945 and section 5 of the Fatal Accidents Act 1976 (contributory negligence) shall have effect as if the defect were the fault of every person liable by virtue of this Part for the damage caused by the defect.

1945 c. 28.
1976 c. 30.

(5) In subsection (4) above 'fault' has the same meaning as in the said Act of 1945.

(6) Schedule 1 to this Act shall have effect for the purpose of amending the Limitation Act 1980 and the Prescription and Limitation (Scotland) Act 1973 in their application in relation to the bringing of actions by virtue of this Part.

1980 c. 58.
1973 c. 52.

(7) It is hereby declared that liability by virtue of this Part is to be treated as liability in tort for the purposes of any enactment conferring jurisdiction on any court with respect to any matter.

(8) Nothing in this Part shall prejudice the operation of section 12 of the Nuclear Installations Act 1965 (rights to compensation for certain breaches of duties confined to rights under that Act).

1965 c. 57.

7. The liability of a person by virtue of this Part to a person who has suffered damage caused wholly or partly by a defect in a product, or to a dependant or relative of such a person, shall not be limited or excluded by any contract term, by any notice or by any other provision.

Prohibition on exclusions from liability.

Power to modify
Part I.

8. – (1) Her Majesty may by Order in Council make such modifications of this Part and of any other enactment (including an enactment contained in the following Parts of this Act, or in an Act passed after this Act) as appear to Her Majesty in Council to be necessary or expedient in consequence of any modification of the product liability Directive which is made at any time after the passing of this Act.

(2) An Order in Council under subsection (1) above shall not be submitted to Her Majesty in Council unless a draft of the Order has been laid before, and approved by a resolution of, each House of Parliament.

Application of
Part I to Crown.

9. – (1) Subject to subsection (2) below, this Part shall bind the Crown.

1947 c. 44.

(2) The Crown shall not, as regards the Crown's liability by virtue of this Part, be bound by this Part further than the Crown is made liable in tort or in reparation under the Crown Proceedings Act 1947, as that Act has effect from time to time.

Glossary

breach of warranty. A failure by a party to a contract to satisfy the standard required by a warranty, common law or statutory, express or implied, applicable to that contract. In general a warranty is an undertaking of a non-fundamental nature for the breach of which an action lies, but for which the contract cannot be declared at an end.

insurance broker. An insurance intermediary who advises clients on their insurance requirements and arranges their insurance.

burden of proof (onus of proof). The question of which party to a dispute on a fact must undertake to try to establish the disputed fact.

captive. An insurance company owned by a company partly or fully to insure the company's risk.

case law. The general term for principles and rules of law laid down in judicial decisions, for generalizations based on past decisions of courts and tribunals in particular cases.

CE marking. The characteristic CE lettering applied to show that a product conforms with relevant directives.

certification. The act of certifying, by means of a certificate of conformity or mark of conformity, that a product or service is in conformity with specific standards or technical specification.

code of practice. A document providing practical guidance for the design, manufacture, setting-up, maintenance or utilization of equipment, installations, structures or products.

common law. The royal justices of the English kings developed and administered general rules common to the whole of England, as distinct from the local customs, peculiarities and variations. The common law accordingly came to mean the whole law of England, including ecclesiastical, maritime and mercantile law, as distinct from that of other countries, particularly those based on Roman law.

contract condition. A clause in a contract prescribing an act or event on which the existence or quality or effectiveness of some obligation or payment is dependent.

cut-off. The period after which proceedings against the producer of a defective product may not be instituted.

damages. Civil court award for monetary compensation for an injury or loss.

damages, exemplary. Intended not merely to compensate the plaintiff but to punish the defendant to mark the outrageous nature of his conduct.

deductible. A provision for reducing an insurance settlement made on any loss by a specified sum.

defect. A product is defective when it does not provide the safety which a person is entitled to expect, taking all the circumstances into account (Article 6, EC Directive on Liability for Defective Products).

Delphi technique. A logical and structured system to examine a state of uncertainty by drawing together information that may be scattered and remote.

development risks. The residual chance that unforeseen failure modes will be revealed in a new product once it has been put on the market.

development risks defence. A producer will have a defence if he can show 'that the state of scientific and technical knowledge at the time when he put the product into circulation was not such as to enable the existence of the defect to be discovered' (Article 7, EC Directive on Liability for Defective Products).

duty of care. The legal duty to take reasonable care to avoid acts or omissions which are likely to injure those to whom the duty is owed. Breach of this duty gives rise to liability for negligence.

exemption clause. One which purports in general terms to limit or exclude the liability of a party which would otherwise arise under a contract.

Fail-to-safer. Strictly speaking, no product can be totally safe under all circumstances. Therefore, when a redundancy system is designed to take over after the failure of the primary system it can only make the product safer – not safe.

Failure Mode Effects Analysis. A study of the potential failures that might occur in any part of a system to determine the probable effect of each on all the other parts of the system and on its operational success.

Fault Tree Analysis. A study of the possible sequence of events constituting the failure of a system using the diagrammatic method of algorithms.

fundamental breach. If a party to a contract failed to comply with his fundamental obligations under it, he would not be allowed by the courts to rely on its terms, and in particular terms excluding or restricting his liability.

Hazard Analysis Critical Control Point. A method of anticipating hazards and identifying the points at which they can be controlled.

hazard operability study. A method of identifying hazards and problems which prevent efficient plant operation.

liability, absolute. In the law of tort liability in damages, imposed by reason of the mere occurrence of the accident of a kind deemed prohibited, without regard to care of precautions taken and without need for proof of negligence or fault.

liability, no-fault. The doctrine that a person who has sustained any stated injuries or losses should have a claim against an injurer or fund, frequently managed by the state, without having to establish that another person was liable for fault in causing him the harm complained of.

liability, product. The issue of whether, on what basis, and to what extent a manufacturer or supplier of some product should be liable to the ultimate consumer or user for harm done by reason of a defect in design or manufacture.

liability, strict. The term in the law of tort for a standard of liability which is more stringent than the ordinary one of liability for failure to take reasonable care, yet not absolute, which is the standard sometimes set by statute, where liability arises if the harm to be prevented takes place, whatever care and precautions have been taken.

liability-sensitive. A product, or a company or an industry associated with it, a defect in which can present grave risks to users.

limitation of actions. The principle in English law that, after the lapse of a fixed period of time, an action is not maintainable.

Lloyd's (of London). A section of the insurance market consisting of individual underwriters (and groups of underwriters working in syndicates) each transacting marine or non-marine insurance on their own account in the City.

negligence. In legal usage the failure to exercise the standard of care which the doer, as a reasonable individual should, by law, have exercised in the circumstances. The name negligence is given to a specific kind of tort – the tort of failing in particular circumstances to exercise the care which should have been shown in those circumstances, the care of the reasonable individual, and of thereby causing harm to another in person or property.
negligence, contributory. A partial or complete defence to liability in negligence when it could be shown that the plaintiff was partly or wholly responsible for his injuries.

New Approach. Based on EC Council Resolution on 7 May 1985, a policy for European product legislation based on mandatory 'essential requirements' backed by harmonized technical specifications which remain voluntary but which demonstrate conformity with the legal requirements. Hence 'New Approach directive' – a Directive adopted under this policy.

notified body. A body authorized to issue marks or certificates of conformity under European directives, details of which are notified to the European Commission and other Member States.

product extortion. The crime in which a product, often food or drink, is contaminated and then made available to the public, or threatened to be made available to the public. In return for information regarding the location of the contaminated packs, or abandoning the threat, there is a demand for a consideration: money, the release of prisoners or the wide publication of radical views. Also the threat to contaminate a product. Akin to blackmail.

product recall. Generally, the action taken to remove, repair, replace, retrofit or correct a defective product. Putting the distribution chain into reverse.

Quality. The totality of features and characteristics of a product or service that bear on its ability to satisfy a need (BS 4778 4.1.1.).

Quality Assurance. All the activities and functions concerned with the attainment of quality (BS 4778 5.1.1).

Quality Control. The operational techniques and activities that sustain the product or service quality of specified requirements (BS 4778 19.1.1).

Regulation. A binding document which contains legislative, regulatory or administrative rules and which is adopted and published by an authority legally vested with the necessary power.

reinsurance. The system by which an insurance company or underwriter, who has accepted an insurance, shares part of the risk with another insurer to lessen his own ultimate liability. The responsibility of the original insurer to the policy-holder for the full amount covered is not in any way affected by such reinsurance.

retrofit. Replacement *in situ* of a defective part.

res ipsa loquitur. Literally, 'the thing speaks for itself' – a principle often invoked in the law of tort, to the effect that the event itself is indicative of negligence. As Thoreau said, some evidence is very strong, as when you find a trout in the milk.

risk. The combined effect of the probability of occurrence of an undesirable event, and the magnitude of the event.

safety. Freedom from unacceptable risks of personal harm.

safety-critical. A component or ingredient which has a significant influence on the overall safety of the end-product in which it is used.

satisfactory quality. The Sale and Supply of Goods Act 1994 revised the old-fashioned term 'merchantable quality' of the Sale of Goods Act 1979. Instead, goods now have to be of 'satisfactory quality', which includes fitness for purpose, freedom from minor defects, appearance and finish, safety and durability.

specification. The document that prescribes in detail the requirements with which the product or service has to comply.

Standard. A technical specification approved by a recognized standards body for repeated or continuous application.

state of the art. A term applied to the cumulative knowledge and experience of an industry at a given point in time about a specific topic, usually with reference to when a product was made. The scientific and technological knowledge available to the prudent manufacturer.

tort. The term in common law systems for the civilly actionable harm or wrong, and for the branch of law dealing with liability for such wrongs.

Total Quality Management. A discipline and philosophy which institutionalizes planned and continuous business improvement.

uberrimae fidei. Of the utmost good faith. A term applied to a category of contracts and arrangements where each party must not only refrain from misrepresenting to the other but must voluntarily and positively disclose any factor which a reasonable person in the position of the other party might regard as material in determining whether or not to undertake the contract.

unavoidably unsafe products. There are some products which, in the present state of human knowledge, are quite incapable of being made safe for their intended and ordinary use. Such a product, properly prepared and accompanied by proper directions and warning, is not defective, nor is it unreasonably dangerous. The seller of such products is not to be held to strict liability for unfortunate consequences attending their use, merely because he has undertaken to supply the public with an apparently useful and desirable product, attended with a known but apparently reasonable risk (US Restatement of the Law of Torts).

underwriter. In an insurance company, the person who accepts or declines risks and who decides the terms and rates which are acceptable. At Lloyd's, a member who accepts risks for his own account as an individual or for a syndicate.

Unreasonably dangerous product. A product which must be dangerous to an extent beyond that which would be contemplated by the ordinary consumer who purchases it, with the ordinary knowledge common to the community as to its characteristics (US Restatement of the Law of Torts).

Index

Concurrent Engineering
What's Working Where

Edited by Chris J Backhouse and Naomi J Brookes

A Design Council Title

Concurrent Engineering aims to maximise profitability through the shortening of new product introduction time. But whilst the overall philosophy may be clear, the precise details of what form of Concurrent Engineering is most appropriate for any given set of circumstances is not so well defined. Specific cases of successful implementation need to be understood within their context to ensure success if repeated elsewhere.

This book addresses this issue by developing a framework within which all the influencing pressures acting on a company can be considered. The framework shows how these pressures can be categorised and then related to the elements which come together to form the Concurrent Engineering solution.

The core of the book is a series of case studies written by senior industrialists. In each chapter companies which have employed similar approaches to Concurrent Engineering are compared. The case studies range from multinationals, such as Rolls-Royce, IBM and Marconi, through to smaller enterprises. By reference to these real examples, executives concerned with evaluating or implementing Concurrent Engineering can see how the most appropriate techniques can be selected and introduced into their own company.

Gower

Design and Corporate Success

Clive Rassam

A Design Council Title

Good product design in terms of both performance and appearance can make an enormous impact on a company's ability to compete in markets around the world.

Design and Corporate Success shows how just influential good design can be from the viewpoint of leading British product designers, corporate identity specialists and senior company executives.

The book includes interviews with a galaxy of the UK's leading designers and corporate identity experts contributions from senior managers at Rover, Black and Decker, Electrolux, international furniture maker Steelcase Strafor, plus four export-led SMEs.

Drawing on their experience, Rassam shows how successful companies use good design to their own advantage and why designing the right product or corporate identity requires changes in approaches and attitudes. For anyone involved in the development of competitive advantage in their product range, this book is an essential guide.

Gower

Concurrent Engineering
What's Working Where

Edited by Chris J Backhouse and Naomi J Brookes

A Design Council Title

Concurrent Engineering aims to maximise profitability through the shortening of new product introduction time. But whilst the overall philosophy may be clear, the precise details of what form of Concurrent Engineering is most appropriate for any given set of circumstances is not so well defined. Specific cases of successful implementation need to be understood within their context to ensure success if repeated elsewhere.

This book addresses this issue by developing a framework within which all the influencing pressures acting on a company can be considered. The framework shows how these pressures can be categorised and then related to the elements which come together to form the Concurrent Engineering solution.

The core of the book is a series of case studies written by senior industrialists. In each chapter companies which have employed similar approaches to Concurrent Engineering are compared. The case studies range from multinationals, such as Rolls-Royce, IBM and Marconi, through to smaller enterprises. By reference to these real examples, executives concerned with evaluating or implementing Concurrent Engineering can see how the most appropriate techniques can be selected and introduced into their own company.

Gower

Design and Corporate Success

Clive Rassam

A Design Council Title

Good product design in terms of both performance and appearance can make an enormous impact on a company's ability to compete in markets around the world.

Design and Corporate Success shows how just influential good design can be from the viewpoint of leading British product designers, corporate identity specialists and senior company executives.

The book includes interviews with a galaxy of the UK's leading designers and corporate identity experts contributions from senior managers at Rover, Black and Decker, Electrolux, international furniture maker Steelcase Strafor, plus four export-led SMEs.

Drawing on their experience, Rassam shows how successful companies use good design to their own advantage and why designing the right product or corporate identity requires changes in approaches and attitudes. For anyone involved in the development of competitive advantage in their product range, this book is an essential guide.

Gower

ISO 14000 and ISO 9000

Brian Rothery

This is a practical 'hands-on' description of how companies can implement a comprehensive system to meet the requirements of the ISO 14000 Environmental Management Standard and the ISO 9000 Quality Management Standard, in addition to the Health and Safety regulations, and other public and product safety and general liability requirements. Written by the leading authority in this field, it anticipates the Phase Two revisions of ISO 9000 and provides complete sets of generic documentation including a Quality Manual and all the environmental registers and manuals.

The author also takes account of the 'backlash' against the ISO 9000 certification process which uses checklists of documents to please inspectors rather than implementing real quality improvement schemes. Throughout the book, advice is given on introducing good, comprehensive systems rather than producing sets of bureaucratic documents.

By presenting an integrated approach to the standards covering quality, health and safety and environmental issues, Brian Rothery has once again provided managers with an important reference and guide.

Gower

Strategies for World Class Products

Mike Farish

A Design Council Title

This book seeks to identify the essential elements of successful product design. A wide range of case studies are presented in order to identify and explore the basic principles involved in developing world class products. The book emphasizes the contribution of enlightened management practices - such as teamworking, Concurrent Engineering and information-sharing, and includes multiple examples of the experience of real companies in applying these principles in the area of product design and development.

Strategies for World Class Products is an essential guide for senior management involved in developing best-practice techniques for product development.

Gower